SEA ROAD TO THE INDIES

AN ACCOUNT OF THE VOYAGES AND EXPLOITS OF
THE PORTUGUESE NAVIGATORS, TOGETHER WITH
THE LIFE AND TIMES OF DOM VASCO DA GAMA,
CAPITÃO-MÓR, VICEROY OF INDIA AND
COUNT OF VIDIGUEIRA

BY

H E N R Y H . H A R T , F.R.G.S.
Member, Sociedade de Geografia de Lisboa
Member, Instituto de Coimbra

THE MACMILLAN COMPANY : NEW YORK

1950

FOR HELEN

PREFACE

EARLY half a century has passed since even a short account of the life of Vasco da Gama and his discovery of the Indies has been written. The book has long been out of print, much has been learned in the interim, and the historical perspective of his age has come into sharper focus.

The documentation of the Emanueline era is scanty, and contemporary accounts of the Portuguese voyages still remain, for the most part, untranslated and unavailable to the student.

The aim of the present volume is to fill this gap, to give a survey of the Portuguese contribution to the discovery of the Eastern world (as far as India), and to include a fuller presentation of the figure of Vasco da Gama * than has heretofore been written. There is little first-hand information of the period of his life; much must be obtained from documents or gleaned from the scanty references of contemporary authors. He left, as far as is known, no record of his voyages. The narrative of the first voyage, written by one of his officers, was first published in 1838. Though one of the two accounts of the second voyage, by a member of the crew, was first published in Italian in the very rare *Viaggi* of Ramusio in 1554, no Portuguese edition appeared until 1812. Neither it, nor a very short Flemish account, has ever been available to the average reader. No eyewitness narrative of the third voyage has ever come to light, and we are dependent on the chroniclers of the period, chiefly Correa and Castanheda, for our information. The accounts and documents have

* The reader using indexes in his search for material must consult entries under "Vasco da Gama" and "da Gama," for few, even of the most meticulous historians, seem to realize that his family name was "Gama," though he is always so mentioned in Portuguese writings.

all been read in the original languages, and no reliance was placed on quotations until they were verified. Except where noted, the author is responsible for all translations.

The author wishes to acknowledge a heavy debt of friendship and gratitude, one which can never be repaid, to Dr. Ruth Fox Wyatt, of Northwestern University, for her constant encouragement, wise counsel, and innumerable suggestions, as well as for a most painstaking reading of the manuscript for publication.

The officials of Harvard College Library, of the University of California Library, and of the Sociedade de Geografia de Lisboa have been most generous in searching for and supplying rare books and documents on the period.

To Miss Marjorie Macaulay French, of San Francisco, go the author's thanks and appreciation for her patient and often difficult task of typing the book.

It is with pleasure that the author expresses his obligations to the officials of the British Museum, the Bodleian Library, and the Hakluyt Society for their active assistance, and for permission to use copyrighted material. Acknowledgment is also made of the generosity and cooperation of the following publishers for permission to quote or otherwise use material: Messrs. B. H. Blackwell, Ltd., of Oxford, England, and A. & C. Black, Ltd., of London.

HENRY H. HART

June 17, 1949

CONTENTS

INTRODUCTION

HEN I was a very small boy, just beginning to read, a beloved girlhood friend of my mother came to visit us from what was then distant Texas. She brought me a book. That book, though it vanished in some unknown manner long ago in those far-off childhood days, has probably influenced my imagination, mostly through its numerous and vivid illustrations, more than any other book I have ever read.

The book * purported to be an account of the men who had opened up the unknown lands of the world—discoverers, explorers, conquistadores. My child-mind registered its exciting, vivid woodcuts and colored lithographs indelibly, and through the years they have never been obliterated or sensibly dimmed.

Among them I remember the picture of the ghost of Vasco da Gama fleeing in full armor through the air, pursued by his victims in hot cry for vengeance—scantily clad men without hands, without arms, with gaping wounds and torture-stricken features, seeking to grasp and punish their mortal enemy.

Still vivid are the gaudy double-page lithographs of his destruction of the Arab ship, his appearance before the Lord of Calicut, and all the other startling pictures illustrating his career. And those pages, fleeting repeatedly through my mind during the years, have caused me to write this book.

A copy of the volume recently came again into my hands. Alas, the disillusionment! Its pages are a crowded procession of inaccuracies and misstatements. Those beloved illustrations were stock cuts brought together from various sources and used in the sub-

* Buel, J. W., *Heroes of Unknown Seas and Savage Lands* (Philadelphia, 1891).

[xi]

scription volume. Dom Vasco, discussing the chart of his projected voyage with Dom Manuel, is shown as a wild-eyed old man with a white spade beard. A few pages further on he is depicted as an Elizabethan gallant with an imperial beard, receiving the envoy of the King of Calicut; and in truth he was hardly thirty when he set out on his memorable voyage.

But, though wiser and sadder for this seeing of the book after more than half a century, none the less I cherish it, for it first fired my imagination and interest in history and travel; and though I have visited and sojourned in many of the scenes in its pages, none of what my eyes have beheld in the flesh is as thrilling as those which I visited on its magic carpet, which annihilated time and space, and gilded all with the aura of the golden age of childhood. And to its giver, Miss Annie Harris, of Giddings, Texas, now long gathered to her fathers, I bow my head in affection and homage.

H. H. H.

PROLOGUE:
THE FORERUNNERS

So I iudge, there is no land vnhabitable nor Sea innavigable.
From "The booke made by . . . M. Robert Thorne in the yeere
1527 . . . to Doctour Ley, Lord Ambassadour for King Henry the
eight."—HAKLUYT, *Voyages* (ed. 1598–1600), I, 219

CHAPTER I

PORTUGAL

O kingdom of Portugal,
Where the land comes to its end
And the great sea begins,
And where, in the ocean,
Phoebus seeks his repose.
—Camões, *Os Lusíadas*, III, xx

NE of the most astonishing achievements of history is the discovery of nearly half of the world by the tiny nation of Portugal, whose people at the time numbered little over a million—an achievement compassed, too, in less than a century. The studies by historians of the voyages of Columbus have overshadowed those of the Portuguese, and many accounts of the Portuguese expeditions have lain forgotten for years, or even centuries, in dusty, unread volumes and unpublished manuscripts. The Portuguese themselves have neglected to spread the story of their own exploits, and the first real movement toward publishing and annotating them has been undertaken only within the last few decades. Much valuable material probably still lies buried in the national and colonial archives. Of many of the voyages—even of some of great importance—we possess mere outlines or brief references by contemporary or later writers. Numerous accounts have probably vanished forever, and "hundreds of 'Rutters' [1] exist in public and private libraries in Portugal and elsewhere, for the most part unread."

A study of the map of Portugal will reveal the compelling reasons that caused her people to take to the sea early in their history. To the east and north lay the kingdoms of Spain, cutting her off by land from the countries in those directions. Situated at the extreme southwestern corner of the Continent, she was the last western outpost of European civilization, and was within close touch with the Moslem coast of North Africa. Her coastline, though only about three hundred miles long, has many deep and safe harbors, espe-

[2]

cially for ships of shallow draft. All of her larger rivers flow into the Atlantic, and at their mouths or farther up on their banks the important cities of the kingdom developed and expanded.

From the end of the eleventh century, when Count Henry of Burgundy answered the summons of Alfonso of León to aid in his struggle against the Moors, Portugal's commercial, social, and political life has been separate from that of Spain. In return for assistance rendered, Alfonso gave Count Henry his illegitimate daughter Theresa in marriage, together with the counties of Oporto and Coimbra as a dowry, and conferred on him the title of Count of Portugal. The history of Portugal as a separate nation dates from 1095, when Henry entered his domain as a feudal lord owing allegiance to Galicia, one of the three kingdoms of Alfonso. But within two generations Portugal had broken away from Galicia and begun its independent career.

We are not concerned with the subsequent history of the development and expansion of the kingdom until the great age of discovery. It need only be noted that the course of events mainly followed that of contemporary Spain: the consolidation of royal power, the subduing of feudal lords, the wars with the Moors, the firm establishment of Catholicism, the gradual development of national and local administrative institutions, the founding of schools—including the famous University of Coimbra—and the development of a truly national sentiment among the people. The population, though of mixed races and creeds, lived happily together—Christian, Mohammedan and Jew—until the Inquisition lit the fires of persecution in the sixteenth century. Then the dominant group turned in hatred, ignorance, and blind fanaticism against the less fortunate minorities and in the end destroyed those very qualities of courage, skill, and industry which had built the country into a stalwart, prosperous nation and brought it to the low estate from which it has not recovered even in our own day.

The geographical position of Portugal has favored constant commercial and social intercourse with North Africa from the earliest times, together with migration and invasion from the southern shores of the Mediterranean. The result has been a blending of bloods—white, black, and brown—so that the Portuguese people are an extraordinary mixture of races. This mingling of racial strains developed in the Portuguese peculiar characteristics, which contributed not a little to the urge for discovery, invasion, exploration, and settlement of lands whose inhabitants were all of the darker groups, with mores and manners far removed from those of Europe.

As a group they were by heredity adjusted to living in the tropics. Sexual intermixture in early Portuguese history, when negro, Phoenician, Berber, and Moorish invaders often raided her shores, tended through the centuries to shake, then to weaken and finally break down the bar of color, making unions with the natives of conquered lands quite acceptable; and the offspring of such unions did not bear the stigma with which the half-caste has been branded in many lands.* The continued presence of large numbers of Moors in the kingdom for centuries brought to the people, besides the admixture of foreign blood, strong Semitic characteristics of mobility and adaptability, both of the group and the individual. To these were added the superior skills not only of the Moors but of the large number of Jews in their midst. Moreover, the Moslem strain contributed easygoing ways, vagueness, fatalism, and the superstitions of ancient pagan cults, together with a strong element of salaciousness and sexual laxity. The blond group from the north could not entirely resist these infiltrations, especially as the southern invaders brought with them superior techniques and skills in agriculture, handicrafts, and the sciences, and among other material contributions, the olive, the vineyard, cotton, the silkworm, sugar cane, and the water wheel.† It is interesting to note with Freyre that all the noble families of Portugal, even those who most distinguished themselves by killing infidels, have Arab or Moorish (and in many cases, Jewish) blood. To these were later added the blood of black and brown slaves, brought to the homeland by priest, trader, and conqueror.

This extraordinary fusing of physical and mental characteristics, in conjunction with its geographical position, its great variety of maritime and trading stimuli, and the economic pressure of an always poorly nourished people, may explain the astonishingly rapid ascent of Portugal to its brief but brilliant maritime and commercial

---

* This phase of Portuguese social mores (in Brazil) is ably presented in a fascinating manner by Gilberto Freyre, in his book *The Masters and the Slaves,* translated from his *Casa Grande e Senzala* (New York, 1946).

† To this day, moreover, countless words and phrases in the Portuguese language attest to the Moorish contributions. Even the word "mourejar"—to labor hard or diligently—meant originally "to work like a Moor."

supremacy in Europe. Its people were beyond a doubt ideally prepared for the great adventure that lay before them. In addition to
all the factors here so briefly stated must be added the preeminence
of the Arabs in nautical science and their development of scientific
aids to nagivation, together with their vast experience in practical
seamanship. Of all of these the Portuguese were able to avail themselves in their close contacts with Barbary.

Though there were early pioneers of other nations—Phoenicians,
Italians, Catalans, English, and Normans—who preceded the Portuguese in daring to sail unknown seas, with their terrible, mythical
monsters and the real dangers of savage lands beyond the horizon, it
was Portugal which first sent out successive and systematic exploring
expeditions into the Atlantic and along the West African coast, and
the Portuguese mariners developed nautical science to the highest
point that it reached until comparatively modern times.

NOTES

[1] Rutters (Portuguese, *roteiros*): the earliest type of seamen's manuals,
traceable to ancient Greek times. They were journals or pilot books of voyages,
containing details of landmarks, anchorages, shoals, watering places, currents,
tides, winds, etc. Compiled gradually, and corrected and supplemented as time
went on, they have never been superseded. The first printed rutters known are
those of Pòrtugal.

CHAPTER II

PRINCE HENRY THE NAVIGATOR

Por mares nunca de antes navegados.
(Over seas that never had been crossed before.)
—CAMŌES, *Os Lusíadas*, I, i

HE one man to whom more than to any other was due the advancement of nautical science in Europe and the systematic expansion of maritime enterprise in Portugal was the Infante Enriques, better known to the world as Prince Henry the Navigator.

Born in 1394, Henry, the third son of King John I and Philippa of Lancaster, daughter of John of Gaunt, as a boy had heard numberless tales of the Moors and his people's wars with them. He had heard as well marvelous stories of Africa—of the caravans that came up out of the Sahara heavily laden with ivory and gold dust, ostrich plumes and skins—and lurid accounts of wild beasts and wilder people. From early boyhood he appears to have had his thoughts ever turned to the Dark Continent, of which only the northern fringe was known to Europe. Winning his spurs in 1415 as a soldier at the siege of Ceuta, in Morocco, his experiences there aroused a deeper interest in Africa than ever. He greedily absorbed every available bit of information concerning the routes followed by the caravans from the far interior, and learned much from the merchants of Oran about articles of trade and the people in the hinterland. He added to his store of knowledge the tales of traders from Timbuktu and Gambia and the Niger country. He studied all the maps that he could find—even though they were very crude, and more often inaccurate than correct. He studied minutely the more scientific charts drawn with care by the Jewish cartographers of Majorca. When finally the expedition returned from Ceuta to Portugal, the prince resolved to bend every effort to seek a road to the rich lands of Guinea by way of the sea, and so to avoid dealing with the Arabs of the African Mediterranean littoral. For the remainder of his life (with the exception of certain political episodes with which we are not concerned here) he concentrated all his thoughts, efforts, and resources to the accomplishing of this end.

Henry's motives in his enterprise were manifold, and historians have not ceased to this day their arguments and disagreements about his character or his aims. According to Henry's contemporary chronicler, Gomes Eanes Azurara, the prince had five reasons which motivated him in his project. The first was "a wish to know the land that lay beyond the Canaries and Cape Bojador, and to this he was stirred by his zeal for the service of God and of the King Edward his lord and brother who then reigned." The second was to develop trade with such lands, especially Christian, "which traffic would bring great profit to our countrymen." The third was to learn as much as possible "how far the power of the infidels extended" in Africa. The fourth was the desire to find a Christian monarch who would aid Portugal in its wars against the same infidels. The fifth was to send out missionaries "to bring to him all the souls that should be saved."

Of these reasons the first was a utilitarian one—to expand and develop a knowledge of geography. The second and fourth were doubtless based on the legends and vague reports of the land of Prester John, supposedly in East Africa or Asia. The fifth reason was a desire to proselytize—for the crusading spirit was by no means dead in Portugal, and played an important part in the early Portuguese maritime enterprises.

It is a strange paradox that the prince to whom history usually refers as the Navigator hardly ever "navigated." The longest voyages that he made were probably never out of sight of land. They were between Portugal and the African coasts about Ceuta and Tangier. None the less he was the initiator of the era of great discoveries by sea.

This does not imply that Henry's ideas, plans, and enterprises were entirely original, for maps, portolanos, sailing directions, rutters, and traditions of the sea had existed from earliest times. Moreover, innumerable merchants, pilgrims, and missionaries had wandered through the Levant and much of Asia during the period of the Crusades, and later had furnished much valuable information, as well as a stimulus, to the search for a direct sea route to the rich

East by way of Africa—provided there was open ocean between—
a point about which there was much doubt in Europe.

Portugal was the logical point of departure for such a quest. Its
harbors had been for centuries ports of call for the traffic between
the Mediterranean and the coasts of the countries in the west, as
well as with the British Isles. Moreover, the land itself faced the
unknown, unexplored, and mysterious Atlantic.

Whether the project of finding a sea road to the Indies was
uppermost or even of great importance in the mind of Prince Henry
in his early enterprises is open to grave doubt. However, it seems
certain that with the passing of the years it eventually became his
most cherished dream and desire. Moreover, as one discovery followed another along the African coast, and as better maps were
made, winds and currents more closely and carefully studied, and
instruments and methods of navigation perfected, the chances of
finding such a sea route became increasingly probable.

The prize promised to be worth the struggle. It meant capturing
at least a large part of the wealth that was pouring into the coffers
of Venice and Genoa, as well as into Moslem treasuries, for it meant
obtaining both the cargoes and the carrying trade of the Indies.
Henry's immediate object, however, was to divert the desert trade
which was enriching the Barbary despots and forcing the galleys
and caravels of the Christians to seek their cargoes in infidel ports.
Then, too, as he was Grand Master of the Order of Christ, the
opportunity of entering new and virgin fields for the conversion of
the heathen was one not to be neglected.

Henry's projects brought in their train many problems of navigation which required solution before any considerable measure of
success was to be expected. The leaders of each expedition brought
back charts of the coasts they visited, sailing directions, notes on
landmarks for taking bearings, on winds, shoals, rocks, safe and
dangerous anchorages, places where water, wood, and food might
be obtained, and so on. For future and repeated voyages all these
data had to be collated and systematized. This brought about careful charting of larger and larger areas and made ventures into more
extensive operations safer. But the most important difficulty in the
prince's undertakings was the finding of solutions of certain astronomical problems the answers to which were all-important for successful deep-sea navigation. It was in this field that Prince Henry,

his collaborators, and successors were eminently successful, raising the Portuguese mariners in an incredibly short time to the position of the foremost navigators of Europe. Other merchant marines, such as those of Genoa and Venice, were indeed very important, but their voyages followed well known and constantly traveled routes, with the object of transporting Oriental goods to European ports and taking back European products to the East. The Portuguese also sailed to the Levant, Normandy, and England, and had warehouses and agents in Flanders. Now, however, they were to strike boldly out into unknown seas and explore savage lands, to struggle not only against the perils of the sea but to throw off the age-old accumulation of superstitions, the imagined terrors and horrors of the world beyond the horizon which had haunted mankind since its childhood.

Henry's real activities began after his Ceuta experience, though contemporaries tell of ships dispatched by him along the African coast as early as 1412. They recount, too, that "he always kept a number of armed ships at sea to guard against the infidels, who then made very great havoc upon the coasts both on this side the straits and beyond; so that the fear of his vessels kept in security all the shores of our Spain and the greater part of the merchants who traded between East and West."

The better to concentrate on his plans and supervise their execution, the prince left Lisbon and settled in or near the town of Lagos, in the southern Algarve region of Portugal. He also established a small town named for him "Villa do Infante," very near Cape Saint Vincent. These havens had already been visited often by vessels of many nations passing in and out of the Strait of Gibraltar, as they were most convenient shelters and well fitted for the watering, provisioning, careening, and repairing of ships. He employed the finest mathematicians, cartographers, and makers of nautical instruments that he could attract to him. The most competent and famous was Jahuda Cresques (better known as Master Jacome), a Jew.

The most difficult mathematical problem propounded to Henry and his collaborators was fixing with certainty the position of a ship at sea or a point on the land. The stars had been used for centuries, and after the twelfth century the compass, brought from China probably by the Arabs, and elaborated by them and their Christian rivals, came into common use. Then came the cross-staff, astrolabe, and quadrant, all of which had been developed to a high degree of efficiency by the Arabs, who for centuries had made long voyages across the seas between Asia, Africa,. and India. These various instruments and their use were for the most part introduced by the Jews of Spain and Portugal, who were often the intermediaries between the Moslems and their Christian neighbors.[1]

As the mariners crept farther down the western coast of Africa, they entered the findings of their instruments on their maps and in their logbooks, so that gradually more or less reliable charts became available to those following them. At the beginning the entries were careless and haphazard, according to the disposition and whim of the individual navigator. The notations were not accurate, nor, as King Affonso V stated in a royal letter of October 22, 1443, "were they [the lands beyond Cape Bojador] marked on sailing charts or mappe-mondes except as it pleased the men who made them." Prince Henry corrected this, and ordered that all information derived from observations of his officers be entered on their navigation charts. Proceeding carefully along these lines, the Portuguese became the founders of the modern science of cartography. Unfortunately, the original maps and instruments used before the sixteenth century have disappeared through fire, loss, carelessness, or in the great Lisbon earthquake of 1755. But the results remain.

Thus the Infante, with dogged and undaunted persistence, led his people on a quest which, before it lost its impetus, had covered the seven seas. The results of his lifetime of planning and effort, examined from the modern viewpoint—when men are equipped with every scientific device for navigation, reliable charts, swift ships not dependent on wind or current, and well provided with food and every protection for the personnel—may seem pitifully meager. But when we consider the tiny tonnage of their vessels, dependent entirely upon sails, the crudeness of their equipment, the comparative ignorance of their navigators, the pathetic inadequacy of their provisions, their ignorance of the seas they sailed and the lands they sought, the achievement of the Portuguese borders on the incredible.

NOTES

[1] The greatest question was that of fixing longitude, for latitude could be worked out fairly correctly by the North Star—at least until the mariners lost sight of it in the south. Later, in the days of John II, a new method of calculating latitude was developed by observations of the noonday sun and the use of tables of declination. The most famous of these tables was the *Almanach Perpetuum* of Abraham Zacuto (published in 1473-1478). He was Professor of Astronomy at Salamanca, Spain, and later became the Portuguese Astronomer Royal. From this almanac simplified, practical manuals were prepared for the use of the often unlettered mariners. It may be added that the problem of fixing longitudes was not entirely solved until the perfection of the chronometer in the eighteenth century. A common practice (said to have been followed by Columbus) was to sail north or south along a coast until the parallel of latitude was reached which it was believed would lead to the desired destination, and to follow due east or west as the case might be.

CHAPTER III

EARLY DEEP-SEA VENTURES

Lands where our fleets
In their wanderings, saw new marvels.
—CAMÕES, *Os Lusíadas,* V, viii

HE first deep-sea voyages of the Portuguese were probably those to the Canaries and the Azores in the early part of the fourteenth century. Though there is no record of any such voyages in the latter half of that century, the silence of the chronicles or other records proves nothing, except perhaps that no discoveries made were deemed worthy of record. During this period Lisbon was a free port, and a contemporary avers that hundreds of vessels, many of them foreign, were always lying in the Tagus, loading or unloading. The king encouraged the merchant marine in numerous ways, such as granting wood from the royal Portuguese forests free to shipbuilders and remitting import duty on other materials used in ship construction. In addition merchandise brought in on the first voyage of a Portuguese ship paid lower duties, owners of ships were partially relieved of military service, official shipping records were begun, and a cooperative system of marine insurance was established. All of these innovations stimulated shipbuilding activity and maritime trade under the Portuguese flag so that when Henry was ready to begin his more ambitious enterprises he had a fine working nucleus of vessels, navigators, and crews ready at hand.

The first ships were sent out by the prince in 1412 or 1415. They reached Cape Bojador (the Bulging Cape), so called because of the great western curve of the African coast at that point. Though twelve years were spent in efforts to round the headland, expedition after expedition turned back, dismayed and baffled by the maze of currents, shoals, and adverse winds that greeted them. Added to these were the imaginary terrors of the deep—very real to the ignorant, superstition-ridden mariners—demons of the storm, fabu-

lous monsters, whirlpools, sirens, mermaids, and all the other creatures of tradition that had been transmitted from the mists of early
time.

In 1433 Henry sent out Gil Eanes with imperative orders to
double the cape. He failed the first time, but in 1434 succeeded in
overcoming all the obstacles in his path. He was able to demonstrate
that open water lay to the south, and that navigation was feasible
where his predecessors had declared it to be impossible. In 1435
Eanes set out once more, and sailed to a point 150 miles beyond
the cape. Baldaya, Henry's cupbearer, following Eanes's lead,
reached the Rio do Ouro, 240 miles south of Bojador, in the same
year, and in 1436 touched a point 50 miles still farther south.

As the ships returned one after another with their tales of adventure by land and sea, Prince Henry's curiosity was whetted as to
the character of the peoples and the lands visited, and he instructed
his sea captains to bring some of the natives back to Portugal with
them. In obedience to the Infante's orders, Antam Gonçalves, one
of his captains, returned in 1441 with

ten blacks, male and female . . . and besides the blacks . . . he got
also a little gold dust and a shield of ox-hide, and a number of ostrich
eggs, so that one day there were served up at the Infante's table three
dishes of the same, as fresh and as good as though they had been the
eggs of any other domestic fowls. And we may well presume that there
was no other Christian prince in this part of Christendom, who had
dishes like these upon his table.*

In 1443 Nuno Tristão sailed farther south to Arguin Bay and
"saw that twenty-five canoes made of wood had set out, and in them
a number of people, but all naked, not so much for the need of swimming in the water, as for their ancient custom." They pursued the
luckless blacks and captured fourteen of them, and later seized fifteen more, all of whom they took back to Portugal.

Meanwhile the Portuguese had been directing an ever increasing
volume of severe criticism and even derision at Henry's expeditions
as a shameful and useless waste of money. When, however, a few
boatloads of negroes had been brought in, they changed their tune,
and even extravagantly and loudly proclaimed that "it was plain
the Infante was another Alexander." Perhaps the arrival on Portu-

* Azurara, I, 57.

guese shores of the captured blacks meant to the prince an opening wedge in the conversion of the African "gentiles," but to the more mundane-minded men who surrounded him these naked savages had a far different significance. In Azurara's words: "Their covetousness now began to wax greater. And, as they saw the houses of others full to overflowing of male and female slaves, and their property increasing, they thought about the whole matter and began to talk among themselves."

The time was ripe for the importation of cheap labor into Portugal. The country had never been densely populated. The toll of wars with Castile, the expeditions against Ceuta and Tangier in Morocco and elsewhere, and the heavy impositions of taxes were such that the people were hard put to it to support themselves. Labor was desperately needed both on the land and in the cities. Henry's enterprises brought opportunity to the very door of the shrewd and calculating.

Slavery was an age-old institution in the world, and little, if any, peccancy or moral obliquity was attached to it.* Moreover, the African natives, being heathen, were, according to Barros, "outside the law of Christ, and at the disposition, so far as their bodies were concerned, of any Christian nation." Immediately applications were made to Henry (who held the monopoly of African commerce) for licenses for the African coastal trade. The first was granted to Lançarote, one of the prince's retainers. His expedition of six armed caravels set out in state for the south, and in due time arrived at an inhabited island just off the Guinea Coast. Azurara tells the story:

The "Moors" † having evidently had unfortunate experience with former white visitors, with their women and children were already coming as quickly as they could out of their houses, because they had caught sight of their enemies. But they, crying "St. James," "St. George," and "Portugal," attacked them at once, killing and taking all they could. Then might you see mothers forsaking their children, and husbands their wives, each striving to escape as best he could. Some drowned themselves in the water; others sought to escape by hiding under their huts; others concealed their children among the seaweed

* Cf. Hart, *Venetian Adventurer,* 3rd ed. (Stanford University Press, 1947), p. 17.

† The general Portuguese term of the period for any people of African descent.

(where our men found them afterward), hoping that they would thus escape notice. And at last our Lord God, who giveth a reward for every good deed, willed that for the toil they had undergone in his service, they should that day obtain victory over their enemies, as well as a guerdon and a payment for all their labor and expense; for they took captive of those Moors, what with men, women and children, 165, besides those that perished and were killed.

Thus the chronicler airily sketches the picture of an attack by heavily armed and armored men on a village of defenseless, naked savages, and in the very simplicity of the narrative reveals the callousness with which the Portuguese regarded the natives.

As soon as the Portuguese had rested and feasted after the "battle," they extorted from their prisoners information about other inhabited islands, "where they would be able to make large captures with little trouble." The episode is but a foretaste of the actions of the Portuguese throughout the whole period of the discovery and exploitation of their empire. The account of the voyage continues with a description of the capture of several small parties of unarmed men and women and of binding and loading them on the vessels—but one notes that the Europeans fled when the natives outnumbered and threatened to overwhelm them. Then the Portuguese would take to their boats and move on to the next place where they might capture more of the helpless people unawares. Finally, after a whole village had fled, "so that they only found one girl, who had remained sleeping in the village, they took her with them," and, returning to the caravels, made sail for Portugal.

The arrival of the flotilla at Lagos marks a turning point in the world's history, for that day saw the beginning of the shameful, inhuman modern European trade in African slaves. It was a trade that was to debauch a nation and drag it down, after a short-lived eminence, to utter impotence in world affairs, a trade that was to sully the flag of every country that engaged in it, and one which not only was to cause the ruthless destruction of countless black men, women, and children but was to be the cause of the greatest and bloodiest civil war in history, and of some of the most serious unsolved problems of modern society.

The prince himself was on hand to receive the ships with their 235 miserable captives. His people swarmed down to the shore, some even went in boats to hail the returning heroes, "and you may

guess what would be their joy among their wives and children."
Not so happy was to be the lot of the poor black folk. Let Azurara
himself speak. His story needs no adornment or commentary:

And next day Lançarote said to the Infante: "My Lord, your grace
well knows that you are to receive the fifth part of these Moors, and of
all that we have gained in that land, whither you sent us for the service
of God and of yourself. And now these Moors, because of the long
time we have been at sea, as well as for the great sorrow that you must
consider they have at heart, at seeing themselves away from the land
of their birth, and placed in captivity, without having any understanding of what their end is to be, and moreover because they have not
been accustomed to a life on shipboard, for these reasons are poorly
and out of condition. Wherefore it seems to me that it would be wise
to order them taken from the caravels at dawn and to be placed in the
field which lies outside the city gate, and there to be divided into five
parts, according to custom, and that your grace should go there and
choose one of these parts, whichever you prefer. . . ."

But before they did anything else in that matter they took as an
offering the best of those Moors to the church of that place, and another little Moor, who afterward became a Friar of St. Francis, they
sent to St. Vincent do Gabo.

O Thou Heavenly Father . . . I pray Thee that my tears may not
wrong my conscience, for it is not their [the negroes'] religion but
their humanity that maketh mine to weep in pity for their sufferings.
And if the brute animals, with their bestial feelings, by a natural
instinct understand the sufferings of their own kind, what wouldest
Thou have my human nature to do on seeing before my eyes that
miserable company, and remembering that they, too, are of the generation of the sons of Adam?

On the next day . . . very early in the morning, by reason of the
heat, the seamen began . . . to take out those captives and to carry
them on shore, as they were commanded. And these, all placed together in that field were a marvelous sight, for amongst them were
some white enough, fair to look upon, and well proportioned; others
were less white, like mulattoes; others, again, were as black as Ethiopians, and so ugly, both in features and in body, as almost to appear to
those who saw them the images of a lower hemisphere. But what heart
could be so hard as not to be pierced with piteous feelings to see that
company? For some kept their heads bowed and their faces bathed in
tears, looking one at the other; others stood groaning very dolorously,
looking up to the heights of Heaven, fixing their eyes upon it, crying
aloud, as if asking help of the Father of Nature; others struck their
faces with the palms of their hands, throwing themselves at full length

upon the ground; others made their lamentations in the manner of a
dirge, after the custom of their country. And though we could not
understand the words of their language, the sound of it right well
accorded with the measure of their sadness. But to increase their sufferings still more, there now arrived those who had charge of the division
of the captives, and who began to separate one from another, in order
to make an equal partition of the fifths, and then was it needful to part
fathers from sons, husbands from wives, brothers from brothers. No
respect was shown either to friends or relations, but each fell where his
lot took him.

O powerful fortune, that with thy wheel doest and undoest, com-
passing the matters of this world as pleaseth thee, do thou at least put
before the eyes of that miserable race some understanding of matters
to come, that they may receive some consolation in the midst of their
great sorrow. And you, who are so busy in making that division of the
captives, look with pity on so much misery, and see how they cling one
to the other, so that you can hardly separate them.

And who could finish that partition without very great toil? For as
often as they had placed them in one part, the sons, seeing their fathers
in another, rose with great energy and rushed over to them; the
mothers clasped their other children in their arms and threw themselves flat on the ground with them, receiving blows with little pity for
their own flesh, if only they might not be torn from them.

And so troublously they finished the partition, for besides the toil
they had with the captives, the field was quite full of people from the
town and from the surrounding villages and districts, who for that day
gave rest to their hands (in which lay their power to get their living)
for the sole purpose of beholding this novelty. And with what they saw,
while some were weeping and others separating the captives, they
caused such a tumult as greatly to confuse those who directed the partition.

The Infante was there, mounted on a powerful steed, and accompanied by his retinue, making distribution of his favors, as a man who
sought to gain but small treasure from his share, for of the forty-six
souls that fell to him as his fifth, he made a very speedy distribution of
these, for his chief riches lay in [the accomplishment of] his purpose,
for he reflected with great pleasure upon the salvation of those souls
which before were lost.

And so the great Prince Henry, Grand Master of the Order of
Christ, a man who had vowed for himself perpetual virginity, who
is supposed to have lived only for the highest of ideals and purposes, sat calmly upon his horse, presiding unmoved over the division of his plunder, the flesh and blood of human beings, tearing

wives from husbands and parents from children, and bestowing them as gifts to his favorites, with never a thought of the sufferings being heaped on the heads of the poor slaves, so intent was he on saving their souls! Strange and unbelievable as it may appear to the modern mind, this was not hypocrisy but the genuine spirit of the age. And Azurara is evidently perfectly sincere when he concludes:

And so their lot was now quite the contrary of what it had been, since before they had lived in perdition of soul and body, of their souls, in that they were yet pagans without the clearness and light of the holy faith, and of their bodies, in that they lived like beasts . . . for they had no knowledge of bread or wine, and they were without the covering of clothes, or the lodgment of houses, and worse than all, through the great ignorance that was in them, in that they had no understanding of good, but only knew how to live in a bestial sloth. . . . And now consider what a reward should be that of the Infante at the hands of the Lord God, for having thus given them the chance of salvation, and not only them, but many others whom he afterward acquired. . . .

And so forthwith he [Prince Henry] made Lançarote a knight, giving him a rich reward, according to his deserts and as his excellence required. And to the other leaders also he gave increased advancement, so that besides their first profit they considered their labor well bestowed.

And thus began in the Vedoria (market) of Lagos in Portugal the modern European trade in black biped animals. Before it ended, the infamous traffic was responsible for the forcible removal of at least twelve million black Africans from their native land, and for the death of as many.[1]

A new era had opened for Portugal. Black ivory and white, gold, and Guinea pepper,[2] these were the attractions that aroused the enterprising Lusitanian spirit to more venturesome voyages, more extensive slave raids, more explorations—and ever growing profits. The resulting influx of negro slaves, together with the governmental policy of encouraging marriages between them and the Portuguese (who responded to the official encouragement with alacrity), slowly but inexorably caused a profound alteration in the characteristics of the people.*

* It should be added that the majority of the slaves were, according to contemporary writers, well treated by their masters. Many learned trades, became freemen, and married Portuguese women; and their descendants were gradually absorbed into the white population.

In 1444 Nuno Tristão reached the Senegal River, and the following year Dinis Dias rounded Cape Verde. As slave raiding was an integral part of these expeditions, the news spread rapidly by native grapevine along the coast, with resultant bitter hostility of the natives and the killing of some of the Portuguese leaders.[3]

By 1446 fifty-one vessels had entered the African trade and had pushed over 450 leagues beyond Cape Bojador. For some unknown reason little is recorded of Portuguese exploration for some years after 1448. Beyond a doubt trade went steadily forward, the bolder mariners adventuring slowly farther and farther southward along the African coast, feeling their way among the unknown winds, currents, and shoals, and ever preying on the natives when they could seize them unawares. The Portuguese, moreover, were gradually consolidating their position on the African coast with fortified settlements and factories. In fact, colonization had begun. The west coast was slowly emerging from the mists of the unknown and the uncertain into the light of day. Little by little the gloom and the dread of fabled monsters and imagined terrors of the old tales were dissipated in the sunlight of experience, knowledge, and common sense.

For the most part, though the Portuguese realized that the goods offered them at their coastal stations were, chiefly, from the hinterland, they were content to confine their trading activities to the immediate vicinity of the shore. The traffic in the interior was in a great measure in the hands of courageous Jews, who penetrated far inland or who even reached remoter sections by camel caravan from the north by way of the oases of the Sahara. Evidences of this are found in the carefully drawn maps made by their coreligionists of Majorca, whence came the finest cartographers of the period. Some of these maps, even those dating back as far as 1375, show Timbuktu, the Atlas Mountains with a caravan pass, and crude pictures of "the Lord of the negroes of Guinea." The goods bartered with the simple natives in exchange for their ivory, ebony, gold, skins, and slaves were glass beads, mirrors, knives, bells, bright-colored cloth, and the like. These are still the "trade goods" exchanged at remote interior points of Africa.

Though the Portuguese ships had probably found their way to Sierra Leone by 1448, the wars with Castile (for possession of the

Canaries, 1451–1454) and with the Moors retarded the progress
of exploration during the remainder of Henry's life.

An account of one voyage made to the African coast during this
period is of great historical and geographical interest, however. It
is that of the Venetian adventurer Alvise Cadamosto,* who has
left a fascinating account of his travels in the service of Henry, and
who probably was the first to sight the Cape Verde Islands. Born
in Venice about 1426, he sailed to Candia (Crete) in 1445. Five
years later we find him a "noble bowman" on a "great galley" of
Alexandria, and still later he sailed on a Flanders galley. From the
few facts to be gleaned from contemporary writers, he had not been
trained as a navigator but was a gentleman trading adventurer. In
1454, because of his father's involvement in extensive litigation,
followed by banishment, Alvise left Venice with his younger brother
Antonio in search of adventure and fortune.

By chance Cadamosto's ship on the way to Flanders from Venice
was delayed by contrary winds off Cape Saint Vincent, not far
from Prince Henry's estate of Reposera. The prince, hearing that
an Italian vessel was offshore, sent a secretary on board with
samples of African coast products. These aroused the interest of
young Cadamosto, who "asked if the . . . lord permitted any who
wished to sail." When he was informed that his services would be
welcome, and learned of the conditions—the division of the cargoes
brought back, and so forth—he decided to fit out a caravel and
go to the African coast, for, as he wrote, "I was young, well fitted
to sustain all hardships, desirous of seeing the world and things
never seen before by our nation, and I hoped also to draw from it
honor and profit."

Cadamosto's galley sailed first to Madeira and the Canary
Islands, and thence down the coast of Africa, making notes everywhere of winds, currents, and places and peoples seen. His descriptions of the tribes visited are especially interesting and contain
much valuable information. The slave trade was in full swing
throughout the coast near Cape Blanco, and "ten or fifteen slaves are
given for one of these [Berber] horses, according to their quality."

* In Venetian, Alvise da Mosto, though the English form is more commonly
used. The house where he was born in Venice still stands on the Grand Canal,
near the Rialto Bridge. It bears a tablet inscribed: "Here was born Alvise da
Ca' da Mosto. He discovered the Cape Verde Islands. He showed the Portuguese the route to the Indies. By decree of the Municipality, 1881."

The Arabs also exchanged Granada and Tunis silk for human beings. "As a result, every year the Portuguese carry away from Arguin a thousand slaves." He also speaks of the desert Tuareg, describes their veiled faces, and calls them

Liars, the biggest thieves in the world, and very treacherous. . . . Their hair is black, and anointed daily with fish oil, so that it smells vilely, the which they consider a great refinement . . . that woman who has the largest breasts is considered more beautiful than the others, with the result that each woman, to increase their size, at the age of seventeen or eighteen, when the breasts have taken shape, draws a cord around her chest, binding down the breasts tightly. In this manner the breasts are stretched, and frequent daily pulling [of the cord] causes them to grow and lengthen so that many reach down to the navel. And those who have the largest hold them dear, as a rare thing.

We are told of the "silent trade" * in salt between the merchants and the blacks, the latter leaving a heap of salt and hiding, the former placing some gold by each heap. If satisfied, the black took the gold, the merchant the salt.

Cadamosto also observed a remarkable custom which has been rediscovered in our own day, and which is used with very salutary

---

* The "silent trade" is very ancient and has been practiced by many primitive peoples since the beginning of recorded history. Herodotus, writing in the fifth century B.C., recounted a tale told him by Carthaginians. They used to sail south beyond the Pillars of Hercules [the Strait of Gibraltar] to trade with the natives. They would unload and spread their goods on the beach, then build a fire to raise a column of smoke, and withdraw to their vessels. The natives would come down to the shore, examine the goods, lay by them what they considered their fair value in gold, and return to their hiding places near by. The Carthaginians would then row to shore and, if satisfied with the price offered, would take the gold and sail away. If not satisfied they would return to their ships and wait until enough gold had been added to satisfy them. "Neither party deals unfairly with the other, for they themselves never touch the gold until it comes up to the worth of their goods, nor do the natives ever carry off the goods till the gold has been taken away." Ammianus Marcellinus, the last of the great Roman historians (*ca.* A.D. 330), wrote of the Chinese that "when strangers cross their river to buy their cloth or any other of their merchandise, they interchange no conversation, but settle the price of the article wanted by nods and signs." Fa Hsien, a Chinese pilgrim who visited Ceylon early in the sixth century after Christ, informs us that the early inhabitants of the land were "devils, with whom the merchants of the neighboring countries traded by barter. . . . The devils did not appear, but set out their valuables with the price attached. The merchants then gave goods according to the prices marked, and took away the goods they wanted." [4]

results, but one which remained unnoted for nearly six hundred years
after Cadamosto was given his information.

The merchants of Mali, near Cape Blanco, could not have clearly
understood one of the causes of heat prostration, yet Cadamosto
records:

It is extremely hot at certain seasons of the year. This causes the blood
to putrify, so that, were it not for this salt, they would die. The remedy
they employ is the following: They take a small piece of the salt, mix
it in a jar with a little water, and drink it each day. They say that this
saves them.

After passing Cape Verde, Cadamosto's ships arrived at the
country of the true negro races, here represented by the Jalofo. The
slave trade was rampant everywhere, and captives were sold to both
Arabs and Portuguese. The customs of the people are described in
detail and make fascinating reading. "You should know too, that
the men of these countries perform many women's tasks, too, such
as spinning, washing clothes and such things." Here Cadamosto
landed and sold some horses and harness to the chief for one hundred slaves, and notes: "As soon as he saw me, he gave me a young
girl of twelve to thirteen years of age, pretty for all that she was
very black, and said that he gave her for the service of my bed-
chamber. I accepted her and sent her to my ship." Thereafter he
recounts an incident which revealed the remarkable swimming
powers of these coast negroes. He found it necessary to send a
message to his vessel standing three miles offshore, with high seas
running, much wind, shoals and sandbanks near the shore, and a
very strong current beyond. Two men volunteered to go. One
could not breast the waves and turned back; "the other stood firm,
struggled at the sand bank for a whole hour, finally crossed it,
carried the message to the ship, and returned with the reply. This
appeared a marvelous thing to me, whence I conclude that for a
certainty these negroes of the coast are the finest swimmers in the
world." And the charge for the service was two bars of tin, worth
a grosso each.

As he traveled along the coast, well received by the friendly
natives, some of whom were nominally Mohammedans, he marveled at many things, too numerous to discuss here—marriage customs, the king's way of holding audiences, the strange foods, palm

wine, snake charmers, poisoned weapons, and so on. He has, among
others, a delightful chapter on the elephant. He enjoyed visits to
the biweekly markets, mingling with the people and watching them
at their haggling and bartering—for they did not use money. He
recounts, too, how "the negroes, men and women both, came to
look at me, as though I were a marvel. . . . They were amazed
no less at my clothing than at my white color . . . some touched
my hands and arms, and rubbed me with saliva, to see if my white-
ness was a dye, or really flesh, and seeing that it was flesh, stood
agape with wonder."

Cadamosto amused himself hugely by inviting some of the
negroes to board his vessel. There they were terrified at the crossbows and the firing of a bombard. When he told them that more
than a hundred men could be killed by firing one shot, they were
astounded, saying that it was "an invention of the devil." One of
the sailors played a beribboned bagpipe, and they thought it a
living animal singing in different voices. When shown its mecha-
nism, they were sure that "God had made it with His own hands,
that it sounded so sweetly, and with so many different voices." The
equipment was beyond their comprehension, and they believed the
painted eyes were really eyes through which the ship was enabled
to see when it passed through the water.[5] Even a burning candle
was a miraculous thing to these simple folk, who knew no other
light than that of a fire. Cadamosto thereupon showed them how
to make candles out of the beeswax which the natives threw away
after extracting the honey. When he lighted one of the candles that
he had made, their admiration knew no bounds.

The vessel continued on its course, always within sight of land.
Other tribes were encountered, unfriendly and cruel and acknowl-
edging no overlord. All along this coast, Cadamosto remarks:

Each of our ships had negro interpreters, brought with us from
Portugal, who had been sold by their lords of Senegal to the first
Portuguese who came to discover this land of the Negroes. These slaves
had been made Christians, and knew the Spanish [6] language well, and
we had had them from their owners with the agreement that for the
stipend and pay of each we would give them [the owners] one head
[slave] for each, to be selected from our whole collection [of captives],
and if each of these interpreters would obtain four slaves for his owner,
the latter would grant him his freedom.

However, when one of these interpreters was hacked to pieces by some natives with their short swords when he landed to obtain information, Cadamosto decided that he had gone far enough in this hostile land, so he ordered anchors weighed and with all haste set sail southward to the river Gambia.

Sailing up the Gambia about four miles, the ships came upon seventeen war canoes with

about 150 [men] at the most, they appeared very well built, exceedingly black, and all clothed in white cotton shirts: some of them wore small white caps . . . on each side [of the caps] they had a white wing, with a feather in the middle of the cap. A negro stood in the prow of each canoe, with a round shield, apparently of leather, on his arm.

The negroes attacked forthwith, showering arrows on the ships, but they were quickly terrified and thrown into confusion by the firing of the bombards. Next, "the sailors began to fire at them with their crossbows; the first to discharge his arbalest was the bastard son of that Genoese gentleman [Antoniotto Usodimare, Cadamosto's partner in the African venture]. He hit a negro in the breast so that he immediately fell dead in the canoe." Though this at first frightened the natives and caused them to withdraw, they soon returned to the attack. "By the grace of God, however, not one of the Christians was hit," though the river was filled with dead and dying blacks. Finally an interpreter was able to persuade a canoe to come within bowshot. When he demanded to know why the vessels had been attacked, the answer was that "they had received news of our coming . . . for they firmly believed that we Christians ate human flesh and that we bought negroes only to eat them, and they did not want our friendship on any terms and wanted to kill us all." When, soon thereafter, the captain wanted to proceed farther up the river, the crews felt that they had had enough, "and with one accord began to cry out that they would not consent to any such thing, and what they had done for that voyage was enough." When the leaders realized that they had an incipient mutiny on their hands, they abandoned their plans, for, as Cadamosto remarked, the sailors were "men pigheaded and obstinate." So they "departed thence, holding their course toward Cape Verde, to return, in the name of God, to Spain."

In the following year (1456) the Italian with his Genoese partner again prepared two vessels to explore the Gambia River farther, and to continue southward along the coast. Prince Henry gave his blessing to the venture and even added a fully equipped caravel of his own. Cadamosto was more fortunate in his relations with the Gambia River natives than on his first visit. He found but little gold, however, and the sailors were attacked by severe fevers; so leaving the river, the ships ventured as far as the Rio Grande. No new lands were discovered except the Cape Verde Islands, but many novel things were seen on the voyage, and Cadamosto entered them in his account. He was a hardheaded man, and his narrative reads more like the report of a nineteenth century explorer than any of those of his predecessors, and may be taken as the first careful and accurate (for the time) description of lands visited and peoples studied. He was courageous and curious and even sampled all the new foods he encountered, from strange birds to turtles, and from odd fish to roasted and broiled elephant. He made notes on the peculiar long native paddles with circular blades, the dress of the natives, the tattooing of their women, and the methods of hunting the elephant. He described the hippopotamus and the giant bats, and numerous other oddities that he saw. He even had an elephant's foot and flesh salted to take home. These "I presented later in Spain to the Lord don Heurich [*sic*], who received them as a handsome gift, being the first that he had had from the country discovered through his energy."

Finally, when the ships reached a land whose people could not understand or be understood by the negro interpreters, Cadamosto gave up, turned back, and returned to Portugal with no further noteworthy incident.

As an appendix to his tale, Cadamosto added a brief account of the voyage of a nameless and otherwise unknown Portuguese friend to Africa. The young man had traveled with Piero de Sintra down the coast as far as Sierra Leone, and told Cadamosto the story of his adventures on his return home. The Italian made notes of his friend's observations on the people, their manners, and customs—among them the "marks made with hot irons on their faces and bodies."

This people have their ears pierced all around with holes, in which they wear divers little rings of gold, one behind the other, in a row, and they have the lower part of the nose pierced through the middle [septum], in which they wear a ring of gold fastened in the same manner as in our buffaloes, and when they wish to eat they pull it to one side.

The traveler told of the nakedness of the people near Sierra Leone,[7] and how, when three of these poor fellows came aboard one of the caravels, the Portuguese captain seized and retained one of them. "This they did in obedience to His Majesty the King." It was a standing order that captains were to "bring away a negro, by force or persuasion," from any land whose people spoke a language not understood by the interpreters. The unhappy man was taken back to Portugal and presented to the king, who tried in every way to find someone who understood his language:

Finally a negress, the slave of a Lisbon citizen, who had also come from a far country, understood him, not through his own language but through another known to both. What this negro told the king through this woman I do not know, save that he said that among other things found in his native country were live unicorns. The said lord, having kept him several months, shown him many things of his kingdom, and given him some clothes, very charitably had him carried by a caravel back to his own country.

So the narrative had a happy ending.[8]

Another account of the period records the voyage of Diogo Gomes to the coast of Senegambia in the caravel *Picanso*—one of the few names of vessels of the period that have been preserved. The ship was fitted out by Prince Henry and set sail in 1456 or 1457. The voyage did no more than fill in details of the descriptions of this portion of the African coast which had already been conveyed to Portugal by earlier explorers. The account of a second voyage made by Gomes two years later contains a bitter complaint that the trade in slaves was being ruined, "For whereas the Moors [on the Guinea Coast] used to give seven negroes for one horse, they gave them now no more than six." The narrative is noteworthy because it contains the first reference to the use of the quadrant in navigation. The tale ends with the return of Gomes to Lisbon, describes a visit of the king to Oporto and the savage and barbarous manner in which a Portuguese who had sold arms to the Moors was burned alive. A furnace of fire having been prepared, "the king ordered that they . . . throw him into it with his sword and gold."

In November, 1460, Prince Henry was gathered to his fathers

and buried in a chapel of the Monastery of Batalha. The founder of Portuguese nautical science, the pioneer in sending out systematic exploring expeditions, the dreamer who kept before him ever the goal of a sea route to the Indies died before his well laid plans came to fruition. But he will ever live in Portuguese and in world history for his great work which, thirty-eight years after his death, was crowned with the successful voyage of Vasco da Gama.

Duarte Pacheco Pereira,[9] a noted navigator and a contemporary of Gama, has written the Portuguese estimate of Prince Henry's achievement:

. . . he sent to Majorca for Master Jacome, a skilled maker of charts . . . and by many gifts and favors brought him to these realms, where he taught his skill to men. . . . All this and many other good things . . . were done by this virtuous prince, besides discovering Guinea as far as Serra Lyoa [Sierra Leone]. We must therefore pray God for his soul. . . . The benefits conferred on Portugal are such that its king and people are greatly indebted to him, for in the country which he discovered, a great part of the Portuguese people now earn their livelihood and the kings of Portugal derive great profit from this commerce; for . . . when the trade of this country [the African coast to Sierra Leone] was well ordered, it yielded yearly 3,500 slaves and more, many tusks of ivory, gold, fine cotton cloths, and much other merchandise. Therefore must we pray God for the soul of Prince Henry, for his discovery of this land led to the discovery of the other Guinea beyond Serra Lyoa and to the discovery of India, whose commerce brings us an abundance of wealth.

The Portuguese were most anxious to maintain a monopoly of their trade on the African coast, especially in view of conflicting Spanish claims. In pursuance of this aim it was the policy of the kings of Portugal, both during the lifetime of Henry and thereafter, to suppress or restrict as much information as possible concerning the seas traversed and the lands visited. Charts, globes, maps, and documents were censored or kept secret in order not to excite the jealousy or cupidity of other maritime powers, or to prevent their making practical use of the results of the Portuguese findings.*

* "She guarded her charts from the foreigner, and kept secret the reports of her master mariners. What Portuguese ship was it that left her carronades in Napier Broome Bay, in northwestern Australia? They are now at Navy Headquarters in Sydney: lean guns of brass, mounted with the P. Crown, dating from the fifteenth or the early sixteenth century."—Paul McGuire, *Australia, Her Heritage, Her Future.*

Sailors were forbidden to discuss their travels, accounts of voyages were tampered with, and an extensive organization of spies was maintained in foreign courts and ports. As late as 1501, Angelo Trevisan, secretary to the Venetian *oratore* in Spain, wrote to the chronicler Domenico Malipiero, who had made inquiries about Cabral's voyage to India, that "it is impossible to obtain a map of this voyage, for the king has decreed the penalty of death for anyone who sends it out of the country." [10]

The first important move made by King Affonso V in furthering the policy of the deceased Prince Henry was to lease the monopoly of the Guinea trade to Fernão Gomes, "a respected citizen of Lisbon," in 1469 for a period of five years, upon the condition that at least five hundred leagues of untraversed African coast be explored during its term. The king himself became a partner in the deal, for all the ivory obtained was to be sold to him at a fixed price, and he contracted in turn to sell it at a profit to Martin Eanes Boaviagen. The investment was a fortunate one for Gomes, as his agents, visiting the Gold Coast in January, 1471, found an abundance of alluvial gold. At the termination of a supplementary year's lease which the king granted him, Gomes (who had been knighted for fighting the Moors in Morocco) was appointed a royal councilor, and was assigned as his coat of arms "a shield with a field of silver, blazoned with three heads of negroes, each with three rings of gold in the ears and noses and a collar of gold around the neck, and also the new surname of 'da Mina' [of the mine] in memory of its discovery." The southernmost point reached by Gomes's pilots was Cape Saint Catherine, two degrees below the equator, and his expeditions had explored the seas from Liberia to the Cameroons. To their surprise they found that the coastline turned again from an easterly and westerly direction to a southerly course, dashing their hope that they had been skirting the southern coast of the continent.

In the quaint language of the chronicler Barros, "as all princes devote the greater part of life to the works of their inclination, King Dom Affonso came to neglect the affairs of this discovery, and to praise greatly those of the African war [in Morocco]." Therefore, at the termination of Gomes's lease, he handed over the direction of further trade and exploration to Dom John, his nineteen-year-old son, and promulgated strict laws, granting him a monopoly on the African coast, together with all the rights and privileges which Prince Henry had enjoyed. At the same time the old inducements of bonuses and rebates for those building and equipping sea-going vessels were renewed. Moreover, all ships in the African trade had to carry the royal licenses to avoid seizure as pirates.

Progress in exploration was greatly retarded, however, by the Portuguese-Castilian war of 1475 to 1479, during which freebooters from Flanders, England, and Spain cut into the trade and raided the coast settlements. The Portuguese held their African monopoly as a sacred possession, and waxed most indignant at such high-handed methods. One of their chroniclers of the period, writing of mariners from Flanders who "dared to sail with their merchandise to Mina" (now Elmina, on the Gold Coast), felt that they were fitly visited by divine wrath, for

as they did not fear the heavy excommunication of the Holy Fathers . . . and as they did not fear the prohibitions of the Holy Mother Church, God gave them a bad end; for on their return voyage from Mina . . . they anchored in twenty-five fathoms; but as the bottom all along this coast is full of rock it cut through their hawser during the night, and a wind blowing up from the sea drove their ship onto the beach, where it was wrecked. The negroes there ate the thirty-five Flemings who formed the crew.

When John II succeeded to the throne of Portugal in 1481, he immediately demonstrated his continued interest and determination to develop further both African trade and exploration.[11] His first expedition of importance was sent out in June, 1482, under the leadership of Diogo Cão, a mariner already familiar with the Guinea Coast.[12]

The voyages of Diogo Cão—of which surviving accounts are very brief—marked the first employment of stone *padrões*. Each was a column surmounted by a cube terminating in a cross, and inscribed on one side with the arms of Portugal, together with the name of the king and that of the explorer and the date of discovery in Latin and/or Portuguese on the other. The use of these padrões was an idea of King John's. They were to be set up on prominent landmarks at various important places visited, with four objectives in view. First, they were a concrete proof that the discoverer had reached the place claimed by him; second, thereafter they would be invaluable as landmarks; third, they would be unquestioned proof of the priority of Portuguese discovery and sovereignty; and finally, surmounted by the cross, they were to be the visible symbol of the Christian faith in heathen lands. Some of these padrões have been preserved or recovered in whole or in part, and representations of them appear on maps of the period.*

Cão proceeded cautiously along the coast, soon passing the most southerly point reached by Gomes's ships. In early August his vessels arrived at a region where the water was discolored and fresh several leagues out at sea, and with every indication that a large stream with a very powerful current was pouring out its waters somewhere in the vicinity. He landed and set up a padrão, calling it "the padrão of St. George," and naming the river Rio do Padrão—the "River of the Pillar." It was the mighty stream now known as the Congo.†

Cão sailed a short distance up the stream, conversing with the natives in sign language, and trading with them. Then the voyage was resumed southward along the coast of Angola to Cape Saint Mary, where he erected another padrão (now in a Lisbon museum). After seizing four natives as hostages for some of his men who had gone ashore into the interior and who had not returned, Cão sailed for Lisbon to report. On his arrival King John knighted him, granted him a pension, and sent him back to the coast in 1484 with the four hostages. When he arrived at the mouth of the Congo, he found his four "lost" men safe and sound, awaiting his return, so the hostages were released with appropriate gifts.

Again turning south along the coast, Cão proceeded nearly 1,500 miles beyond Cape Saint Catherine as far as Cape Cross.[13] From this point on the narratives differ. One states that Cão died near Cape Cross; another claims that he returned to Portugal. An undated carving on a rock on the bank of the lower Congo at Ielala would indicate that he reached a point some distance up the river. It is interesting to note that with his name on the rock appear those

* Before the introduction of the stone padrões perishable wooden crosses or inscriptions roughly carved on trees were used to mark important positions along the coast and to prove Portuguese priority of discovery and possession.

† This is the first mention in history of the Congo. In early documents and narratives it is often referred to as the Zaire.

of Pero de Escolar, who was later the pilot of one of Gama's ships, John de Santiago, who rounded the Cape of Good Hope with Bartholomeu Dias in 1487, and Gonçalo Alvares, the master of the *São Gabriel* in Gama's fleet.*

The reports of the various expeditions sent out by King John only whetted his appetite for more discoveries and more trade. Moreover, interest in Prester John, the legendary Christian monarch of a land situated somewhere in Africa or Asia, had been stimulated by stories brought to John by a visiting king from the Bight of Benin, in West Africa. The descriptions of the ruler bore a fancied resemblance to the stories that had filtered through Europe of Prester John, and his country and India gradually became the twin centers of the king's attention. Two expeditions were presently sent out in an effort to find both lands speedily. The former was that of Pero de Covilhan † by land, the latter under the leadership of Bartholomeu Dias by sea.

* The four padrões erected by Cão on his two voyages still survive either whole or in fragments, and the inscriptions on two are legible. The pieces of one were preserved as fetishes by the local natives until 1887, when they were recovered.

† See Chap. V.

NOTES

[1] A ghastly detailed eyewitness narrative of the trade as it was carried on as late as 1788 is given by Alexander Falconbridge, a surgeon on one of the ships, in a rare pamphlet entitled *An Account of the Slave Trade on the Coast of Africa* (London, 1788).

[2] At first, the Guinea Coast was called the Malagueta Coast, but in the middle of the sixteenth century English corsairs began to speak of Malagueta pepper as "Guinea grains," and the coast thereafter was referred to as the Guinea Coast. Guinea pepper—also called "Grains of Paradise"—the pungent seeds of *Amomum Melegueta,* was much used in early days as a substitute for pepper.

[3] Many of the African tribes were themselves addicted to slavery, and joined the Portuguese in their nefarious traffic.

Roger Barlow, in his *Brief Summe of Geographie,* written in 1540, recounts of the tribes of the Guinea Coast: "In this countrey one take another, as the brother the sister or brother and the father the sone, and sellis them to the shippis of Portugal that comes theder for pecis of clothe of colours and for rynges of latyn [brass], and so thei brynge them into speyne to selle for slavys."

[4] The "silent trade" in what is now Rhodesia is described by Gaspar Veloso in a report made to King Manuel about 1513 and very recently discovered by

Dr. Eric Axelson in Lisbon. See *Transactions of the Rhodesia Scientific Association*, Vol. XI, April, 1945, p. 73.

[5] Eyes have been painted on ships of many countries through the centuries. See C. Daryll Forde, *Ancient Mariners*, Chap. IV.

[6] Cadamosto uses "Spanish" for "Portuguese" and "Spain" for "Portugal" very often in his narrative.

[7] It is a common occurrence to see the magnificently built men and boys of the coast villages in this region swimming or running entirely naked on the seashore, as the author can attest from personal observation. This seems in no way to detract from their native dignity or self-respect. They appear more like nude bronze statues than like naked men. They are still splendid swimmers and boatmen.

[8] Cadamosto left Portugal in 1463, three years after the death of Prince Henry.

[9] Duarte Pacheco Pereira's book, *Esmeraldo de Situ Orbis*, though written in the first decade of the century, is still a most valuable volume of eyewitness information on the sea, the coast, and the peoples of the west coast of Africa as far south as the Cape of Good Hope. Only three books and a part of the fourth out of five projected books are extant. Unfortunately, the original manuscript was lost in the 18th century, but two copies lay in Portuguese libraries unnoticed until 1892, when the book was published in commemoration of the four hundredth anniversary of Columbus's voyage to America.

[10] "Da carta de qual viazo non è possible haverne, che il re ha messo pena la vita a chi la dà fora."

[11] As purely local developments in West Africa—interesting though they are—lie outside the purview of this book, they are for the most part omitted.

[12] During this period the whole of the West African coast was called "Guinea" by the Portuguese.

[13] The padrão set up by Cão at Cape Cross was found there in 1893, and is now in Germany.

CHAPTER IV

BARTHOLOMEU DIAS AND THE DISCOVERY OF THE CAPE OF GOOD HOPE

O sea of dread, with gloom o'erspread,
Fathomless sea!
Endlessly rave, endlessly rave
Thy waters black, and in many a cave
Green monsters will ever howling be.

Sea by night sobbing, through the night throbbing,
Loud-thund'ring sea!
In wind and cold, through wind and cold,
On thy waters dark go ships untold,
With sailors singing as in glee.
—GUERRA JUNQUEIRO, "The Voices of Fishermen's Huts."
  Translated from the Portuguese by Aubrey F. G. Bell.

O original report of Dias's memorable voyage has survived, some of its dates are unsettled,[1] and we are dependent on a few scanty chapters and references in contemporary chronicles for information on one of the most important events in maritime history. The results of the voyage were the first consequential factors in the broadening of Europe's world at the end of the fifteenth century. Though Columbus's voyages were to have more important and far-reaching effects on world history, the rounding of the southern end of Africa had more immediate consequences.

Of Bartholomeu Dias—or, to give him his full name, Bartholomeu Dias de Novaes—little is known prior to the time he set out on his momentous voyage of discovery. Speculation makes him one of the family of João Dias, who first doubled Cape Bojador, and of Dinis Dias, who discovered Cape Verde. An experienced navigator and a cavalier of the royal house, he had commanded a caravel in the expedition of Diogo d'Azambuja in 1481 to the African coast. He also had been at one time the superintendent of the royal warehouses in Lisbon. He received his appointment as commander of the fleet in October, 1486, but for some unknown reason the departure of the ships was delayed until August of the next year.

The ships were better and more carefully prepared and equipped than any that had been sent out before. With the definite goal of finding and rounding the southern point of Africa, this was not to be a mere coasting voyage, with frequent landings en route, but a determined effort to find a sea route to India. The Portuguese mariners were by now familiar with the Guinea Coast, and progress in the navigational sciences and shipbuilding had been phenomenally rapid in the preceding half-century. Moreover, a new and wise plan had been adopted. Many ships had been forced to land on hostile coasts or to return to Portugal prematurely because of the lack of provisions. Often, too, voyages as planned took the ships far out to sea, where the obtaining of much needed stores or fresh water was impossible. To correct this there was added to the two caravels (woefully small and inadequate by modern standards) a store ship, designed to carry extra food, water, spare stores, and equipment for replacements and repairs.*

The chief pilot was Pero d'Alenquer, one of the best known mariners of the period. He was close to the king and had been granted by royal patent the right to wear garments of silk, together with the adornment of a gold neck chain, to which was suspended the whistle of his office. Resende, the chronicler of Dom John's reign, in giving an account of a dinner of which D'Alenquer partook with his sovereign, refers to the mariner as a "muito grande piloto de Guiné." The following episode indicates the secure and confidential position of D'Alenquer, and also throws a significant side light on the strict secrecy with which the Portuguese crown endeavored to safeguard the African trade. D'Alenquer was seated at table with the king in the presence of a roomful of courtiers. A discussion arose as to the comparative merits of various types of vessels sailing the seas between Guinea and the Peninsula. The king remarked that *navios redondos* † could not make the voyage suc-

* Though it is by no means certain, Dias's flagship was probably called *São Cristovão*. Her commander was one Leitão, of whom nothing is known; his name may be a nickname, as "leitão" means "suckling pig" in Portuguese.

† *Navios redondos*—ships with square sails. John made this statement, averring that caravels (rigged with lateen sails) alone could navigate the African coast because of the winds and currents. Only Portugal had these caravels.

cessfully. D'Alenquer, who was familiar with the coast, declared that he could make the voyage in any sort of vessel, irrespective of size. The king replied that it was impossible, as he had ordered it tried many times, but that every attempt with "round vessels" had failed. Whereupon D'Alenquer hotly insisted that he would guarantee to make such a voyage at any time, if called upon. This so angered the king that he rose from the table and left the room with the cutting remark: "There is nothing that a common fool does not think he can do, but in the showdown he does nothing." A little later D'Alenquer was summoned before the king in private. Dom John asked the pilot's pardon for speaking sharply as he did, but explained that he did so in order to cut the discussion short, as he desired to keep information of value concerning the Guinea voyage as secret as possible.

João Infante, a knight, was captain of the second vessel, the *São Pantaleão*, with Alvaro Martins as pilot, and João Grego as sailing master. The provision ship was captained by Diogo Dias, brother of Bartholomeu, and the pilot was João de Santiago, who had been in Cão's expedition, and who was familiar with the African coast. In fact, we are assured by Barros, "todos cada hum em seu mister mui espertos" (and all of them very expert in their craft).

The fleet set sail in August, 1487. There must have been at least six happy people on board the ships sailing down the Tagus and out to sea. Two of them were negroes who had been carried off forcibly by Cão to Lisbon, and four were negresses seized on some earlier voyage to the Guinea Coast. All six, well fed and clothed in European dress, were to be landed at various places along the coast, with specimens of gold, silver, spices, and other African merchandise desired by the Portuguese, and with orders to encourage the natives to trade. They were also to spread everywhere the story of Portugal's power and wealth. It was hoped, too, that their talk might reach the ear of the much sought for but elusive Prester John. The negresses were selected with special care, for it was believed that, being women, "with whom men do not wage war," they would come to no harm, and, since they were not natives of the regions where they were to be put ashore, they would soon return to the neighborhood of the coast, where the ships could pick them up on the return voyage and convey them back to Portugal.* Dias set his course for the mouth of the Congo, and thence proceeded with great caution down the unknown coast. The two negroes were put ashore, without incident, at a place called Angra do Salto. Though putting "safe" negresses ashore among unknown peoples may have been excellent in theory, it did not work out well in practice. One was landed in the Bay of Islands (Angra dos Ilhoes, identified as Angra Pequena), where Dias set up the first of his padrões. The second was put ashore at a bay called Angra das Voltas. The third negress died aboard ship. On arriving farther down the coast at a bay named by Dias the Angra dos Ilhoes de Santa Cruz, the sailors seized two native women whom they found gathering shell fish in the shallow water off shore. The last of the four negresses was landed with them and all three were turned loose. As far as is known, none of the six thus used as involuntary Portuguese agents was ever seen or heard of again.

Shortly after this incident Dias's ships ran into heavy weather which rapidly increased to a gale, so that the vessels were forced to run before it for thirteen days with close-reefed sails.[2] The crews were terrified at the height of the waves, "and as the ships were tiny, and the seas colder and not such as they were in the land of Guinea . . . they gave themselves up for dead." But at last the storm abated, and Dias, realizing that he had been driven far off his course, gave orders to steer eastward in search of a landfall. He naturally assumed that the coast ran from north to south, as he had found it heretofore in this region. However, after they had made a run of several days without sighting land, he ordered the course changed to the north. At last high mountains came into view over the horizon, the ships approached the coast, and on February 3, 1488, the weary sailors dropped anchor in what is now Mossel Bay. They had rounded the Cape of Good Hope during the tempest without knowing it!

The shores of the bay were sloping green pastures, and from the decks herdsmen could be seen tending large numbers of grazing cattle. Dias and some of his men landed with trinkets for the natives, in order to learn from them something of the land which they had reached. The naked blacks were terrified at the sight of the ships

* On board the ships were carried three padrões, to be erected as Dias's best judgment dictated along the coast which he was to explore.

with their great sails, and when the strangely clothed white men—
like no human beings whom they had ever seen—approached them,
they drew away. Hastily they gathered their cattle together and
drove them off to the hills, refusing to look at the gifts held out to
them. When Dias saw that he could learn nothing from the herdsmen, he ordered his men to look for drinking water, of which the
supply on shipboard had grown scanty and stale. A stream was
found near the beach at the foot of a hill. Casks were sent ashore
and the men started filling them. Meanwhile, some of the natives
had crept back to the top of the hill above them, and with shouts
and gestures tried to drive them off. As the sailors paid no attention
and continued with their tasks, the blacks, growing bolder and
angrier, began showering stones on them from the hilltop. Dias
threatened them with a crossbow, but as they had never seen such a
weapon it did not frighten them. Finally Dias, in desperation, pressed
the trigger and killed one of them with an arrow, whereupon the rest
fled.* Thus nothing was learned of the inhabitants of the region
except that they kept cattle and that "they were woolly-haired, like
those of Guinea." This bay was named Bahia dos Vaqueiros (Herdsmen's Bay) because of the cattle and drovers encountered there.

Still ignorant of where he was or to what shore he had been driven
by the terrific gale, Dias gave orders to follow the new eastern course
along the coast, "with which the captains were very satisfied." From
this point they progressed slowly, struggling with difficulty against
the Agulhas Current and the prevailing winds. Finally a landing
was made in Algoa Bay, and a padrão was set up on the shore.
And now

here, as everyone was weary, and terrified by the great seas through
which they had passed, all with one voice began to murmur, and to
demand that they proceed no farther, saying that the provisions were
being consumed [before they would be able] to return to find the
supply ship, which had been left so far behind that when they reached
it all would be dead of starvation, if they went on farther. That it was
enough for one voyage, that they had discovered such an extent of
coast, and that now they were bearers of great news [namely], that
that discovery had revealed that the land ran in general to the east,
whence it appeared that behind them was some great cape, and that it
would be a better counsel to turn back from their path to find it.

* The native who was killed by Dias's crossbow has been called "the first
victim of white aggression in South Africa."

On this, Dias went ashore for a private conference with his captains, officers, "and some of the chief sailors," for the general complaint could not be ignored.[3] He asked them to state under oath what they thought best to do as men in the service of the king. They with one accord agreed that a return to Portugal would be wise. In order to place them on record and thus protect himself later on, Dias requested each man to place his name on a document to this effect. When the paper had been signed, he begged one favor of them, that he be allowed to proceed on his course just for two or three days, after which, he solemnly promised, he would turn back and set a course for Portugal. His captains agreed, anchors were weighed, and again the ships moved slowly along the coast.

Just before reaching the limit of the short time accorded him, the ships arrived at the mouth of a large river, which he named Rio de Infante,[4] after João Infante, captain of the *Pantaleão,* the first man to set foot ashore. No sooner did the anchor touch bottom than the crew again began to murmur. There was nothing for Dias to do but to accede and keep his promise. So, here, where the coast begins to turn from east to northeast on the very threshold of the Indian Ocean, the commander, bitterly disappointed, gave the order to turn the prows of his ships to the west, and the long voyage home to Lisbon began. On the return journey, as the ships slowly passed the padrão set up on the island in Algoa Bay, Dias sadly bade farewell to the column "with as much sorrow and feeling as though he were taking his last leave of a son condemned to exile forever, recalling with what danger to his own person and to all his men they had come such a long distance with this sole aim, and then God would not grant it to him to reach his goal."

Hardly had the voyage homeward begun, with favoring winds and fair weather, when before their eyes in the distance rose "that great and famous cape, hidden for so many hundreds of years." Dias gave the cape a name, but here, too, the records differ. Barros, who wrote about sixty-five years later, records:

Bartholomeu Dias and his company, because of the perils and storms [tormentos] through which they had passed while doubling it, bestowed upon it the name of "Tormentoso" [Stormy]; but the king D. John, when they arrived in the kingdom, gave it a more illustrious name, calling it "Cape of Good Hope," for that it promised the discovery of India that was so much wished for, and sought over so many years.

Duarte Pacheco, writing within twenty years after the discovery of the cape, notes:

It was with good reason that this headland was called the "Cape of Good Hope," for Bartholomeu Dias, who discovered it at the order of the late King John in 1488, observed that the coast here turned north and east toward Ethiopia . . . giving great hope of the discovery of India called it the "Cape of Good Hope."

These conflicting reports together with a brief note made by Columbus are all that we have of this momentous discovery.

The first view of the cape and (a little to the north and west of it) Table Mountain is a sight never to be forgotten, the point sought for in vain for nearly a century, the headland where one world ends and another begins. The landfall of the cape has enthralled travelers and mariners for all the years that have passed since the Portuguese first sighted it. In the words of Sir Francis Drake, who doubled it in June, 1580, "This cape is a most stately thing, and the fairest Cape we sawe in the whole circumference of the earth."

Dias landed, took readings for his chart and log, and set up a padrão which he called São Gregório,[5] but, since time pressed, he could not explore inland, and left at once in search of the supply ship. They finally sighted it after exactly nine months of separation. Of the nine men whom Dias had left aboard, only three were alive:

And of those one, whom they called Fernão Colaço, a native of Lumiar, a district of Lisbon, who was a clerk, was so overcome with joy at seeing his companions that he died of a sudden, being very weak through illness. And the cause of the others being dead was that they had put their trust in the negroes of the land, with whom they came into contact, and who, because they coveted some of the things which they possessed, killed them.

After the food and stores were removed, the supply ship was burned, as it was in very bad condition and "much worm-eaten." Then the two remaining vessels sailed along the west coast of Africa, rescuing Duarte Pacheco Pereira at the island of Principe, where he had been shipwrecked. With him and the survivors of his crew on board they continued on to Rio do Resgate, where some slaves were purchased, and thence the fleet proceeded to São Jorge da Mina, on the Gold Coast. There gold bought from the natives by the king's resident factor was taken on board, and they proceeded on their way up the coast.

Finally the coast of Portugal was sighted. The weary crew, rejoicing that at last the long and trying voyage was over, slowly sailed up the Tagus and dropped anchor off Restello "in December of the year 1488, it having been sixteen months and seventeen days since they had departed. And Bartholomeu Dias had discovered in this voyage 373 leagues of coast."

It is of particular interest to note that Christopher Columbus was present at the Portuguese court when Dias made his report to the king. It impressed Columbus so forcibly that he made the following interesting and valuable entry concerning it on the margins of folio 13 of his copy of Pierre d'Ailly's *Imago Mundi*:

Note: that in December of this year 1488, Bartholomaeus Didacus [Bartholomeu Dias], commandant of three caravels which the King of Portugal had sent out to Guinea to seek out the land, landed in Lisbon. He reported that he had reached a promontory which he called Cabo de Boa Esperança [Cape of Good Hope]. . . . He had described his voyage and plotted it league by league on a marine chart in order to place it under the eyes of the said king. I was present in all of this.*

Dias's feat was one worthy of a far more extensive account than has thus far been obtainable from available records. His expedition had discovered over 1,400 miles of coast beyond the farthest point visited by Diogo Cão. He had rounded the Cape of Good Hope and proceeded far enough east and north to prove that there was open, unobstructed sea between Africa and India. He had brought back data and detailed charts, that they might be used by his king in sending out later voyagers. He had accumulated invaluable experience, which was used to good advantage by Vasco da Gama on his voyage to India. Yet no word is recorded of a fitting—or any—reward or honor conferred on him by his sovereign. For some unknown reason he was not included in the personnel which sailed with Gama, though King John employed him to supervise the building of the ships for the great adventure.

* A second marginal entry to this same effect was made by Columbus on a page of his copy of Pope Pius II's *Historia Rerum Ubique Gestarum.*

History recounts but one more—the last and the most tragic—chapter in the life of Bartholomeu Dias. Together with his brother Diogo he sailed from Portugal for India in the fleet of Pedro Álvares Cabral in March, 1500, and took part in the discovery of Brazil. Setting a course from South America for Africa at the beginning of May, Cabral's fleet of thirteen vessels ran into a very heavy storm about the 24th of the month:

Suddenly appeared a black cloud in the air, which the sailors of Guinea call *bulção,** on the appearance of which the wind died down as though those black clouds had engulfed it all within themselves . . . but only to spew it forth more furious than ever. Then the hurricane swept down in an instant, bursting so furiously that it gave [the crews] no time to furl the sails, and sank four [of the ships] of which the captains were Aires Gomes da Silva, Simão di Pina, Vasco de Taide, and Bartholomeu Dias, to whom, having suffered so many perils by sea in the discoveries which he made, and above all of the Cape of Good Hope, this fury of the wind dealt his end, and to the others, casting them into the abyss of that great ocean sea . . . human bodies as food for the fish of those waters, which bodies we can believe were the first, since they were navigating in unknown regions.

Thus, almost within sight of the padrão of which he had taken despairing leave twelve years before, perished miserably Bartholomeu Dias de Novaes, fidalgo of Portugal, faithful servant of his king, on his second vain attempt to reach the India of his dreams, to the discovery of which he had contributed so much, but on which he was destined never to set his eyes.

The brief comment of Galvão (whose book was published posthumously in 1563) is perhaps the most fitting close to the story of the courageous Dias who had, until the voyage of Vasco da Gama, ventured farther than any other man out into the unknown African seas in search of the riches of the East:

It may be said that he saw the land of India, but, like Moses and the Promised Land, he did not enter in.†

---

* *Bulção:* a dark cloud forecasting a thunderstorm.
† "Q se pode dizer qvia terra da India, mas nã entrou nella, como Mouses na terra de promissam."

NOTES

[1] Discussion of the disputed dates of Dias's voyage has been omitted. Details may be found in Richard Hennig, *Terrae Incognitae,* IV, 387ff.

[2] Ravenstein questions the type of the gale and its duration.

[3] It was customary for the captains of Dias's day to consult with their officers when matters of policy were in question.

[4] There is no way of absolutely identifying the Rio de Infante with the Great Fish River, as the contemporary writers disagree on the location.

[5] A full discussion of the padrões erected by Dias and the fascinating story of the recovery of the padrão of São Gregório may be found in Eric Axelson, *South-East Africa, 1488–1530* (London, 1948).

CHAPTER V

THE MISSION OF PERO DE COVILHAN

He [King John] sends his messengers. . . .
People unknown and strange their eye surveys,
Beholding various customs, various ways,
Creature and product of each region's race.
But paths so harsh and of such length of days,
Alas, they could not easily retrace;
There did they die, in fine, and there remain,
Their longed-for land they never saw again.
—CAMÕES, *Os Lusíadas,* IV, lx ff.
Translated by J. J. Aubertin.

RINCE HENRY had been dead twenty-seven years, but the work that he had begun, the inspiration, the encouragement and impetus that he had given to mathematical and nautical science had continued. The Portuguese were slowly but steadily pushing their explorations farther and farther south along the west coast of Africa. New and better charts were being drawn, more accurate data concerning winds and ocean currents were being accumulated, and nautical instruments, tables, and almanacs were being improved.

Henry's nephew, King Affonso V, had also died, and his son, Dom John II, the "Perfect Prince," had mounted the throne of Portugal. To the task of ruling the destinies of his people he brought wisdom, patience, and vision, together with a firm resolve to push ever further the plans of his great-uncle Henry. Combined in him were the steadfastness and persistence in the face of obstacles of his English great-grandfather, John of Gaunt, and the lively imagination of his Portuguese forebears. His aims in encouraging the full realization of Henry's dreams and plans were many: to break the strangle hold of the Venetian and Genoese trade with the Moslems, to develop the foreign trade of his own kingdom, to forward the conversion of the "heathen," and to resist the ever growing political power of Islam and the Turks.

[43]

To combat the Moslems he resolved to try to reach, and to form an alliance with, the semilegendary Prester John, a Christian prince whose kingdom was reputed to be somewhere in East Africa. Its exact location was vague, and varied with each report and rumor.

An interesting description of King John and his court at this time has come down to us in a manuscript recording the observations of one Nicholas, a braggart Pole of Popelau, who arrived in Portugal in the month of July, 1484. He visited John at Setúbal, where the monarch was holding court, and wrote concerning John and his people:

The King is of medium height, a little taller than I. He is beyond a doubt the wisest and most virtuous of his people. He should be about twenty-nine years old. And he had with him his heir of nine years, of an English cast of countenance, and him he always kept at his side at table. The king partakes of only four or five dishes at meals, and drinks only well water, without sugar or spices. His son drinks wine with water and eats the same food as his father, but from a special service. At table there are usually ten servants, who push the king about with their hands, and jostle him with their stomachs, a vulgarity which the king inexplicably permits. Below the table and at the feet of the king are always six or eight pages, and one more on either side of him, to drive away the flies with silken fans.

There are Portuguese endowed with much subtlety, but I could not find any who could rival me in this particular. In general the nobility, the citizens, and the peasants of this country are like those of Galicia, that is, coarse, poor, lacking in good manners and ignorant, in spite of their pretense of wisdom. They remind one of the English, who do not admit any society equal to theirs. The Portuguese have more loyalty among themselves and also for their king—more loyalty than the English. They are not as cruel and insensate as these. They show themselves more sober in eating and drinking. None the less they are ugly, dark, and black, almost like negroes. They wear cloaks black and voluminous, like those of the Augustinians. As for their women, few are beautiful; almost all look like men, though in general they have lovely black eyes. In love they are ardent, like Englishwomen when one has once gained their confidence. They dress their hair with no exaggerated adornment and wear scarfs of woolen cloth, or a neckerchief of silk. They allow one to look upon their faces without hindrance, and also upon much of their bosoms, for which purpose their shifts and outer dresses are cut generously low. Below their waist they wear many skirts so that their posteriors are broad and beautiful, so full that I say it in all truth in the whole world nothing finer is to be seen. They [the women] are for the most part sensual, fickle like the men, lewd and greedy for money . . . and they are in no way generous as the women of France and Lombardy. The women are so dissolute that rarely can one meet a young girl of "guaranteed" virtue. To satisfy their desires they suffer no scruples to stand in their way. Besides all this, both husbands and wives have lovers, and it would be an illusion to travel among [them] to learn good manners or virtue.

Evidently Herr Nicholas was no lover of the English, nor of women either—unless mayhap he was unsuccessful in his experiences with both the one and the other.

Two "Moorish" * slaves had been promised to Nicholas to take to the German emperor. The traveler selected them personally from among fifty who had arrived in Portugal the week before. He tells how he watched the sale of these slaves, who were exhibited and offered in public naked, like animals. He remarked that the first thing he found necessary to do after he received his two slaves was to buy clothes for them, for when delivered "they were naked as God made them."

Hieronymus Münzer, a German physician of Nuremberg, has also left us an account of his visit in 1495 to John's court, whither he had fled from his native city with three of his fellow countrymen to escape the plague that was raging there:

King John is a most learned man, and one very wise in all things. He governs his kingdom in peace and tranquillity. He is most affable and keenly desirous of acquiring knowledge of many things. He ships to Guinea woolen goods of various colors, like the carpets which are woven in Tunis, also cloth, horses, varied wares of Nuremberg, quantities of copper kettles and brass basins, weaves of vermilion and yellow cloth, English and Irish cloaks, and many other things. Thence he has brought home gold, slaves, pepper, grains of Paradise, innumerable tusks of elephants, and so forth.

And now this King John had decided that not only should explorations by sea be pushed ever farther south, but that emissaries should be sent by the Mediterranean route to the kingdom of Prester John, to seek an alliance with him against the infidel, and, if possible, to open up trade relations with him. Efforts were to be made, too, to learn everything possible of India and the other lands whence

* Probably negroes.

the Italian trading cities drew their fabulous wealth. Barros, "the Livy of Portugal," recounts that "it seemed to the king that by way of Prester John he might find an entrance into India, because by Abyssinian friars who had come to the Peninsula and by other friars who had gone from Portugal to Jerusalem with orders to get news of this prince he had learned that his country was over Egypt and stretched to the southern sea."

King John first dispatched on this important mission Pero de Monterroyo, "a man of the house of Monterio and a friar of Lisbon, Antônio." They traveled as far as Jerusalem but, after some investigation, returned forthwith to the king, reporting that it was not possible to travel farther, either toward India or into the land of Prester John, without a good working knowledge of the Arabic language.

The king then cast about him to find men properly equipped to perform this mission of great political and commercial import, and one fraught with perils by both land and sea. At last, after much searching, two men were chosen and summoned to court. One of these is little known to us. He was Affonso de Paiva, a gentleman of the court and a native of Castelo Branco. His family is mentioned as being of Canarian origin,* and we are told that he spoke Spanish and Arabic. More than that, nothing is known. The other of the two was Pero de Covilhan,† the leader of the mission, whose story has come down to us. Covilhan was a man of action. He wrote but little—only a few letters, as far as is known—and unfortunately those have been lost to us. We can, however, piece together his life and his character from the reports that have been preserved by other hands.

He was a native of Covilhan, in the mountains of Beira. His origin was obscure, as is evidenced by our having the record only of his Christian name and the place of his birth, but not of his family name. He had spent six or seven years in Spain. There he had been a participant in the quarrels of the group around Ponce de León and took an active part in the frequent ambushes and night attacks on the street corners and in the narrow alleys of Seville. He had fought in the battle of Toro and had sojourned in France, where he had come into close contact with both Louis XI and the Duke of Burgundy, the king's most powerful vassal. He had also spent a year

* This is stated by Correa, I, 6, without proof.
† His name is spelled variously: Covilhan, Covilham, Covilhã, and Covilhão.

in Castile at the court of Ferdinand and Isabella the Catholic as a
secret agent of Portugal, with special orders to spy on the Portuguese
exiles and their political machinations. He was said to have been
able to speak "Andaluz" as well as though he had been born on the
banks of the Guadalquivir.

About 1474 Covilhan returned to Portugal and served as an
esquire to King Dom Affonso V, on whose death he entered the
service of King John II. Later he was sent on two diplomatic missions to Barbary. Probably he had learned Arabic ere this, or such
missions would not have been entrusted to him.*

His two visits to Barbary increased his knowledge of Arabic, as
well as of the habits, manners, customs, and dress of the Moslems,
all of which differed but little from Morocco to Calicut in India.
This broad experience had made of him a rare adventurer even at
a time which was rich in adventurers. His African mission was to
Tlemcen, then a great city, and the capital of Maghreb-el-Ansat.†
Tlemcen was a picturesque place, surrounded by orchards and olive
groves and irrigated by springs and watercourses. It was a city of
palaces, mosques, and richly endowed schools, and its opulence and
fame had caused it to be known as "the Granada of Africa." Its
leather work and saddles and harness were much sought after by
the Barbary horsemen. Its woolens and its cotton cloth, known as
Lambeis or Alambeis, were shipped in large quantities for the
coastal trade with the African negroes, being carried by caravan to
the seaport of Oran.

Covilhan's mission took him next to Maghreb-al-Aksa, the Kingdom of Fès, where he added to his knowledge of Moslem life and
learning, as well as of the commercial and social customs of the
people.

These travels to a man of his mind—keen, decided, and courageous—combined with a phenomenally retentive memory, had endowed Covilhan richly with the very qualities and resources which
were indispensable to the mission for which he had been chosen by
King John. No one could have been better equipped, physically or

* It must be remembered that at this time there was a large Arabic-speaking
population in both Spain and Portugal. Alvares states: "Este Pero de Covilhan
he homen que todas has lingoas sabe que se fallar podem asy de christãos como
mouros e gentios" (This Pero de Covilhan was a man who knew all the languages which may be spoken by Christians, Moors, or the heathen).
† Now western Algeria.

mentally, for the task entrusted to him. He was mature, too, a man of forty, with a wife and children living in Covilhan.

The scene enacted in the town of Santarém on May 7, 1487, was little noted at the time and is given scant mention by historians. But like many another obscure event, it probably influenced profoundly not only the destiny of the people of Portugal, but also that of the other nations of Europe and Asia.

Dom John sat surrounded by his advisers and councilors. Spade-bearded, clad in red velvet, black hose, white shirt, a heavy gold chain about his neck, a dagger thrust through his belt, he looked every inch the king. The men whom he had gathered about him this day were his "technical" advisers—Moyses (also known as Joseph) Vizinho, the learned Jew from Viseu, who had translated a summary of the *Perpetual Almanac* * from the Hebrew into Latin and Spanish; Mestre Rodrigo de Pedras Negras, and the wise Bishop Ortiz. Among the fidalgos at his side was his cousin Duke Manuel of Beja, later to succeed him and become known in history (largely as the result of John's plans and labors) as "Manuel the Fortunate." The council was held in great secrecy, for spies from Italy and Castile and perhaps from other jealous European powers swarmed at the Portuguese court.

Pero de Covilhan and Affonso de Paiva listened attentively as the king discussed his project and told them of the long and perilous road that lay before them. Their mission had two objectives: the first was to proceed by the Mediterranean route as speedily as possible to the country of Prester John, to seek him out and endeavor to bind him to an alliance against the infidel with his most Christian and royal brother of Portugal; the second was to investigate thoroughly the spice trade—its sources, its routes, means of transport, its value, and methods of packing and other important details.

Their journey would take them to far distant lands which no Portuguese—and perhaps no European—foot had trod before, lands beyond the rising sun, lands largely unknown to the West, lands whose very outlines were dim and shadowy, save for the tales of Marco Polo and the Arab wanderers. They were countries of whose inhabitants dread and weird tales were told and believed, lands of fabulous wealth in gold and precious stones, where strange practices and customs prevailed—the storied Indies and the country of Prester

* See note, p. 11.

John, that legendary Christian monarch of whom rumor and fragmentary tales had come through desert and sea into Europe for long
centuries.

The king sat grave and pensive, his eyes fixed as those of a man
absorbed in an inward vision, the pageantry of an unknown Asia
and East Africa, a vision of sunlit sea and waving palms, a vision of
the Cross vanquishing the Crescent, of the nations bowing before
the might and riches of Portugal. It was that same vision which had
gripped the imagination and guided the life of his great-uncle, Dom
Henry, who was to be known to future generations as Prince Henry
the Navigator, though he himself was no traveler, but only the
inspired guide and leader of others.

John's eyes saw, as in a vision, the fall of Venice and Genoa, those
greedy republics whose harbors had been too long the crowded
emporia of the trade of the East, and whose warehouses and galleys
were bursting with the spices and sandalwood, the silks and brocades, the carpets and drugs of Asia. He saw the camel caravans
and Arab dhows bearing this wealth toward Italy, and the coffers
of its merchants overflowing with the profits of the trade. All this
would change when his dreams came true and his carefully laid
plans had come to fruition with the years.

The king and his councilors, both Gentile and Jew, had studied
well and carefully their problem, and the means of solving it. They
had the rich fruits of Prince Henry's life work to aid and to guide
them. Their store of maps and portolans, charts and crude globes
was growing ever larger. Rutters of their captains who had sailed
out on the unknown Atlantic and crept down the feared and treacherous west coast of Africa were accumulated, together with narratives and letters of the explorers of coastal terrain and river mouth.
All these added to their store of knowledge, together with the improved instruments of navigation and mathematical tables—the
majority of which were the result of the labors of Abraham Zacuto
and other Jewish savants of the realm.

The king was recalled to realities by the low voice of Covilhan.
Down the centuries we still hear his murmur of protest, "his fear
that his knowledge would not be as great as his desire to serve His
Highness." The king impatiently waved the objection aside and
proceeded to give more explicit instructions.

The details of the preparations for the journey are given variously by different chroniclers, but we can fit the pieces together and

can know what was done. After the royal audience the two men met with the advisers of Dom John in the house of Pero de Alça-cova, Secretary of Works, near the Alfofa Gate in the old city wall of Lisbon. At the meeting was present Dom Diogo Ortiz, chaplain to the king and Bishop of Tangier, one of the most powerful men in the kingdom, and one especially learned in geography. With him came Mestre Rodrigo and Mestre Moyses. Both of them were physicians, mathematicians, and geographers, and, like Ortiz, were high in the councils of the king. They had collaborated in the preparation of a "Table of the Declination of the Sun," and had labored with the German Martin Behaim in the construction of an improved astrolabe. They had also carefully studied the plans presented in Portugal by Christopher Columbus and had abstracted for their use what they considered of value.

It is not known whether the instructions given by these men to Covilhan and his companion were oral or written. Ramusio, the famous editor of an Italian collection of voyages (Venice, 1551), states that they were directed to learn "if there was any information in the seas [of Prester John] by which it would be possible to pass into the eastern sea, because the said doctors told that they had found I know not what note of it." This statement is very questionable, and may be only a gloss written after the event.

We are told that they were given several aids for the projected journey, including a *carta de marear* (navigating chart) made by the licentiate Calçadilha. Gaspar de Correa (*Lendas da Índia*), who is a very unreliable authority in the matter, adds that the two were promised by the king

large recompense for such a great service as they were rendering him, and that as long as they were in this service he would take care of the maintenance of their wives and children, and that if they died in the said service the rewards would be given to their children and wives.* And he gave each of them a plaque of brass like a medal, and on it were engraved letters in all languages which read "King Dom John of Portugal, brother of the Christian Monarchs," that they might show them to Prester John. The king gave them precious stones—"some jewels of price" which they should sell for their expenses.

---

* There is no other record of Dom John's pledge, and certainly none of his ever having fulfilled it.

The two envoys set out from Santarém on their momentous mission on May 7, 1487. From this day all dates of the journey are conjectural, being calculated as closely as is possible from the meager accounts surviving.

Aside from the tales of later chroniclers, the sole detailed story of the travels of Covilhan and his companion has been preserved for us in the strange recital of the embassy of Dom Rodrigo de Lima (which was sent by King John III to Abyssinia in 1520), as narrated by Francisco Alvares. He was a priest of the expedition who wrote an account of it entitled *Verdadeira Informaçam das Terras do Preste Joam das Índias*, first published in Lisbon in 1540. The eventful tale of Pero de Covilhan was told by Alvares many years after Covilhan's death in Ethiopia, and it is very short and slight. Fortunately, we are able to fill in many gaps and reconstitute the story from other contemporary material.

From Santarém the travelers proceeded to Lisbon to arrange for receiving money en route. They presented themselves at once at the countinghouse of Bartolomo Marchioni, a Florentine merchant and banker of the city. The Florentines were the most numerous group of Italians in Lisbon. They had important business dealings with the Portuguese, which increased with the years, especially after 1494, when the Florentine merchant marine was destroyed by the Pisans. Records indicate that the Florentines had a large carrying trade between Italy (especially Lucca) and Portugal, and that they brought to Lisbon fine woolen cloth, leather goods, and silk, and took back for resale in Italy preserved fish, cork, ivory from the Guinea Coast, and imports from Morocco, principally leather (Moroccan leather was even then famous in the world's markets) and feathers.

Of all the Florentines in Portugal, Bartolomo Marchioni was the best known and most influential. He had been established in the country for many years and was engaged in large financial transactions with and for the government of King John. In fact, he was the acknowledged leader of the Florentine colony in Lisbon, and to him, probably acting under their secret instructions, Covilhan and his companion turned their steps. Most of the money given them by the king's agents was deposited in Marchioni's countinghouse, and they received in exchange a letter of credit acceptable throughout the Peninsula. Marchioni had agents and banking correspondents throughout Spain and Portugal, and issued a letter drawn on his Valencia house.

On Covilhan's arrival at Valencia the letter was presented and cashed, and the overland journey was continued to Barcelona, where ship was to be taken for Italy. Even as early as 1487 Barcelona was a flourishing seaport, linking Spain, Barbary, France, Italy, and the Levant. Its hardy Catalan sailors had navigated the sea for centuries and were reputed the best and most reliable in the Mediterranean.

Arriving in Barcelona on the *dia de corpo de Deo,* the two men presented their credentials to another Marchioni branch. Having received in exchange for their money another order drawn on Naples, they departed on a small sailing vessel. The voyage of ten days proceeded with no untoward incident, Vesuvius was duly sighted, and a landing made in Naples on St. John's Day, June 24.

By 1487 the De' Medici family of Florence had extended its financial operations throughout the length and breadth of Italy and had established branches in all the cities of commercial importance. Naples was not the least of these, and the bank of Cosimo de' Medici at once honored the letter presented by Covilhan.

After a short stay in Naples the travelers sailed for Rhodes, where they had orders to present themselves to two Portuguese friars dwelling there. The island was then under the rule of the Knights Hospitalers of St. John of Jerusalem (the Grand Master of the order being a cardinal, Pierre d'Aubusson), and the two friars Frey Gonçalo and Frey Fernando were Knights Hospitalers. They were thoroughly conversant with the politics and commerce of the eastern Mediterranean, and Covilhan and Paiva had been directed to consult them before proceeding farther, for on leaving Rhodes they were bidding farewell to the outposts of the West and Christendom. Henceforth their path would lead through the lands of Islam and the Turks and even farther, to the cities of farthest India, still all but unknown. Perils of every kind would threaten them, from man, beast, climate, and disease. Yet these two adventurers never appear to have faltered, but bravely prepared for the ordeal.

They were advised that it was no longer wise or prudent to travel as messengers of the King of Portugal. They were about to enter the dominions of fierce and fanatical Mohammedans, who, moreover, were in many cases closely allied to Venice and other Italian trading cities, whose representatives everywhere, but more especially in the Levant, were suspicious, jealous, and distrustful of all Europeans except their own fellow countrymen. Their native language would seldom be heard on other lips than their own, and they were to meet few, if any, Portuguese. So, acting on the advice of their two compatriots, Covilhan and Paiva bought garments similar to those of the Levantines and prepared to travel thenceforth as merchants. Rhodes did not offer much in the way of products or manufactures, so they were advised to invest in a cargo of honey. After buying their merchandise and putting on their new garments, they boarded the ship of one Bartholomeu de Paredes, bound for Alexandria, in Egypt.

The ancient seaport at the mouth of the Nile was again regaining the important position that she had occupied when the Romans were the masters of the eastern Mediterranean. From the time of Constantine the city by the Golden Horn had held or controlled the greater part of the commerce of the East, and was the chief entrepôt through which poured the goods of Asia moving westward and the gold and other commodities of the West in demand by the dwellers in Eastern lands. In turn she had had Roman and Greek masters and even rulers from the West. Venice and Genoa had vied for her richly laden argosies and maintained vast enterprises and warehouses within her walls. Keels of every country plowed her waters, and, even after she had lost the proud crown of her Roman rulers and was gradually shorn of land and power and prestige by the infidels, she was still the natural center of the trade of the Levant. Greek-speaking travelers venturing thence seldom used the name Constantinople, but said simply that they were going "εἰς τὴν πολίν" (is tin polin—to the city), until the expression became a word—Istamboul—the name by which the city is still called in the East.* But now all was changed. The invading Turk had seized more and more of the dying Byzantine Empire, until little was left but the city itself. And that city vanished in smoke and flames, slaughter and blood in 1453, when Mohammed II and his hordes swept down upon it. His soldiers swarmed over its walls in an all-engulfing wave, and he marched down its broad streets as a conqueror, turning loose his barbarians to loot and rape, murder and destroy as they would. Then he ordered the summons of the muezzin to prayer to be sounded from Saint Sophia itself, and with that call

* See Hart, *Venetian Adventurer,* 3rd ed., Chap. I.

from the venerable building erected by Justinian nine centuries
before, Constantinople ceased to be a Christian city and the eastern-
most bulwark of the peoples of the West.

But though the world had changed, men's activities remained the
same. They must eat and drink, be clothed and housed. They must
have grain and meat, cloth and iron, and after these necessities they
demand comforts and luxuries, that life may be more than mere
existence. Barter and selling, trading and commerce must go on, for
these are the means of bringing to men what they need and conveying elsewhere that which they have in abundance and can offer in
exchange. And so, with Constantinople lost to Europe, and even
long before that catastrophe, the keen traders of Italy, especially
the Genoese and the Venetians, had turned to the great port of
Alexandria. There they had developed an outlet for the goods of
Asia, one where they could load their galleys with spices and silks,
printed cottons and skins, ivory and slaves. These cargoes were all
to be found in Alexander's great city. Caravans converged from
inland Asia to bays and roadsteads on the Red Sea. Others came
up from the south, and loads of precious goods traveled up the Nile
from Nubia and the Sudan and from far in the heart of the unknown and unexplored Dark Continent. Still more came by Arab
ship and dhow from the shores of Arabia, from Hormuz in Persia,
from Zanzibar and Sofala and other ports on the East African coast,
and still more poured in from the far cities of Ceylon and India, and
even from China and the unvisited, unknown islands of the East
Indies. This trade caused Egypt to wax rich, and her power gradually spread until the sultan ruled as lord over Lesser Armenia and
Syria, as well as over the valley of the Nile.

Tor and Kosseir and other ports, now little more than names,
were then busy, bustling, populous harbors, and in them jostled
crowds from every land and port in the Eastern world. In them
every tongue of Asia and Europe and Africa was to be heard. In
them were to be found every luxury and every vice—and in them
life was cheap, and men disappeared and vanished forever. Moreover, to a Moslem a Christian was no better than a dog; and to the
pious but ignorant European in turn, the followers of Mohammed
and the other heathen were beasts without souls, to be slaughtered
without mercy or afterthought. Yet it was a strange world withal,
for in spite of such fierce and irreconcilable antagonisms, in spite of

racial and religious hatreds, all these Eastern folk met on common ground to transact business one with the other, to cheat, to rob, or to be honest traders with each other, but always with the common aim of making a profit from the contact. Even the Church used its mighty power to aid and abet this trade, and Rome issued a bull allowing the Italians to deal directly with the infidel. The Circassian Mameluke sultans of Egypt, more tolerant than the earlier Moham-medan rulers, and impelled by a self-interest which overcame their religious scruples, accepted the overtures and threw open the gates of their country to the hated unbelievers, first of all to the Venetians. Then Cosimo de' Medici himself sent an ambassador to Cairo, and obtained from the sultan the same trading privileges as those granted the Venetians. It was into this seething and dangerous whirlpool of international trade and politics that the Portuguese emissaries were entering with their innocuous cargo of *muito mel* (much honey), as Francisco Álvares calls it.

Covilhan and Paiva found the city crowded as it had never been before. The fall of Constantinople in 1453 had dealt a fatal blow to the Genoese trading colonies in the Black Sea, and by 1475 nothing was left of them. Many of these dispossessed traders had turned the prows of their ships toward Alexandria, and, with a trade as great as or even greater than that which Egypt had possessed when it was the granary of the Roman Empire, the city had grown far beyond its ancient boundaries. It had an unhealthful climate and was thor-oughly unsanitary, for whatever the Pharaohs, Greeks, and Romans had constructed of a drainage system and pure water supply had long since deteriorated and fallen into disrepair. Alexandria, though a great metropolis, was a danger spot, a plague center of the world, whence diseases were spread everywhere by trader, traveler, and sailor.

The two Portuguese were not molested in any way when they landed. Italians, who constituted by far the most numerous foreign colony, swarmed everywhere. Some of them had even traveled the long road to India by the Red Sea route as early as 1320, and had returned in safety. To these Italians, holding as they did the trade of Asia and Africa in the hollow of their hand, Covilhan and Paiva offered no threat and gave no cause to arouse suspicion or even to draw the slightest attention. They were simply two petty merchants with an unimportant cargo of honey, and as such not worthy of a glance. As the Moslems were accustomed to the presence of numerous Italians among them, and as probably they could not distinguish between them and other Franks, it was not even necessary to conceal their religion. But the advice given at Rhodes to travel as merchants was wise. Neither Italian nor Moslem dreamed that these men were emissaries of far-off Portugal, seeking to learn about trade routes and trade secrets, in preparation for world-shaking moves that were to bring about the commercial ruin of the one and to sweep the other and his ships and trade from the Eastern seas.

The beginnings of the sojourn of the two lonely wanderers in Egypt were not auspicious. Sanitation and health conditions in the Europe of the late fifteenth century left much to be desired, but the East was far worse, and Alexandria received her Portuguese visitors grimly. Hardly were they settled in their lodgings, than both were suddenly smitten with fever and for some time hovered between life and death. Then, while they were tossing helplessly on their beds, Fate dealt them another hard blow. It was a pleasant custom of the rulers of the country to seize the possessions of any stranger who happened to die in the land and who was not fortunate enough to have relatives or friends to protect his property. The plight of the two men came to the ears of the Naib (acting governor) of Alexandria. After ascertaining that they had neither kith nor kin in the city, he decided that, since he was sure that they were going to die, there was no use wasting any time. So he seized the cargo as his right and declared that the goods were forfeited because "the travelers had no sons or brothers with them."

Unfortunately for the Naib, they recovered. We are not told what representations, pressure, or threats they brought to bear on the zealous Naib, but simply that they were able to reclaim part of the money value of the confiscated goods and immediately invested it in more merchandise. Probably not honey this time.

The next city visited was Cairo—El Kahireh (the victorious)— ruled over by Quat Bey. Here Covilhan and his companion were to begin their real mission, for in Cairo they found themselves in the full current of the trade with India. The Portuguese marveled at the great city, so different from any in the West, though rendered a bit familiar to Covilhan, at least, by his visits to the ports and souks of Barbary. There were great broad thoroughfares, crossed by narrow streets and still narrower lanes. The narrower cross streets were closed at night at either end by guarded wooden gates, and the lanes, usually culs-de-sac, were closed at the open end at nightfall. Most of the better private houses were of stone, windowless on the street floor, and the courses painted with crude red ochre and whitewash. The upper stories projected over the street and were usually of dull red brick. Often the upper floors almost touched in the middle of the street, furnishing protection from rain and sun. The entrances, guarded by porters, were usually highly ornamented and carved or sculptured, with heavy wooden doors, mostly unpainted, but decorated with Arabic inscriptions to keep off the evil eye. The usual inscriptions were "O Allah!" or "He is the Great Creator, the Everlasting One." The doors had iron knockers and heavy wooden bars and locks, like prisons, and, to accommodate horsemen or those alighting from donkeys or camels, the richer houses had mounting stones at the side. The first tiers of windows were high above the heads of passing horsemen, and to make a view of the interior more difficult, were covered with heavy wooden gratings. The upper windows were of close latticework which, while concealing the occupants, admitted a certain amount of light and air. On the larger thoroughfares shops occupied the street floors. Most of the houses on the narrow streets and twisting, tortuous lanes were miserable structures of unbaked bricks and mud. The streets were for the most part only earthen paths, hard and dusty in the dry season and deep in mud in times of flood.

As in most Eastern cities, the various trades and crafts were crowded into separate streets or quarters. These were known as the Street (or Market) of the Copper Workers, of the Ivory Workers, the Weavers, the Jewelers, the Leather Workers, and so forth. Most of the shops were small, with open fronts, shaded with matting or boards, often extending across the street. There were usually two rooms—the salesroom in the front, the storehouse in the rear. All this has changed but little in the bazaars of the Levant, and in all Asia from Arabia to Japan. Bargaining and haggling went on everywhere, for few sales were consummated without wrangling and dispute over the price or the quality of the goods. *Dellals* (auctioneers) shrieked the virtues of their wares up and down the busy streets. Goldsmiths and silversmiths and makers of copper and brass basins filled the air with the sound of their clanging hammers. Strange sweet scents and less welcome odors mingled in the heavy air—

perfumes and drugs, coffee and the aromas of cooking from open-air food shops and the emanations from heaps of garbage and open sewers. Hawkers of bread and vegetables elbowed their way through the crowds. The vendors of limes and roasted melon seeds vied with the peddlers of sherbet, figs, and grapes. Flower sellers, bearing on their shoulders great bunches of henna flowers, attracted their customers with their weird call, "Buy roses, roses which were once thorns, which blossomed from the sweat of the Prophet." Water sellers pushed their way through the throng, their goatskins swollen with Nile water, and crying "Ya owwad Allah" (May Allah recompense me). They offered skinfuls to the housewives or brass cupfuls to the passers-by. Competing with them were the sellers of licorice or raisin water, advertising their wares by clicking together their brass cups. The purveyor of boiled starch jelly tried to cry down the itinerant cake seller, and the sweet-rice peddler to outshout them both. And everywhere, in the streets, at the corners, before the shops, and against the houses were the filthy beggars—men, women, and naked children, together with young girls often in no better state. Many of them, crippled, leprous or eaters of hashish, lay on doorsteps or at the backs of the shops. The beggars' call could be heard at every turn : "O God of Mercy," "For the sake of Allah," and the like. Always the call to the Almighty to help—instead of working for their bread.

Into this maelstrom of Cairo the Portuguese plunged—into the heart of this city whose streets were crowded, throbbing, ever moving streams of people from every nation, every race, and every religion. From the minarets came the call of the muezzin five times a day, summoning the faithful to prayer. In the synagogues of the crowded Jewish quarter the rabbis chanted the age-old liturgy of their fathers, and in their churches the Copts, descendants of the ancient Egyptians, performed their Eastern rites. The colonies of Greeks and Italians and Ethiopians each had their churches and services. Hindus jostled Nubians, Arabs from Mecca and Yemen quarreled with wily Turks and shrewd Egyptians, wild-eyed dervishes from the desert strode challengingly through the crowds, and slaves and eunuchs, black and white, hastened on errands for their masters. Of women there were few on the streets, and these were of the lower classes. They hurried past, veiled to the eyes, escaping from the crowded hot streets and from the no less hot and greedy scrutiny of the crowds of men, womenless men, gathered from every corner of the earth to bargain, buy, and sell—and often to prey upon their fellows.

And when they had walked the city's streets and beheld its strange sights and talked with many people and were full to satiety with the noise and smells and dust, the two Portuguese sat down to decide on their future course. Here they were in the flowing turbid current of the trade with India, and here in Cairo was more exact knowledge of the land and the people of Prester John. They had met many traders who dealt with India, or who had even been there themselves. Moreover, they had become acquainted with several Moslem merchants who were preparing to travel to India by way of Arabia. A decision was quickly reached. They would remain in Cairo until these newly made Moorish friends were ready to depart and then they would travel with them, taking advantage of their knowledge of trading customs, of the countries they desired to visit, and of the peoples they would meet on the way. Covilhan discussed ways and means with the North Africans, who were natives of Tlemcen and Fès. He had been drawn to them and they to him because he knew their dialect and customs. It was decided that they should take ship at Tor, on the eastern coast of Egypt, and proceed to Aden, on the southwestern tip of Arabia, at the entrance to the Red Sea.

The year 1487 had drawn to a close, and the spring of 1488 had come when their caravan set out, winding through the narrow streets, thence passing out of the ancient city gate and into the desert, headed for Suez. As had travelers for thousands of years before them, they too passed in the shadows of the great pyramids and the Sphinx, which still held intact the secrets of Egypt's great past, those secrets which were not to be wrested from them until the coming of Napoleon and the English to the Land of the Pharaohs over three hundred years later. From Suez they traveled on across the sands, continuing the long desert journey to the port of Tor. They camped by Ayin Musa (the Well of Moses), in sight of Horeb and Mount Sinai, which the Arabs called Jebel Musa (the Mountain of Moses). At last they arrived at Tor, a miserable cluster of hovels on the Red Sea, where stood the Maronite Monastery of St. Catherine.

The vessel which they boarded—a *djelba*—was a rude, flimsy

structure of rough planks shaped into a hull and sewn together with cords. The sails were woven grass mats. The *djelbas* were unseaworthy and leaky; they clumsily wallowed in the slightest swells and were difficult to steer. The voyagers traveled by day but put into port at night. It was too risky to chance being wrecked on the reefs or coral shoals, for the boat sailed as near to shore as possible. The last stop on the African coast was at Suakin, still a port of the Sudan. At Suakin the Portuguese, together with their Moorish companions, transferred to an Arab dhow, and the run was made across the Red Sea.

At last, after having passed a thoroughly uncomfortable two months en route from Cairo, they passed through the Strait of Bab el Mandeb (the Gate of Tears) and in due time sighted the peak of Aden. The vessel entered the bay and passed the ancient volcanic crater, and the Portuguese landed in the town nestling at its foot—a town older than Cairo by hundreds of years, a town old when the Prophet Ezekiel wrote in the sixth century B.C. The city of Aden, situated on the arid plain, received part of its water then, as now, from the descending chain of tanks built in a ravine in the crater wall, partly by hollowing out the solid rock, partly by erecting massive masonry walls. Each tank was filled by the overflow of the tank above, the water being collected from the various gullies which converge into the ravine. Tradition had it that the tanks were built by a Persian ruler at the end of the sixth century—but they might be centuries older.

The city the Portuguese found beautiful, with its walls and towers, its rising terraces of houses and its mountain ridge. A Spanish account of 1518 (translated into English in 1540) has picturesquely described it:

> The citie of Aden is stronglie walled wt towres of lyme and stone and faire howsen and is of grete trat out of ethiope and the indies, and is plentifull of all maner thinges.

The great importance of the town at the time of Covilhan's visit may be judged from the description by Tomé Pires, Portugal's first emissary to China, which was written in 1515: *

---

* Though Pires finished his account about 1515, and a portion appeared in an Italian version in 1550, the complete book, of prime historical importance, was not published until 1944.

This city . . . is one of the four great trading cities in the world. It trades cloth to Dahlak and receives seed pearls in exchange; it trades coarse cloths and various trifling things to Zeila and Berbera in exchange for gold, horses, slaves and ivory, it trades with Sokotra, sending cloth, straw of Mecca, Socotrine aloes and dragon's-blood, it trades with Ormuz, whence it brings horses, and out of the goods from Cairo it trades gold, foodstuffs, wheat and rice if there is any, spices, seed pearls, musk, silk and any other drugs; it trades with Cambay, taking there the merchandise from Cairo and opium, and returning large quantities of cloth, with which it trades in Arabia and the Islands, and seeds, glass beads, beads from Cambay, many carnelians of all colours, and chiefly spices and drugs from Malacca, cloves, nutmeg, mace, sandalwood, cubebs, seed pearls and things of that sort. It takes a great quantity of madder and raisins to Cambay, and also to Ormuz; it trades with the kingdom of Goa, and takes there all sorts of merchandise and horses both from [Aden] itself and from Cairo, and receives in return rice, iron, sugar, fine muslins and quantities of gold; it trades with Malabar and India . . . whence it took pepper and ginger; and it traded merchandise from Malacca with Bengal in return for many kinds of white cloths, and it traded musk and precious stones, rice also from Bengal, rice from Siam, and merchandise from China which comes through Ayuthia. And in this way it had become great, prosperous and rich. The merchandise of Aden consists of horses, madder, rose-water, dried roses, raisins, opium. . . . It [Aden] is a thing worth seeing . . . although its drinking water has to be brought in a cart.

There in warehouses, awaiting transportation to Egypt for the European trade, were heaped vast quantities of merchandise. Because of the dangers of Red Sea navigation, the large Arab ships from India unloaded their cargoes in Aden, where they were reloaded on the slower, shallower-draft dhows plying between Aden and the Egyptian coast, and also through the Strait of Bab el Mandeb to Jidda, the port of Mecca. Because of the routes thus followed, both the larger and smaller Arab vessels were often referred to by the Portuguese as *nàos da Meca* (ships of Mecca).

In Aden the two voyagers again took counsel and decided to separate, and that each should pursue a different route. Paiva was to make his way to Ethiopia, the land of Prester John, and thence to return to Cairo at a set date. There Covilhan was to join him on his own return journey. Covilhan himself was to go to India. The two voyagers bade each other farewell, and at this point Affonso de Paiva disappears from the story forever, nothing more being known of his travels or adventures.

After leaving Paiva, Covilhan sought passage on an Arab vessel bound for the Indian coast. It was a venturesome journey, one never made by a Portuguese before and one from which he might never return alive. The ship which bore him to the unknown land whither his king's orders directed his steps was larger than that on which he had traveled to Aden. It was of two hundred to three hundred tons burden, badly built of planks sewed together with coconut fiber. It had no deck, the cargo being merely covered with thick mats to protect it from the weather. The passengers shifted for themselves as well as they were able.

For all their clumsy ships, however, the Arab mariners were no mean navigators. They were skillful in the use of the compass and other nautical instruments and, moreover, knew the Indian Ocean well—its winds and its currents and its dangers. Covilhan had arrived in Aden at a most opportune time, the beginning of the monsoon, the favorable wind which would bear his ship to the southwest coast of India. The slow, monotonous voyage with its burning, sticky heat, bad food, and vile water, lasted a month, and all on board greatly rejoiced when the lookout at last sighted Mount Dely—the same Indian landfall to be sighted by Vasco da Gama ten years later.

A landing was made at the ginger port of Cannanore, and there "the first Portuguese trod the soil of India." * Cannanore was a very important shipping point in the trade with Cambay, Hormuz, and Aden. It was the port of entry of Vijayanagar, a now vanished but then flourishing Indian kingdom of the interior, rich in spices, especially in cardamom and ginger.

From Cannanore King John's secret emissary, ever alert, ever observant, ever noting all details of trade—values, standards, ways of packing and shipping, customs of the merchants and the like— proceeded to Calicut, his farthermost goal and one of the two objectives of his long journey. In Calicut, of which we shall learn more anon, Covilhan found himself in the heart of the fabled land of India, that India which had fired the imaginations of the peoples of the West from earliest times. Throughout human annals it has

---

* "O primeiro portugues pisava o solo da India" Ficalho, *Viagens de Covilhan,* p. 87.

ever been a fateful magnet, drawing to it mariner and explorer, soldier, and adventurer, a country whose subsequent history was to be inextricably woven into that of all Europe, with results neither clear nor certain even in our own day.

To the Portuguese traveler Calicut was far more exotic, more unfamiliar, and more incomprehensible than Alexandria or Cairo or Aden. Fortunately, his knowledge of Arabic and of Moslem customs stood him again in good stead. He could easily find his way about, converse with the Moors, who had a large colony in the city, and learn those secrets so eagerly desired by his royal master.

He found the Hindu city a strange mixture of barbarism and civilization, simplicity and opulence. The dress of the Samorin (the ruler of Calicut) was a perfect example. Naked from the waist up, and barefoot, he wore garments of cloth of gold, and on his fingers were heavy gold rings set with rubies. Surrounded by bodyguards, he reclined on a couch of gold and silver. The perfumed women— always near him—were almost naked. In the streets swarmed an unbelievable crowd of low- and high-caste Hindus, elephants, horses, and litters. Coconut palms grew thickly everywhere; temples and the houses of the rich rubbed elbows with the miserable palm-leaf huts of the poor. In tiny open shops half-naked men trafficked in diamonds, sapphires, and rubies from Ceylon and Burma, or weighed pearls in tiny scales—and drove sharp bargains in loud voices. Down on the shore were Arab ships, whose sailors swaggered through the town, seeking to make the most of their shore leave, and about them clustered women, eager to relieve them of their hard-earned wages. Rice was being unloaded from the Coromandel Coast, and cinnamon from Ceylon. Boats were in from Malacca, bearing camphor from Borneo and Formosa, lac from Pegu, nutmegs and mace from Banda, and cloves from the Moluccas. Bags of pepper, product of Calicut itself, were heaped high in the warehouses or were being loaded onto the ships of Mecca. And over all the heavy air was filled with the odors of sandalwood and palm oil, cooking and temple incense, the flower of the areca, and the spices lying in the hot sun. Covilhan knew he was now at last in that India of which Prince Henry and his own King John had for so long dreamed and planned and fought. But he, Pero de Covilhan, was the first of his people to see it all.

He had arrived in India with the southeast monsoon in August

or September, 1488, as was the custom of the Arab mariners. Now
he hastened to acquire all the information possible before the winds
changed, for the ships of Mecca usually sailed with their Indian
cargoes at the changing of the winds after the beginning of the year.
During his stay at Calicut, Covilhan saw the large, lumbering
yellow junks of the Chinese traders sail into the harbor, the great
staring eyes painted on their prows making them look like fearsome
sea monsters. From their holds he saw disgorged amazing cargoes
of porcelain, silk, tea, tin, lacquer ware and embroideries. What he
witnessed was probably the last of this Chinese maritime traffic with
India, for the competition of the swifter Arab carriers put an end
to such long voyages by the junks at the end of the fifteenth century.

From Calicut, Covilhan proceeded north in a small vessel which
touched at various ports. As he wandered from town to town and
saw everywhere vessels being loaded, boxes and bales of merchandise transported by oxcart and donkey and on the backs of sweating
coolies, or carried swung on poles borne on the shoulders of other
human draft animals, and the great quantities of goods displayed
in the warehouses and shops, he realized how great the trade was
between India and the West. He made careful note of what the
Hindus and Moslems of the Malabar Coast were importing: copper, mercury, vermilion, coral, saffron, printed cloth, rosewater,
gold, silver (of which India has literally swallowed up more than
any other country), and cutlery. He saw displayed for sale merchandise manufactured in "Bruges in Flanders and Venice in Italy,"
as the words of a letter of King Manuel have it. He met merchants
from these European cities, also, some of whom had, before his
arrival in India, written of their visits to the country and of what
they had seen. He met, too, men from far-off lands of which even the
names were unknown to him, travelers from Banda, Sumatra, Java,
Cambay, Pegu, Tenasserim, and Siam. But strangest of all, he
found fellow Christians on the Malabar Coast. They claimed descent from the communities established by St. Thomas, who, tradition had it, traveled this far east to make converts. An early Italian
visitor, Santo Stefano, wrote that there were in Calicut "indeed a
thousand families of Christians." True, their ritual was strange and
unlike that of the Portuguese Church, but at least they were different from the heathen who surrounded them. Often on his journey
he would come upon Italians—mostly Venetians and Genoese—

and even Frenchmen and merchants of the Low Countries, but never did he meet a fellow countryman or hear the Lusitanian speech on the lips of any man.

Covilhan was a loyal subject of his king. He saw how the Italian cities were drawing off the lifeblood of all this trade and jealously keeping it for themselves, and more than ever he realized the magnitude and the aim of King John's dreams and plans. He resolved that he would do all in his power to see the proud Italian cities dethroned from their eminence and his own beloved country set high in their place. This goal was to be reached within a few years, but he, poor man, was not to see it.

From Calicut, Covilhan took a small coasting vessel, sailing north to another important seaport, the island of Goa. Here he found, not a Hindu city with a Moorish colony, but an independent Moslem state, carved out of the Empire of Delhi by the vigorous warriors of Bijapur, and governed in 1388 by Mahmud Shah Balmahi II. Though he could not know that the island itself and part of its hinterland were to be the seat of a great Portuguese empire in the East within a few years, Covilhan did realize its prime importance in Indian trade. The future capital of the Indies was already a bustling center for traffic between the East, Arabia, and Persia, particularly with Hormuz, at the mouth of the Persian Gulf. It still was, as it had been reported two centuries earlier by Marco Polo, the main Indian market for horses. These were imported from Arabia for the use of the potentates and nobles of all India. Horses did not breed well in the Indian climate, and the highest prices were paid for fine animals shipped in open vessels, loaded on top of other cargo, from Aden, Schehr, Sohar, Kalat, Masqat, and Hormuz. From Goa they were distributed by boat along the coast, and so inland to their ultimate buyers throughout the peninsula. When Albuquerque took Goa years later, he found in the city 120 of the finest Arabian horses.

With the thorough investigation of the Goanese trade, Covilhan had accomplished his Indian mission. The monsoon had changed, the Arab ships were preparing for their western voyage, and the Portuguese emissary took passage in one of them. It was February or March of 1489 when the ship set its course for Hormuz.* It was

* For a description of the Hormuz of the period, see Hart, *Venetian Adventurer*, pp. 100–102, 152–159.

laden to the gunwales with pepper, ginger, cinnamon, cardamom, mirolabane, tamarind, rhubarb, aloes, porcelain, and fine cotton goods (calicoes), and, safely guarded by the vessel's captain, valuable bundles of musk, amber, and precious stones. This time the voyage was shorter and less tedious than the eastern passage had been, and with favoring winds was made without any recorded incidents.

We have only vague information as to Covilhan's movements between his departure from Hormuz and his arrival back in Cairo. He probably visited the East African port of Sofala, where dwelt an Arab colony engaged in the lucrative trade in gold brought by the natives from the mines in the interior. Though Alvares makes only a passing reference to such a visit,* Ramusio in his Italian version states:

> He went in a ship to the Red Sea and proceeded to Zeila [on the coast of Somaliland] and with some Moorish merchants went and passed over those seas of Ethiopia, which were shown him in Lisbon on the navigation chart, for he was to do all things [necessary] to obtain information, and so he journeyed westward until he reached the place [called] Sofala, where he learned from some Arab mariners that from everywhere on this coast one could proceed by sea to the West, and that its [the sea's] limits were not known, and that there was a very large island more than nine hundred miles from the coast which was called the [island of the] Moon. And having ascertained these things he, very happy, decided to return to Cairo, and so he went again to Zeila, and thence to Aden and then to Tor and finally to Cairo.

As many other early narratives assert that Covilhan did visit Sofala, it may well be that Vasco da Gama's knowledge of the port was derived directly or indirectly from Covilhan's report. In any case such a voyage would not have been very difficult. The Arabs of the east coast of Africa were renowned for their skill in navigation. They had made a careful and detailed study of the coast, its islands, reefs, landmarks, and shoals, and of its winds and currents and their variations.

The next definite information we have concerning Pero de Covilhan is that he arrived back in Cairo at the end of 1490 or the beginning of 1491. Having been away from home for more than

---

* "Ha costa de Çofala em que elle tambem fora." Ramusio, I, 129.

three years, he was eagerly looking forward to keeping his appointment with Paiva, returning with him to Portugal, and to seeing his wife and family again. To his dismay, after much waiting and fruitless inquiry, he finally learned that his luckless fellow traveler had died, probably while endeavoring to enter Ethiopia.* How, when, or where we know not, nor have we knowledge of what Paiva's movements had been, what lands and peoples he had visited, or what information he had accumulated for his sovereign.

Covilhan had efficiently fulfilled the mission entrusted to him. His work had been profitable, enlightening, and thoroughly successful. He had carried out his instructions directly and with dispatch, allowing nothing to stand in his way or turn him aside. He had crossed the Eastern Sea and visited the western coast of India and had brought back full and accurate information concerning them. And now he was weary and saddened and felt that he had well earned a rest from his labors in behalf of King John. But he was never to see his native land again.

As the lonely traveler sat in his lodgings, pondering his next moves, two strangers sought him out and greeted him in Portuguese, a language to which he must have been almost a stranger for some years. They introduced themselves as messengers from Portugal, presented their credentials, and informed him that the king, knowing that this was the appointed time and place of the rendezvous between him and Paiva, had sent them to Cairo.

One was Rabbi Abraham of Beija, the other, Joseph of Lamego, a Jewish shoemaker.† The rabbi had been to Hormuz (here the accounts are at variance) and on his return had appeared before the king with an impressive account of his journey. Joseph of Lamego, humble though his occupation appears to have been, had traveled extensively in the East, to Baghdad and Basra as well as to Hormuz. He, like the learned rabbi, had returned to Lisbon and laid his report before the king. Since more than three years had elapsed without news of either Covilhan or Paiva, Dom John had commissioned the two to proceed secretly to Cairo to find them. He had furnished the two with the proper credentials and funds,

---

* Several modern English historians state, with no supporting authority, that he was murdered.

† Every original authority stresses the fact that he was a shoemaker.

together with a letter to be delivered to Covilhan and Paiva, or to either of them when, and if, found.*

The two royal agents arrived safely enough in Cairo but found much difficulty in locating their fellow countryman in the crowded city without revealing their own identity and mission. At last, by exercising the greatest circumspection, adroitness, and patience, they located Covilhan. On learning that Paiva had died, they followed their instructions and delivered to Covilhan the letter bearing the seal of the king—the letter which they had so carefully and secretly carried with them all the way from Lisbon to Egypt.

Covilhan read the king's message with a sinking heart. He was tired and homesick. His assignment had been an arduous one. He had carried out his orders, had covered thousands of weary miles by land and sea, had traversed burning deserts and tropic seas, and now he longed for his home, for the heather and pine-clad slopes of the Serra da Estrella, where his wife and family were awaiting him. Again he read the letter of his king. It contained most specific and unequivocal instructions: If he and Paiva had completed their mission, they were to delay no longer but return forthwith to Portugal. If, however, they had failed in anything, or had not obtained all the information required of them, they were to continue on their journey until they reached their goal. He referred especially to Prester John, demanding full and precise information concerning him and his kingdom.

There was nothing for it but to obey. It would be impossible to return to Portugal, even though he had done all that the king had required of him personally. But now poor Paiva was dead, and Covilhan felt it his bounden duty to assume his mission as well— to proceed to the Kingdom of Prester John and acquire all the information desired by the king. There was no other course open to him. So, miserable, homesick, and exhausted, he bowed his head and obeyed.

The letter contained further instructions, given we know not why, that Covilhan was first to accompany Rabbi Abraham (who

* It is of interest to note at this point what an important part the Jews played in the early voyages and discoveries of the Portuguese. They appear again and again as trusted councilors, as brilliant geographers and mathematicians, compiling invaluable navigational and other data, as devisers of nautical instruments, as cartographers, as members of expeditions, and, as in this case, in the role of trusted agents and emissaries of the government.

"had sworn to the king that he would not return to Portugal without seeing Ormuz with his own eyes") to Hormuz and thence, after leaving the rabbi to return to Portugal, to proceed on his journey. But Joseph of Lamego was to return forthwith to Portugal from Cairo.

Before leaving for Hormuz, Covilhan wrote a detailed letter to King John, telling him at length of what he had seen and learned about the lands of the East and of India, of its people, its products, and its cities, and of the navigation of the Indian Ocean by the Arab ships. This letter he entrusted for delivery to Joseph, who departed with it at once. Though much has been written about this letter, all search for it has thus far been unavailing, and little is known of it. That it was written and sent is, however, of enormous importance in the history of discovery and exploration. It was the first report from a Portuguese giving his government full account of the west-coast cities of India from personal observation. The Italians had sent letters to their principals in Europe, but Covilhan's communication was all new and fresh to the Portuguese and was designed to take the place of the fragmentary, inaccurate, and often false information then current among them.

Alvares states simply that Covilhan told him personally that

here [in Cairo] he at once wrote by the shoemaker of Lamego as to how he discovered cinnamon and pepper in the city of Calicut, and that cloves came from [a country] beyond, but that all might be had there [in Calicut], and that, moreover, in the said cities of Cananor and Calicut and Goa, all on the coast, and that to this one could navigate by the coast and seas of Guinea, coming to make the coast of Sofala, to which he had also gone, where was a great island which the Moors call the "Island of the Moon." * They say it is three hundred leagues from the coast, and from each one of these lands one could set a course for Calicut.

The Italian version of Alvares outlines the contents of the letter:

concluding that his [the king's] caravels, which carried on trade in Guinea, navigating from land to land, and seeking the coast of this island [Madagascar] and of Sofala, could easily penetrate into these Eastern seas and come to make the coast of Calicut, for there was sea everywhere, as he had learned.

* Madagascar; in Arabic, Jezer el Qomr.

A map may have been sent to King John with the letter, but it is questionable. The very rare first edition of Castanheda's *History of the Discovery and Conquest of India by the Portuguese* (1551) states that Covilhan also sent "a map on which were placed the names of the places where he had been." This sentence was eliminated by Castanheda himself in the second edition of 1554. Evidently the author questioned the authenticity of his information on the matter and deemed it wiser to omit the statement. At any rate the passage was suppressed, though it was copied into the Italian translation of the work made in Venice in 1578.* If the map was sent, it, like the letter, has disappeared.

The question as to whether or not King John ever received Covilhan's letter entrusted for delivery to Joseph of Lamego has been much debated by historians, because of the great importance of its contents to the Portuguese. That no reference is made to it by Resende in his *Chronicle of John II* is no proof that it was not received, nor is the absence of mention of it by other contemporaries conclusive. The letter was entrusted to Joseph of Lamego, an experienced and shrewd traveler. The voyage from Cairo to Lisbon was a simple and comparatively safe one. There does not appear to be any reason to argue from silence that the letter was not delivered.† King John, moreover, was a shrewd and prudent man. His court swarmed with spies, and trade rivalries and diplomatic plottings were ever at the fore. It can easily be comprehended that the precious secret report would be communicated to but a very small circle about the king—among them the Duke of Beja, who later succeeded John on the throne as King Manuel. Under such circumstances it is readily understood why the knowledge of the letter's receipt or its contents was not permitted to extend beyond John's council chamber.‡ From this we may conclude at least that Covilhan's report might have been one of the cogent reasons for the

* This translation, *Historia dell' Indie Orientali, comp. dal Sig. Fernando Lopes di Castagneda,* translated by Affonso de Ulloa, evidently followed the first Portuguese edition.

† Castanheda is noncommittal, saying only, "and if the King Dom John received the letters which Pero de Covilhan sent by the Jews [*sic*], I did not learn."

‡ The silence concerning the letter may also have been a measure of protection for Covilhan himself.

king's preparations for a maritime expedition to India and for King
Manuel's carrying out of his predecessor's plans.*

After seeing Joseph of Lamego well on his way back to Lisbon,
Covilhan and Rabbi Abraham departed for Hormuz. For the third
time the king's emissary wearily crossed the desert and the Red Sea.
At Aden the two men boarded a small Arab coasting vessel, skirting
the shores of Hadramaut, Oman, and Masqat, and finally reached
their destination.

Hormuz has been delightfully described by an Englishman, Ralph
Fitch, who visited it in the next century, before the city had changed
much—except that it had passed under the control of the Portuguese. His account is worth repeating:

> Ormuz is an island in circuit about five and twentie or thirtie miles,
> and is the driest island in the world, for there is nothing growing in it
> but onely salt, for their water, food or victuals, and all things necessary,
> come out of Persia, which is about twelve miles from thence. All the
> ilands thereabout be very fruitfull, from whence all kinde of victuals
> are sent to Ormuz. . . . In this town are marchants of all nations, and
> many Moors and Gentiles. Here is very great trade of all sortes of
> spices, drugs, silke, cloth of silke, fine tapestrie of Persia, great store of
> pearles which come from the Isle of Baharim, and are the best pearles
> of all others, and many horses of Persia, which serve all India. Their
> women are very strangely attyred, wearing on their noses, eares, neckes,
> armes and legges many rings set with jewels, and lockes of silver and
> golde in their eares, and a long bar of golde upon the side of their noses.
> Their eares with the weight of their jewels be worne so wide that a
> man may thrust three of his fingers into them.

Covilhan recounted nothing to Alvares of what transpired in
Hormuz. In due time the two men separated and Rabbi Abraham
set out on his return journey to Portugal. Castanheda avers that
when Abraham left Covilhan he, bore "another such letter for the
king Dom John as Joseph had carried." That the same information
was sent to John at two different times by two trusted and sagacious
agents justifies one in assuming that at least one of the reports

* We shall find that Vasco da Gama set out directly for Calicut. We are told
that he carried a letter from his sovereign to the Samorin (ruler) of the country.
"All his inquiries en route were for Calicut, not for ports en route. It may be
only coincidental, but it seems to me legitimate to draw the conclusion from
these considerations that the letter was the base, or at least one of the bases, of
the instructions given later [to Gama]." Ficalho, *Viagens*, p 122

reached the king's hands, and that the information therein played an important part in the preparations for Gama's voyage.

Being evidently a man who ever sought to acquire information and to see new lands, Abraham probably returned overland by caravan by way of Basra, Damascus, and Aleppo, and thence by one of the much-used and centuries-old trade routes to the west, and so home. He, too, was the bearer of valuable information to the king, for it is difficult to conceive of the latter's sending two men to Cairo, as he did, without instructing them to obtain data which would make the long journey worth while to him.

From Hormuz, Covilhan proceeded to Jidda, the port of Mecca, and thence to the holy city itself, and to Medina. No order to visit these cities appears in the report of the instructions given by King' John. It may be that he was near enough—perhaps traveling on a Red Sea coaster—to have been seized with a desire to see the holy places of the Moslems. For him it was a simple undertaking. His Arabic was probably perfect after all the years he had spent in Mohammedan countries, and he had a sufficient knowledge of the ritual and ceremonies of the mosque. He had adopted the Arab garb for its comfort and convenience. Beards were commonly worn, and his complexion, burned for years by the sun and winds of the East, made it unnecessary to adopt any disguise. We are not here concerned with his sojourn in Arabia or with what he saw in the sacred places, except to note that he appears to be the first Christian—surely the first Portuguese—to visit the forbidden shrines of the followers of the Prophet.

From Arabia, Covilhan's journey led him to Sinai, where he rejoiced in worshiping in the Christian church of the Monastery of St. Catherine. Thence he proceeded again to Tor and so through the Red Sea and the Strait of Bab el Mandeb to Zeila, where he landed, to proceed thence westward overland into the Kingdom of Prester John.

The peoples of Ethiopia whom he met on the coast were a strange lot. Correa thus describes the group (probably Somalis) who greeted the Portuguese embassy of 1520:

They are a poor civil people with miserable clothes, and they come into the water uncovered, a black, tall people with thick matted locks, which from their birth they neither cut nor comb, so that they wear their hair like a lump of wool, and they carry pointed oiled sticks with which they scratch the vermin which crawl beneath, because they cannot reach their scalps with their fingers, and scratching their heads is their sole occupation.

Alvares adds his comments about the people:

The country people . . . kept fields of Indian corn, and . . . come from a distance to sow these lands and rocky ridges which are among these mountains: there are also in these parts very beautiful flocks, such as cows and goats. The people that we found here are almost naked, so that all they had showed, and they were very black. These people were Christians, and the women wore a little more covering, but it was very little.*

It was 1492 or 1493 when Pero de Covilhan set foot in Ethiopia, the land of Prester John, where reigned Alexander, "Lion of the Tribe of Judah, and King of Kings," † the land where Dom John had ordered him to go. A few brief pages must suffice to sketch the further adventures of the Portuguese agent. Traveling to the capital with a caravan of merchants, he was well received at the emperor's court. Covilhan presented to the emperor his engraved plate of brass and the letters from the Portuguese king, written in Arabic—those letters which he had probably carried on his person all the seven long years that he had been traveling. Alexander received the letters "with much pleasure and joy," and promised to send the emissary back to his homeland "with much honor." However, as has ever been the way in the East, time dragged on; and the weeks passed into months, with no move made to dispatch the Portuguese to the coast and home. Then came bad news. Alexander, while on an expedition to stamp out a rebellion, was killed by arrow-fire in a night attack. This occurred on May 7, 1494. Alexander was succeeded for a short time by his very young son Amda Syon (Column of Zion). During the chaotic seven months of his reign no attention could be paid the unfortunate Portuguese and his mission, and he was forced to wait and twirl his thumbs in impatience. But at least he turned his time to good advantage by learning to speak and write the language of the Ethiopians—and it was well that he did so.

The boy emperor died in October of 1494 at the age of seven;

* Recent personal observations of the author have revealed no great change in many of the customs of these people.

† "Negus Negasti," still a title of the Emperor of Ethiopia.

and as Alexander had left no other children, the crown passed to his brother Naod (called Nahu by Alvares), who ascended the throne without delay. As soon as was feasible, Covilhan presented himself before the newly crowned Negus, petitioning that he be allowed to depart in peace. Naod received him "with much favor," but flatly refused to grant him permission to leave the country.

One may picture the consternation and despair of John's emissary. He had traveled thousands of miles to visit the Ethiopian court, had been well received and entertained; but he had been away from home for almost eight years and had every reason to want to leave the barbarous Abyssinian land and return to his beloved Portugal with the valuable information he had gathered. But it was not to be, so the Portuguese, schooled and disciplined by years of adventure and trials, appears to have taken the decision of the emperor philosophically and to have made the best of his misfortune. Thereafter Covilhan occupied positions of ever increasing importance at court and acquired extensive lands and other property.*

He was not by any means the only European dwelling in the land: There was Nicolò Bianca Leone, once a friar, later a painter, who had lived among the Ethiopians for more than forty years—or so he said—and who initiated the Portuguese into their strange manners and customs. Alvares remarks drily of him that "he was a very honorable person, and a great gentleman, although a painter." And there was another white man, whom Covilhan never met. He told Alvares many years later that this man had lived in a grotto in a deep ravine for over twenty years and had finally sealed himself into it from the inside with a solid wall, and there he had died. During his long residence in Ethiopia, Covilhan met other Europeans, some of whom came voluntarily from other lands and some of whom were refugees from Moorish forays on the Red Sea. None of these, having once entered the land of Prester John, was allowed to depart.

Though their ritual and practices were far removed from those of

* It would appear that, as in the case of the Mongol emperors of China, the rulers of Ethiopia were most anxious to engage the services of Westerners in their government. Having little knowledge of foreign countries, the advice and guidance, as well as the manual skills of the Europeans, were most valuable to them. This would seem the logical explanation of the refusal of successive rulers to Covilhan's pleas for leave to depart. See Hart, *Venetian Adventurer,* 3rd ed., p. 143

Catholic Portugal, Covilhan was not difficult to please in religious matters. Being among Christians after so many years with the infidels was sufficient for him. The one thing he refused to do was to go to confession, as he told Alvares that the priests of Ethiopia did not preserve its secrecy. The Ethiopian abstention from pork and their observation of Saturday instead of Sunday disturbed him not a bit.

As the years came and went, Covilhan became ever more useful to Naod and was even appointed governor of a district. It was also early intimated to him that the Negus desired him to take to himself an Ethiopian wife and beget "sons and a lineage." * Though Covilhan rebelled at first against this arrangement, he finally, of necessity, capitulated. His wife and family in far-away Portugal had probably long given him up for dead. He had been a wanderer without a home for years and perhaps welcomed a fireside of his own. Although we know that his wife was dark—perhaps black—we also know that many of the Ethiopian women are beautiful. As a prominent and rich man, high in the favor of the emperor, he probably could select a wife from the highest class. Moreover, the Portuguese, both in their colonies and in their homeland, have never, from the very earliest times, drawn a strict color line in their social or marital relations. That the union was a fertile one admits of no doubt. Alvares tells us that Covilhan came to him once "with his wife and some of his sons." Correa speaks of one of his sons as "gallant and a gentleman," in spite of being dark. It may be inferred from these few details that Covilhan became reconciled to his fate and may even have been happy in his exile, though he must have ever looked . forward to a day when he could return to Portugal.

Many years passed, until on July 30, 1508, Naod was gathered to his fathers and his young son David † came to the throne. Covilhan, though aging, still lived in the hope of returning home, and he petitioned the newly crowned Negus for leave to depart. But even though he enjoyed the friendship and the strong support of the Empress Dowager Helena, his request was refused. David answered that "he had not come during his [David's] time, and that his ancestors had given him so many lands and lordships, which he should govern, and he had not lost any, and inasmuch as they [his ances-

---

* "Que fizesse filhos e geração," Correa, I, 1, 7.
† So called by the Portuguese. His Ethiopian title was Lebna Dengel.

tors] had not given him this permission, he was not in a position to grant it, and so the matter stood." *

More years passed and more and more Europeans arrived in the country of Prester John: Genoese, Catalans, a Greek of Chios, a Basque, and a German. Then there were two Italians, Tommaso Grandini and Nicolò Musa. One Portuguese priest, John Gomes, also had visited the country in the company of a "Moor," but in some unknown manner had been permitted to depart.

So passed six and twenty years, and life went on for Covilhan with little change. Then suddenly (about May, 1520) came news that a Portuguese embassy under Rodrigo de Lima had landed at the port of Massaua and was approaching the capital. Covilhan hastened to meet it and was overjoyed to find a friar, Francisco Alvares of Coimbra, one of the party. He could at last confess as he desired; and it was in the course of his many conversations with the priest that he told piecemeal the story of his adventures which Alvares has preserved for us—and some of which he probably related later to Correa, who has given us further details.

The chroniclers make it plain that Covilhan was of inestimable service to Dom Rodrigo throughout the stay of the embassy in Ethiopia, as interpreter, guide, and adviser. He even assigned one of his sons, "já casy homen" (already almost a man), to serve the envoy while in the land.

After a lengthy stay in Ethiopia the embassy prepared to depart for the coast. Covilhan, his wife, and some of his sons, together with their attendants and slaves, accompanied it two days' journey. Now seventy-three or seventy-four years old, Covilhan had abandoned any idea of ever returning to Portugal. The narratives differ as to his final renunciation, one stating that it was voluntary, "he being much at peace in the many lands he held," another averring that David again withheld his consent. However, he persuaded Rodrigo de Lima to take with him one of his sons—probably the one who had served the ambassador during his stay at the court— a young man of twenty-three years, a mulatto "dark as a russet

* The quotation is from the Ramusio version, which is slightly fuller than the Portuguese. Purchas (*His Pilgrimes,* XI, 18) quaintly translated it, "Neyther would his successors permit that Ulysses to returne, a man of many languages, and much usefull for his experience in the world "

pear." Covilhan entreated the ambassador to present him to the Portuguese king, that he might be rewarded in Covilhan's stead for the great services he had rendered his country. He also requested "that he might be permitted to return to recount to the Prester what he had seen in Portugal, for his mother and the relatives whom he had in the Prester's land would have pleasure, and that if his wife who lived in Covilhan had any son or daughter he should give her twenty ounces of gold, the which he handed over to his son." Covilhan gave to Dom Rodrigo one hundred ounces of gold for his son's expenses, and to his son a letter for the king, together with the plaque of copper which the King Dom John had given him when he had instructed him as to his orders, "because the king, seeing the plaque, would give him credence. But this son died of an illness on the road, so Dom Rodrigo returned to Pero de Covilhan the large amount of gold which the son had carried with him."

This is the last record we have of Covilhan. We do not know when, where, or how he died, or the fate of his Portuguese or Ethiopian families. He had served his royal master well—too well for his own good. The mission that was to have been accomplished in two or three years had lasted the greater part of a lifetime and was to terminate finally in death in a foreign land, far from his beloved Portugal.

Covilhan's name and story well deserve to be rescued from oblivion. A humble servant of government, he devoted himself fearlessly, tirelessly, and without stint to the fulfillment of his promise to his king. He gathered and sent invaluable information concerning India and the Levant to his sovereign. He sacrificed retirement and ease, honors and rewards, to the accomplishment of that part of the mission entrusted to the companion who had died. There is nowhere to be found any acknowledgment of the royal debt, any record of any recompense to his family, or an official statement of the indebtedness of his fellow countrymen for his invaluable reports of the East—those reports which, if received in Lisbon (as there is a great likelihood they were), aided materially in the preparations for the voyage of Vasco da Gama.

All in all, Covilhan was a fine example of the spirit of the age: a soldier and an explorer, keen of mind, acquisitive of every sort of knowledge, brilliant as a linguist, resourceful and tactful as a traveler in those parts of the world where travel was most difficult and most hazardous. As one of his fellow Portuguese has written of him, "the keynote of his character was 'obedience.' " Perhaps the words of Francisco Alvares, who knew him well, best and most succinctly characterize him: "This Pero de Covilhan is a man who knew all that he was ordered to do, and gave an account of them all." *

* "Este Pero de Covilhan he homem que todas as cousas a que o mandaram soube e de todas dá conta."

'.

CHAPTER VI

THE BUILDING OF THE ARMADA

In far-famed Ulyssias * port now stand
The ships all, ready.
—Camões, *Os Lusíadas*, IV, vi

1

HE record of the return to Lisbon of Dias and his ships is the last notation for some years of the Portuguese search for a sea road to India. Though the reports of both Covilhan and Dias had demonstrated the feasibility of the route, no further known move was made to take advantage of it for nearly a decade. These accounts, however, aroused great hopes in Dom John that at last he was to reach his goal—the control of the trade of the Indies—and he set about putting his plans into execution. But time and events were against him, and another, King Manuel, less worthy than he, was to reap what he had sown and gather the fruits and the glory of his toil.

One obstacle to implementing Dias's discoveries was that of obtaining crews willing to follow their commanders on such long, venturesome voyages, whose end was unknown and whose dangers, both real and imaginary, increased with every mile traversed. Dias's voyage itself had demonstrated this difficulty, for he had been forced by the threatened mutiny of his men to turn back at the very gates of India. Moreover, "a new conceit possessed most of the mariners, as had done before touching Bogiadore [Bojador], that there was no sayling any further."

From the account of Covilhan's travels we may infer a long delay in the king's receipt of his letters (if they were received), with their information and their discussion of the wisest route to follow after doubling the Cape of Good Hope. This delay may have been one of many months, or even of years. Meanwhile, Portuguese relations

* Legend has it that Ulysses was the founder of Lisbon.

[79]

with Morocco had taken a turn for the worse, and much time and money were expended in an expedition across the Strait of Gibraltar. There was, too, the fear of the hostility of Venice, the Turks, and the powerful Sultan of Egypt, nor were relations with the Spanish monarchs too settled or happy. Moreover, the king had not been in good health since the year 1490. The internal affairs of the kingdom and a personal bereavement served but to aggravate his illness, interfere with his plans, and bring them to naught during the last years of his reign.

King John had devoted himself wholeheartedly to the welfare of his country. He had broken the power of the nobility and strengthened the influence of the throne. He had been successful in his struggle with the Spanish crown. He had extended the Portuguese dominions in Africa and vastly expanded its trade. And when ten years of his successful reign had passed, he dreamed of uniting his country with Spain and of seeing his only legitimate son, Affonso, on the throne of the Peninsula. After much negotiation a marriage between Affonso and Isabella, eldest daughter of Ferdinand and Isabella of Spain, was arranged in the year 1490. The union was celebrated with extraordinary pomp and ceremony, such as had never before been witnessed in Portugal. The plague was raging in Lisbon, so the festivities were held in Évora, second city of the kingdom, where a great wooden pavilion was erected for the occasion. But even in Évora "there were outbreaks of the plague, for which the king was very sad, because it would not be well for the feasts if they could not be given with that perfection which he had ordered." After the celebrations the King and Queen of Castile escorted their daughter to the city of Borba, where "with many tears and great sadness the princess kissed their hands and took her leave of them, and they gave her their blessings, and the princess began her journey [to Badajoz], and with her were nine ladies, daughters of great and noble men of Castile and Aragon, and there came as her duenna and chief lady-in-waiting Dona Isabel de Sousa, a Portuguese, a proud and prudent woman, and of most honest life, and other women and servants of her household." The chronicler Resende waxes eloquent for entire chapters in his descriptions of the princess's triumphal journey through the country and of the state banquets, pageants, and theatrical performances that marked the coming union of the two kingdoms.

The rejoicing of the king and the happiness of the young pair were of short duration. On July 12, 1491, the king rode with some guests to swim in the river Tagus, as he was accustomed to do often in the hot summer months. He invited his son Affonso to go with him, as was usual. At first the prince sent word that he was tired, but he later decided to follow. When he was ready to leave, his riding mule had not been brought up, so he mounted a handsome cream-colored mount belonging to his equerry. After he had started, he changed his mind about swimming and went instead for a gallop through the fields. Suddenly his horse stumbled and threw him. He was carried senseless to the nearest house, that of a fisherman. There, in spite of the ministrations of the royal physicians and the prayers of those who crowded around his bed, the young man expired without regaining consciousness.

"He died, being of the age of seventeen years and twenty days, appearing in body, in countenance, in wisdom, in judgment and in poise like a man of twenty-five. He had been married seven months and twenty-two days . . . and he who on that day and on all other [days] had dwelt in regal halls, hung with rich brocades and tapestries, had only (nor could they find other for him) the sad hut of a poor fisherman. . . . And his eyes, once so happy and full of beauty, were in that hour blinded and forever without sight . . . and his sweet mouth, whence had issued so many gentle, tender, and welcome words and from which many had received kindness and happiness, at this moment ceased forever to speak, and his beautiful royal hands, kissed each day for the great and many favors which he bestowed, were in this brief space of time turned to naught. And the ears that were so wont to hear matchless and sweet music and pleasant discourse, how they have become deaf to the lamentations of the king and the queen and the princess, and the multitude of loud cries and hopeless weeping which all offered for him! . . . O Lord God Eternal, how incomprehensible are Thy secrets. Oh, would that one might know Thy judgments. And what sins could such an angelic creature have committed, one of such a tender age, to die such an unhappy and so sudden a death without benefit of confession or of Communion?"

So from the dusty pages of a half-forgotten chronicle comes echoing the sobbing threnody over the long intervening centuries that lie between us and the untimely death of the heir of Dom John, "the Perfect Prince."

The king, whose health had already begun to fail, never recovered from the loss of his only legitimate son. Grief and disappointment began to affect him visibly. There was no longer hope of transmitting his expanding dominions to a child of his body, for his efforts to secure the crown for his illegitimate son George were frustrated by the opposition of both Queen Leonor and the court. With a heavy heart he was forced to name as his heir and successor his first cousin, Emanuel, Duke of Beja, and brother of the queen.

In addition to this sore trial, disputes with Spain after the return of Columbus from his first voyage of discovery disturbed the king greatly. Indeed, it is very possible that his fear that the Spanish would win in the division of newly discovered lands stimulated him finally to make a move in the direction of further exploration and discovery.[1] Therefore, shortly before his death he roused himself from his ever increasing gloom and apathy sufficiently to give orders for the preparation of a fleet for the Indian venture and to name a commander to lead it on the greatest quest of his dreams, the voyage from Portugal to the shores of Calicut.

It was too late. Fate intervened, and John never saw his fleet launched or the ships sail down the Tagus and out to sea. Shortly after work had begun on the vessels, Dom John began to have fainting spells and was increasingly prevented by illness from carrying on state affairs. Rumors (which have never been either confirmed or disproved) spread at court that he was being slowly poisoned. There were grounds for the reports, for he had laid his hand heavily on his nobles and grandees—and even Queen Leonor is suspected by some historians. He had made many bitter and determined enemies, and he was the first King of Portugal who was forced to employ a personal bodyguard. As the months passed the king grew ever worse and finally gave visible signs of uremic poisoning. He recognized his condition and calmly called his entourage about him to inform them that he knew the end was near.

Resende, his personal friend and chronicler, was at his side during his last hours and has described the scene in great detail: "Though the king was suffering much, the Bishop of Tangier reminded him of his many pious and necessary deeds left undone." The Bishop of Algarve, who was also present, was a worry to the king even at that hour:

For, though a right good man, very liberal and a spender of money, he had been but a poor priest of God, and never said mass or paid attention to the divine offices. . . . And now in his last hour the king said to him: "Bishop, I depart bearing a heavy burden on your account; for love of me live well henceforth, and for the service of God, and give me your oath so to do." And the bishop gave it to him, and he took him by the hand [as a promise] to keep his word. . . . And when they called him "Highness," as was their custom, he said, "Call me not 'Highness,' for I am but a sack of earth and worms." . . . He sent to ask at what height the tide stood, and when they told him he said, "Two hours hence I shall reach my end." And so it was. . . . And at the last . . . his soul departed from his body on Sunday, when the sun was about to set, on the 25th of October 1495 . . . at the age of forty years and six months, of which he had been married to the queen, D. Leonor, twenty five years and had reigned fourteen years and two months. And since he had been most virtuous in his life, he reached his end in this manner, which is one greatly to be envied.[2]

Thus passed away at an early age the man who had done much in fostering and furthering the plans of Prince Henry, and one whose reign had witnessed the completion of the discovery of the West African coast and the doubling of the Cape of Good Hope. By his efforts Portugal had reached the Indian Ocean and the information had been gathered which made possible the glories of his successor, in truth surnamed the Fortunate. And Manuel was indeed most fortunate in having had the groundwork of his enterprises so wisely and substantially laid by Dom John. How he pursued those enterprises and what was the eventful outcome is the tale that this book seeks to recount.

2

The discovery of the southern coast of Africa and of the Cape of Good Hope at first aroused but little enthusiasm or interest in Portugal. News of discoveries and explorations of hitherto unknown lands had poured into the country so steadily for nearly seventy-five years that they were no longer a novelty. Except for the slaves, Guinea pepper, ivory and gold—all won with fighting or toil under hot suns and on barbarian shores—nothing had been discovered to fulfill the promise of the fabulous treasures of spices and precious stones believed always to be lying just over the horizon. Duarte

Pacheco Pereira well expressed the sentiment of his age when he wrote: "Although the coast discovered at his [King John's] command yields no profit, we must not blame him for this; the blame lies with the land, which is almost deserted and produces nothing to make the heart of man glad." And this was written of the land which was the cradle of the great, fertile, and prosperous Union of South Africa!

John had made substantial progress in preparations for the expedition designed to complete and crown the work of Dias. It was to cover the entire distance between Portugal and the shores of India. The king had commanded suitable timber to be felled in the crown forests of Leiria and Alcácer. "One John of Bragança, a young man of the mountains [and said to be Dom John's Master of the Hunt], was appointed overseer of the work. It [the timber] was conveyed to Lisbon in the year 1494." And Bartholomeu Dias, selected because of his long and successful experience in the sailing of ships, was made superintendent of construction.[3]

Damião de Goes, chronicler of the reign of Dom Manuel, tells of the way in which the newly enthroned king took up John's enterprises of discovery:

And since, with these realms and seignories he also inherited the prosecution of such a high enterprise [as this] on which his predecessors had embarked, which was the discovery of the East by this our ocean sea, on which so much industry, so much labor and expense had been bestowed for seventy and five years, he [Manuel] wished to show immediately, in the first year of his reign, how great a desire he cherished to add to the crown of this kingdom new titles, even higher than that of "Lord of Guinea," which, by reason of this discovery, King D. John had taken.[4] Whereupon, in the following December, the king, being in Montemor-o-Novo, held several general councils in which the wisdom of sending a fleet to India was discussed. The majority of his advisers opposed his policy, and made every effort to dissuade him from his intention. They declared that "the hope was doubtful, while the perils were great and certain; navigation was most difficult, and India very far from our climes, with the immeasurable distances of remote regions lying between; that there were no advantages which equaled the risks and insupportable hardships of such dangerous voyages. That he should take into consideration that he might become engaged in war with the Emperor of Egypt [called the Sultan] most powerful in that part of the East, and that if he should insist on going on as he wished to do, how great an envy he would bring upon himself from the other Christian princes."

Other voices were raised in opposition to Manuel's proposal because of the small population of Portugal and the insufficiency of her finances. He was warned more specifically that the opening of a sea route to India could not fail to precipitate bitterness and quarrels with other European sea powers, especially if he tried to enforce his idea of establishing a monopoly of the seaborne trade. The Egyptian difficulties were analyzed, and it was argued that the sultan could not look with favor—to say the least—on the resultant deprivation of transit and other revenue if and when the Persian and Red Sea routes were cut or blockaded by the Portuguese. The Venetians, so powerful in the Alexandrine trade, would aid and abet the sultan and might even join him in a war against Portugal. In a word, if Manuel's proposed plans were pushed through to completion, he would bring the whole world down upon his head—and upon Portugal's.

All arguments were in vain, even though they had good common sense and much historical experience to back them. Dom Manuel's decision had already been reached. He knew well that all these objections had already been made to the aims and expeditions of both Prince Henry and King John, and also that they had not been in the least deterred by them. The enterprise, moreover, had been developed too far to be abandoned. It had become a historical necessity. The stone had started to roll, slowly at first, but ever gaining momentum, until nothing could restrain or slacken its speed thereafter. It had to run its course. The councils were adjourned, and Manuel began to act vigorously. Later events proved that in the long view his opponents were right and he was wrong.

The king's first move to put his and John's ideas into execution was to order active work to be resumed on the ships in the dockyards. He directed Bartholomeu Dias to see to it that all were built with great care, "following what he knew was required, in order to resist the fury of the seas in the vicinity of the great Cape of Good Hope."

The fleet fitted out for the voyage consisted of four vessels. Though the records are not unanimous as to their names, the great weight of authority gives them as the *São Gabriel* (the flagship), the *São Rafael,* the *Berrio,* and an unnamed store ship.[5]

The *São Gabriel* and the *São Rafael* were the ships whose construction had been ordered and begun in Dom John's lifetime. Dias had taken advantage of his long experience in sailing the African coasts and buffeting the gales of the Atlantic, and designed the vessels accordingly. He abandoned the lateen-rigged caravels as being too frail and too low in the water * and built instead sturdier, heavier, square-rigged vessels called *naus.* They were of greater draft and were slower, but gained in space, comfort, safety, and general seagoing qualities.

Compared to modern vessels the tonnage of the two was ridiculously small—roughly 100 to 120 tons,[6] though it must be noted that the ship's ton of the fifteenth century was perhaps double that of today's measurement. The classic rule in shipbuilding—one followed until recent times—was that a vessel's length should not exceed four times her beam, and drawings and paintings of the period indicate that the shipbuilders of the "age of discovery" generally followed this rule. The ships were intentionally built small, to facilitate maneuvering in shoal waters or rivers.

Though they were thoroughly seaworthy, the ships were not built on beautiful lines. They were flat-bottomed, with high square stern and bows, the latter so greatly elevated that the bowsprit could (and did) serve as a fourth mast for the spread of a square spritsail. The bowsprit bore—carved in wood—the figurehead of the ship's patron saint. Wales were fastened along the hull near the waterline to check or reduce excessive rolling. To minimize the inevitable fouling by barnacles and marine borers, the bottoms of the ships were plentifully daubed with tallow and pitch or with *cifa,* a thick mixture of tallow and fish oil.[7] In spite of this precaution it was necessary to beach and careen vessels very often for scraping off barnacles, weeds, and so forth, and repitching and recalking the hulls. The ships were calked with a mixture of quicklime and oakum, kneaded with oil to protect the wood from worms, and strips of wood were nailed over the seams on the inside. In addition on the inside, over the calking and strips were nailed plates of lead as a protection against the battering of the waves. The portion of the hull above the water line was painted black—probably with some

---

* Lateen sails may have also been part of the equipment.

tarry mixture—as a preservative.* Heavy planks "two fingers thick" were attached to the sides of the hull for protection in fighting.

When vessels were not sufficiently laden to ride properly they were ballasted by sand, stones, gravel, and so forth, shoveled into the lowest part of the hold. This ballast was gradually removed as the ship was sufficiently laden to ensure stability. Leakage was an ordinary and expected occurrence in such ships, and wooden pumps were installed to keep it at a minimum. In addition to the ever present vile-smelling bilge water, the seamen often carelessly threw all sorts of refuse into the hold, so that it rapidly became a foul and noisome place. When it became unbearable, the ship was beached, everything unloaded, the inside of the hull washed down, and new ballast placed aboard. Rats, lice, fleas, cockroaches, and other vermin swarmed everywhere under these conditions and were a veritable plague to the ship's company.

Six anchors were usually carried on Portuguese ships of the time, as they were often lost in storms. Those not in use were stored in the hold, ready at hand in case of need. A single capstan with four bars was used, and the anchors were raised to the tunes of sea chanteys that have been traditional for hundreds of years. Hawsers and rigging were of flax rope, though after India was reached cordage of coir (coconut fiber) was introduced. The rudder post of this type of ship was carried high up the stern, and the heavy wooden tiller was fitted to a hole in the post. The helmsman was stationed under the poop deck. His vision was usually obscured or cut off by sails, deck obstructions, or towering forecastle, so he steered by his compass and by instructions shouted by the officer of the watch.[8] As an aid during calms and to resist contrary currents, long and sturdy sweeps were carried and when necessary were worked by the crew through ports in the bulwarks. In the waist of each vessel was carried a long boat (*batel*) and a lighter yawl rowed by four or six men.

The armament of each vessel consisted of twenty guns, the heavier ones made of wrought-iron staves bound together with iron hoops. They were mounted on clumsy forked bases. The lighter guns were bombards, one-pounder matchlocks, and the like. The crew carried no firearms, but used crossbows, spears, axes, swords, javelins, and

---

* After 1516, when the Portuguese saw its use on Chinese junks, their hulls, both above and below the waterline, were painted with *galagala*, a coat of hair mixed with tar.

boarding pikes. Some steel armor was worn by the officers, but most of the men contented themselves with leather jerkins and breast-plates. In time of battle the men in the waist of the vessel were shielded from arrows by heavy strips of canvas. Shields with the arms of the owners were fastened along the bulwarks of the "castles" and the arms were also emblazoned on the flags flown on setting sail or on approaching land.

The hold was divided by bulkheads into three compartments. Amidships was stored the water in casks, together with extra cables, all of rope, as wire was not yet employed for the purpose. In the afterhold were the powder, shot (stone balls for cannon were still in common use), and firearms and other weapons, while the forward hold was used for food and spare equipment. The ships were constructed with two decks, the lower one, like the hold, divided into three sections, in which were stored more provisions, as well as trade goods, presents, and sundry merchandise.

Both the *São Gabriel* and the *São Rafael* were three-masters, each mast surmounted by a crow's-nest for lookouts and, in time of battle, for men armed with crossbows, grenades, spears, and other missiles. The foremast and mainmast were square rigged, while the mizzenmast carried a large triangular sail. On each sail was painted in red a large cross of the Order of Christ. The third ship, the *Berrio* (*Birrio* in Castanheda), was not built on the king's stocks, but in Lagos. It was purchased from one Berrios, a pilot, after whom she was named.[9] She was a swift caravel carrying lateen sails, but was very small—of only fifty tons burden. The fourth vessel was that designed for carrying the extra stores necessary for the long voyage. She was bought by the king's order from one Ayres Correa, a shipowner of Lisbon. Her name is nowhere mentioned and her build and rigging are unknown. Her tonnage is also doubtful, but was somewhere between 120 and 300 tons.[10] The average speed of Gama's vessels in a fair wind was from 6½ to 8 miles an hour.

When the *São Gabriel* and *São Rafael* were completed and the other two vessels had been delivered, Dom Manuel summoned before him one of his favorites, Fernão Lourenço, factor of the House of Mines and "a person in whom he had confidence, and one of no small account, and ordered him to equip the armada and provide it with every thing necessary, as speedily as ever he could."

The plans called for a voyage that might last three years, and stores for this period were loaded on board. Great ovens were set up at the king's command in the Valle de Zebro, for vast quantities of sea biscuit (hardtack) had to be baked. Each man was allowed as a daily ration 1½ pounds of these biscuits, 1 pound of (salt) beef or ½ pound of pork, 2½ pints of water, ⅓ gill of vinegar and ⅙ gill of olive oil. For fast days ½ pound of rice, codfish, or cheese was substituted for the meat. A plentiful supply of wine was put on board, stored in pipes or barrels,* and each man was allowed the generous amount of 1¼ pints a day. Then, as today, wine was the common drink of the Latin peoples and could not be stinted if the men were to be kept contented. For occasional variety in the diet, beans, flour, lentils, sardines, prunes, onions, garlic, sugar (white and brown), almonds, and honey were carried. Fish could be caught by the men themselves. It might be noted that the conveniences for cooking must have limited the menus to a minimum number and variety of dishes. The food was slung in wooden bowls at the men, and they ate from trenchers with their knives and fingers. Forks had not yet come into use on shipboard—for that matter, but few, if any, were in use at table anywhere on land. The men slept where they could.[11] Mariners on royal expeditions probably fared as well as, or even better than, their fellows ashore, though then, as in all times, it has been the privilege of sailors to grumble.

Little, if any, provision could be made to combat scurvy, the curse and scourge of seafarers through the ages. Its real causes and cure were not understood until much later. It had been observed, however, that fresh vegetables and fruits, especially citrus fruits, were of value. The accounts of numberless voyages, including that of Gama's first passage, are filled with the sufferings and horrors of the dread disease.

, In addition to the stores of provisions, the king ordered spare sails, tackle, and equipment of all kinds "and in each vessel all kinds of drugs for the sick, a surgeon and a priest for confession." Storerooms in each ship were filled with

"all kinds of merchandise, of what was in the kingdom and what was outside it, and much gold and silver coined into moneys of every king,

* One authority states that the casks for water, wine, oil, and vinegar were lined with earthenware and reinforced with iron hoops.

both of Christendom and of the Moors, and cloths of gold and silk, and of wool of every sort and color, and many jewels of gold—necklaces, chains, and bracelets, and hand basins and ewers of white silver and of gilt, swords, daggers, plain and engraved and embellished with workmanship of silver and gold, and spears and shields, all ornamented, so that they might be presented to the kings and lords of the countries where they might land—and a small quantity of every kind of spice."

Despite this lengthy list given by Correa—a list written either from hearsay or else evolved from his very vivid imagination concerning affairs about which he had little or no first-hand information—the truth is that the goods intended for gifts and barter were sadly lacking in quantity and quality. They were not such as would tempt wealthy civilized peoples like those of the Indian States. The storerooms contained articles good enough for the savages of the west coast of Africa, but otherwise the goods were worthless. A partial list makes this self-evident: striped cotton goods, sugar, honey, coral and glass beads, hand basins, red hats, trousers, bells, tin jewelry, and the like. Of gold and silver money there was practically none.

As the preparations for the voyage neared their completion and the ships were being loaded down at the quays by the river's edge, King Manuel was called upon to make a most momentous decision—the selection of a leader for the expedition. The voyage was to be no ordinary one. It was to be the most important ever planned or undertaken by the Portuguese crown. The first two voyages of Columbus had revealed hitherto unknown countries, and the Portuguese king was determined that the rich lands of the Indies were not to be discovered, possessed, or exploited by Spain or any other country if he could forestall their attempts.

If the need were only for a skilled navigator, Bartholomeu Dias would probably have been the man chosen. He had taken Portuguese ships farther on the sea road toward India than had any navigator before him. He knew intimately the coasts of Africa, their winds, currents, and weather phenomena, and he had personally supervised the building of the ships for the proposed undertaking. But the present expedition called for more than a skilled navigator. Its leader must be a man of affairs, a diplomat, and, if need be, a soldier.[12] He must be a person not only capable of taking his ships to India and bringing them home safely but one equipped by training and experience to deal with men of many races and characters, be they African tribal chiefs or Arab or Indian princes and potentates. He must be a man of quick decision in affairs of state and of business, and one able to stand his ground and enforce the instructions of his king, either peaceably or with his sword.

Finally King Manuel announced his choice. The commander in chief (*capitão-mór*) of the Indian fleet was to be Vasco da Gama, native of Sines and a gentleman of the royal household.

NOTES

[1] On June 7, 1494, John had signed with the Spanish monarchs the famous Convention (or Treaty) of Tordesillas. It divided the lands and seas that had been or might be discovered between the two countries. The line of demarcation was one drawn from pole to pole 370 leagues west of the Azores and Cape Verde Islands. The treaty was confirmed by a bull of Pope Alexander VI.

[2] The worthy chronicler glosses some of the less praiseworthy acts of the "virtuous Perfect Prince" Dom John. The king openly boasted that he was a disciple of Machiavelli and imitated the policies and methods of wily Louis XI of France. Not satisfied with crushing the power of his great nobles, he coveted their lands as well. To obtain those of Ferdinand, Duke of Bragança, his brother-in-law (and because of an ancient family feud), he had the duke arrested and executed at Évora in 1483, after the mere pretense of a trial. To complete the defeat of the nobles, he stabbed with his own hand his wife's brother Diogo, Duke of Viseu, in his palace at Setúbal, on Aug. 23, 1484. When Queen Leonor lamented loudly the murder of her brother, John silenced her by threatening to have her tried for treason also. (Fate was to overtake him in this, for, following the death of his only son, he was forced to name Manuel, the murdered man's brother, as his heir to the throne of Portugal.) Not satisfied with these two killings, he had the Bishop of Évora, his father's favorite, thrown alive down a well Next he executed with or without trial eighty of the leading Portuguese grandees, and made the crown wealthy by confiscating their estates. Thence came at least some of the funds that outfitted and sent forth the ships of the discoverers!

[3] Correa (not a reliable authority at this point) informs us that John Infante (the second in command of Dias's expedition) was in charge of construction, and that when he died in the course of the work Dom John ordered the shipbuilding to be discontinued until he could find another master shipbuilder to his liking.

[4] Correa states that Manuel's enthusiasm for the voyage was fired by his discovery and examination of a chest belonging to Dom John, which contained plans and documents concerning the undertaking.

[5] The favorite names for Portuguese ships of the period were predominantly religious, such as "God of Portugal," "If God Wills," "Queen of Angels," "Our Lady Mother of God and Man," "Our Lady of the Rosary," etc.

[6] Tonnage meant originally the cubic capacity of a ship below decks in terms of wine tuns, and varied considerably

[7] It will be recalled that Dias's supply ship was so riddled by "worms" that he had to destroy it on the homeward journey.

[8] The modern steering wheel was not invented until the eighteenth century.

[9] As two authors call this ship the *São Miguel,* it may be that she had been rechristened *São Miguel.*

[10] "The money spent on the few ships of this expedition was so great that I will not go into detail for fear of not being believed." Pacheco, *Esmeraldo* (Kimble transl.), p. 166.

[11] Hammocks were first brought back to Europe by Columbus, whose crew learned their manufacture and use from the natives of the Antilles.

[12] Perhaps, too, Dias's failure to persuade or force his men to proceed farther than he had on the momentous Cape of Good Hope voyage militated against his selection for an expedition which was to treat the cape as a mere way station on the road to India.

VASCO DA GAMA,
THE CAPITÃO-MÓR

Wil you see what wise and experte travaylers, skilful in geometry and astronomye (for that is to be a Geographer in deede), be able to doe? Looke you on the King of Portingales title: the two partes, of the three therein, were achieved by Vasques Gama, and other travaylers adventurers.

—RICHARD WILLES, from the Dedication of his *History of Travayle,* 1577

CHAPTER VII

VASCO DA GAMA'S EARLY LIFE

And this Vasco da Gama was a prudent man, one of good counsel, and of great spirit for all high adventure.
—GASPAR DE CORREA, *Lendas da India*

N THE west coast of Portugal, halfway between the
river Tagus and Cape Saint Vincent, sixty miles from
Lisbon as the crow flies south, lies the little seaside
town of Sines. It snuggles close behind the cape of
the same name and possesses a diminutive harbor. A
high rocky spit juts out like a finger from the side of the headland
and unites with the cape itself to form a narrow bay, too small for
craft of any considerable size but large enough to receive and shelter
the picturesque fishing boats that for centuries have sailed out and
brought home their rich finny harvests from the sea.

The little haven, warm in the southern sun, is rimmed with a
curving sweep of golden sand, and from the shore the land rises
rather sharply in a rocky slope. It has a wide curve, like that of an
ancient Greek theater, and is clothed in dark-green undergrowth
and the flaming yellow flowers of the *tojo*, a gorse that grows here in
brilliant patches, but which is seldom found elsewhere. On either
side of the point dark pines creep down almost to the water's edge,
and on the brow of the slope inquisitive palm trees lean far over,
as though to watch the ebb and flow of the tides beneath.

A sandy road winds up from the shore to the crest of the hill, and
there the little town of Sines lies, sheltered from the winds that
sweep in from the western sea. Red-tiled and gaily painted in whites,
ochers, greens, and pinks—colors so dear to the Portuguese heart,
and which they use wherever they dwell, from inland Brazil to far
Macao—the houses nestle close to the hillside, some of them straggling down the slope toward the shore, others wandering out toward
the white sand dunes that are everywhere hereabouts heaped up by
the winds of the coast. In contrast to the colors, softened and faded

by time and wind and sun and mist, are the gray battlements and turrets of Sines's ancient castle, up to the very walls of which the houses have crept, as though seeking protection from the elements. The houses are for the most part low and of stone, and many of them are hundreds of years old. Here and there are meager garden patches, enclosed in woven-reed fences. With great effort straggling vegetables are grown in the sandy soil. At the west of the town the aged, modest church of Nossa Senhora das Salas stands apart. Its white roofs and façade—strangely reminiscent of the Alamo and the missions of California and the Southwest—are visible from many miles out at sea, and for over six hundred years it has been a welcome landmark for fishermen and mariners straining their eyes for the first sight of the homeland.

The view from the town itself is entrancing. At the foot of the slope, near the natural rock breakwater, flows a clear shallow stream over water-worn boulders. There for countless years the women have gathered of a morning to wash their linen, and their merry laughter and birdlike chatter come up on the wind as they stoop and rise to scrub and rinse and wring, or spread the clothes out in bright patches of blue and red and white and green on the rocks to dry in the warm air. When the sun is on the bay, the water sparkles and glows in pale green and amethyst, turquoise and pink, and the surface is sown with sapphires and diamonds and emeralds. The waters in the deep-blue pools inshore swirl about the black rocks that raise their sharp heads, while further out the great Atlantic rollers roar and exhaust themselves in angry frustration in spume and spray against the rocks, and masses of purple and jade-green seaweed float and sway in the current. In the bay lies the little isle of Pessegueiro, covered with the ruins of a forgotten fort and chapel. To the north stretch the bare sand dunes of Praia do Norte, and to the southeast rise misty and vague the far-off peaks of Cercal and Monchique and São Domingos. And when the weather is clear, the point of Cape Saint Vincent is visible far to the south, last western guardian of the Continent, lifting its rocky head in defiant challenge to the wild storms of the Atlantic.

In Sines all life is open to the sea, whence it draws its life's blood, for the great stretches of sand make agriculture unprofitable. For hundreds of years, perhaps even before the Phoenicians in their great galleys skirted the shores on their way to the Tin Islands three thousand years ago, the men of this peaceful haven have sought their livelihood in the ocean. They still sail out with their nets into the sunset, while their sturdy women watch over the homes and the children; and when the boats return to shore, heavy-laden with their silvery cargoes, the wives and daughters troop down to the water's edge to lend a hand at hauling on the ropes and unloading the catch. And, as in all the years that have passed over the land, the sun-bronzed fishermen still spread their red-brown nets to dry in the sun, and mend them where rock has torn them or fish have forced their way through. They talk of tides and winds and wrecks, and tell the tales that are as old as seafaring itself, and as the generations of men that have gone down to the sea in ships.

Here all is primitive, all is simple, all is unchanged. Kings have come and gone, and a republic has been in the land for many years. Great wars have crashed their way through the world, but Sines has not changed. Only one road—and that an unkept track—links it to the neighboring towns; and despite its warm sun, its perfect beach, and its haunting beauty, it has dreamed undisturbed and at peace through the years and the centuries.

There is one small house in Sines, humble as the rest, and marked by no special size or elegance or distinction. It is one of a row of dilapidated cottages on the road between the town and the church of Nossa Senhora das Salas. Its lower courses of rough stone have clung firmly to their foundations these five hundred years and more, and for all the restorations that were made some fifty years ago, it cannot be distinguished from its neighbors.*

Yet this small house can lay great claim to renown; it has even become the object of pilgrimage, for in it was born, somewhere about the year 1460 [1]—we know neither the exact year nor the day —a man-child for whom destiny had planned great deeds. He was to trace a course from the coast on which he first saw the light to the far-off shores of India, and his exploits were to change the course of world events and reshape the ways of mankind. Into the tiny hands Fate pressed a key, the magic key, by which he was to unlock and throw open to the Western world the gates of the sea road to India. The baby born that far-off day in the sunny, windswept town of Sines was Vasco da Gama, later Dom Vasco, Captain-General of

* It lies opposite a truck garden called da Borroca, but usually referred to as "a horta da Dom Vasco" or "a horta do Almirante."

the Fleet, Count of Vidigueira, Peer of Portugal, and Viceroy of India.

Gama's family came from Alemtejo. Though it was neither rich nor aristocratic, it had a long and honorable history. The genealogists trace its descent from one Alvaro Annes da Gama, who fought with distinction in the wars of Affonso III, when the province of Algarve * was wrested from the Moors. Another ancestor, Vasco da Gama, carried the royal standard in the wars of Affonso V against Castile. This Vasco had three sons of whom one, Estevão, was appointed alcaide mór of the towns of Sines and Silves. Estevão da Gama married Izabel Sodré, daughter of one João de Rezende and Maria da Silva. There was a strong strain of English blood in Izabel's family. "Sodre" is a Portuguese corruption of "Sudley," for Izabel's grandfather was Frederick Sudley, an Englishman of the family of the earls of Hereford. Of this marriage there were born four children, three sons and a daughter. The eldest son was Paulo da Gama, who sailed to India as captain of one of his brother's ships. The second son was named Ayres. He also went to India, but not until April, 1511, when he sailed as captain of the *Piedade* in the fleet of Garcia de Noronha. The only daughter was named Thereza. Vasco was the third son.

Little is known of the early life of Vasco da Gama. Born on the seacoast, growing up with the sons of sailors and fishermen, he learned early to swim, row, and man a sailboat, as well as to haul in the nets with his companions. Like them he looked naturally to the sea for his career. The call to adventure must have been irresistible, for in his early years everything about him spoke of the sea. Not only was he familiar with the fishing craft of Sines and the other scattered towns on the coast, but he soon became acquainted with the build and rig of the clumsy caravels and "round ships" that wallowed in the offing on their way up to Lisbon and Oporto, and even farther along the coast to France and the Low Countries and England. Often would he see on the far-off horizon at dawn or sunset the heavily laden ships sailing south to Mediterranean ports or to Morocco and the strange and little-known coast and islands of West Africa. Some of the old fishermen had sailed on these vessels, and they related to Vasco and his brothers and the other small boys who gathered around them at their work weird and unbelievable

* The southernmost province of Portugal.

stories of what they had seen and heard. The little fellows sat open-mouthed and wide-eyed at the tales of storms, calms, and ship-wrecks, and of landings on unknown coasts. They heard of black people with huge mouths and bloodshot eyes, scantily clad men with rings in their ears, noses, and mouths, of naked man-eating savages with cruel filed teeth, of huge hairy apes who beat their breasts like drums, apes who could kill a man with a single hug of their great arms. They heard of many strange trees, plants, and foods, and of how gold was found in the river sands by the black men; of great elephants and the tusks that the men of Guinea hacked off and sold to the captains of King Affonso. They held their breath in excitement when the grizzled old sea dogs told of landing and raiding peaceful villages, shooting the poor, helpless blacks who tried to resist the mail-clad Portuguese. They heard of the callous indifference with which the old, weak, and sick were left behind to starve in the villages; and how the strong men, women, and children were bound and driven like cattle, taken out to the boats and dumped into the 'tween decks, as well as of the neglect of the prisoners while on board the ships. They were told how many of the blacks died and were thrown overboard to the hungry sharks, which never ceased to hover about the slave ships, as though knowing that they would never want for food.

So did Vasco and his brothers learn the ways of the sea, its ships, and its men; and so did Vasco begin to acquire the rudiments of practical navigation, to read the stars and the winds, the clouds and the currents, to steer a boat and to handle a sail.

It is believed that the boy Vasco, when he was ready for schooling, was sent to Évora, a town in the hills and some seventy miles northeast of Sines, for the ignorant fisherfolk of Sines could offer little in the way of formal education to one who was the son of a gentleman and an officer of the crown.

Évora opened a new world to the boy, when first he glimpsed its white walls and church towers reaching high toward the heavens. It was then, for all that its inhabitants numbered only about ten thousand, the second city of the kingdom, and it was the favorite residence of the king. It was an ancient town, founded by the Celts, who settled there because it was easily defended. They called it Ebora. The Romans had occupied it, too, and Julius Caesar had granted it the pretentious name of Liberalitas Julia, a name never accepted by the natives.

Vasco marveled at the beautiful undulating plain through which the road wound upward toward the city. Everywhere about him was vegetation: plantations of cork trees, orchards, olive groves, fertile farms, and fields of rye, interspersed with vineyards and chestnut groves. All this was new to the lad, for it was far different from the dreary wastes of sand, scrub, and sea that surrounded and pressed in on little Sines. On the road he passed peasants in knee breeches, woolen leggings, and black peaked caps, men hauling wood, grain, casks, and vegetables in heavy oxcarts or donkey carts with great solid wooden wheels that creaked and squealed as though in pain as the carters urged on their beasts with goad and curse.

He saw the corn being reaped by long lines of men and women, or being threshed by beating the sheaves against a stone, or by driving oxen or donkeys over the grain. He saw the olives harvested in the wasteful way that still persists—by beating them from the trees with sticks—and watched boys like himself heap up the ripe olives in *tulhas* (circles of stone) to await the pressing for oil. On either side along the road were great stretches of wild lavender, white and yellow and pink cistus, cornflowers, daisies, deep purple bugloss, and asphodels; and in the meadows browsed brown sheep and wide-horned cattle, their bells tinkling as they moved. Windmills with pointed roofs of tile and thatch were on the hilltops, and here and there stood low cottages with high chimneys. Évora lay in a beautiful, happy, prosperous land!

When he entered the city, Vasco no longer had the soft sand or turf underfoot. He found himself in steep narrow streets with strange names: the Street of His Highness's Cousin, the Lane of the Cats, the Alley of the Little Devil, the Street of the Maids of Honor, the Road of the Ax. Paved with rough cobblestones, they were streets that were old when the clanking Roman legions marched away a thousand years before, gloomy streets with arches flung across from house to house, many of the latter with low wooden arcades. The high stone buildings with green shutters allowed but little light to filter through. The stones underfoot irked the boy's feet. Once inside the walls and through the first streets, Vasco came upon the highest and greatest building he had ever seen. It was the palace built by the King Dom Duarte, who married his Queen

Leonor there with great pomp and ceremony in 1421. As the boy gazed at the building in amazement and looked with awe at the guardsmen in glittering helmets and cuirasses on the walls and at the gates, he little dreamed that one day he would spend much time within those grim halls in attendance on his king; and that these stout guardsmen who disdainfully ignored the presence of the little country lad would one day bow low before him as he passed, proudly wearing the Cross of the Order of Christ and bearing the title of Count of Vidigueira and Admiral of the Fleet.

Just beyond the palace he saw building going on, men on scaffoldings and ladders, busy with chisel and mallet, trowel and plumbline, clinging like flies to the sides of a structure that seemed, with its battlemented roof, pinnacles, and slender windows, to be reaching toward Heaven itself. He was told it was the new Church of São Francisco and that it had been abuilding for many years. In fact, the workmen did not cease their labors for forty long years, for the church was not finished until 1500, after Vasco had returned from his first voyage to India. The church still stands as it was, but there is one later addition which all morbid-minded visitors insist on seeing. In the seventeenth century a charnel house was added at one side of the church. It was soon filled up, and its walls and ceilings are lined with bleached human bones, while on it is the inscription, "Nos ossos, que aqui estamos, Pelos vossos esperamos" (We bones, who are here, await the coming of yours).

The boy wandered on through the tortuous, narrow streets, past the great square Gothic-Moorish towers of the nobles, until he finally reached the crowded central square, a broad area surrounded by low, arcaded houses. While still a lad, Vasco was to hear of—perhaps even to witness—the beheading of the Duke of Bragança, the most powerful noble of Portugal, by order of Dom John II in this very square. And later its arcades were to echo to the chants of the priests and the shrieks and moans of the dying, for here the victims of the Inquisition were burned at the stake; and 22,000 of those victims, men and women, were condemned in Évora alone. The Judgment Hall of the Inquisition still stands, and under the dungeon whitewash can still be traced the bloodstains of the innocent.

Wandering east from the square, perhaps even finding his way through the street named after him in later days, Vasco came to

another church, one of the greatest and most beautiful in all
Portugal, the Sé (cathedral) of Évora. With its gray-brown walls
it was old and gloomy then, as now, for its building had begun in
1186, and it was consecrated in 1250. It was in appearance as
much like a fortress as a church, with its crenelated walls and towers
with their conelike tops. The boy entered through the high-arched,
gloomy porch to pray like the pious Portuguese he was, and to stare
about him, as boys will, at the vast interior. He noted the strange
accentuation of the lines of mortar where the stones were joined—
peculiar to the architecture of Évora—and the high-springing
arches, the rose and gray marble, and the sunlight pouring in
through the beautiful rose windows in the transepts. Later in life,
after he had become acquainted with the architecture of the Moors
and Arabs, he would recall some of the patterns of the stone carv-
ings of the Sé, and realize that the long residence of the Moors in
Évora had left indelible traces in the minds and the handiwork of
the builders of the cathedral, which sat like a crown atop Évora's
hill.

As time passed and Vasco had leisure from his studies—and we
know not what he studied, or under whom, or where, except that
he learned mathematics and navigation—he saw more of the city
and learned something of its history. The Romans had left much
behind them; and in Évora stood—and stand—not far from where
Dom Vasco lived in later years, the granite and marble ruins of a
Roman temple of the second or third century—the so-called Temple
of Diana. Moreover, here and there were standing, as today, parts
of walls and buildings erected by men of that far-off time. Visigoths
and Moors had occupied the hill after the Romans, and the native
Iberians and Phoenician sea rovers before them. Vasco's Évora
friends delighted in poking about the old streets and squares with
him, pointing out aqueducts and Moorish windows and strangely
carved stones which had played their part in the forgotten life of old
Évora. The city had not been under Portuguese rule for long. It was
only in the year 1165 that an outlaw, one Geraldo (after whom the
central square of the city is named), stormed the town, wrested it
from its Moorish masters, and presented it to King Affonso Hen-
riques. The gift was a liberal one. It added territory to the kingdom
and secured a pardon for Geraldo, but it marked the end of Évora's
importance. The northern coast cities of Lisbon and Oporto grad-

ually drew away the town's men and its industries, until it sank and dwindled into insignificance. Now it is but a shadow of its former self, a sleepy and decaying city, dreaming of its vanished glories in the golden southern sunshine.

The country lad was fascinated by the people on the streets, for their faces and clothes were different from those of the sun-bronzed, roughly clad folk of his home town. The men and women were— and are—taller and leaner than other Portuguese, and had much of the Arab in their dignified bearing and long swinging walk. Many of the men wore odd brown sheepskin coats, often with the wool outside. Their trousers were split up inside the leg and then laced with cords, or, for those who could afford it, with silver clasps or buckles. The hats, too, were odd—a sort of Phrygian cap, with the long end hanging over the eyes to keep off the sun. Vasco would often stand by the ancient fountains of gray stone in the squares and watch the water sellers come down with their empty casks and the women fill their heavy jars of unglazed red clay, which they then carried off, balancing the great vessels gracefully and with no seeming effort on their heads. In Évora, too, he became acquainted with the men and ideas of other countries, for many Flemings and other foreigners passed through the city on their way to Algarve, whose grapes were famous throughout Europe.

Sometimes, too, the lad would climb the winding granite staircase of the cathedral tower and look southward over the hill town of Évora, across the sunny, fruitful plain to the misty, purple-blue horizon beyond which lay his boyhood home of Sines. Or he would walk in the shady cloister of the Sé, fragrant with heavy-laden lemon trees and golden-fruited medlars. There was a wealth of ways in which to spend one's time in lovely old Évora.

The years rolled quickly by in Évora, and Vasco grew from boyhood to young manhood. Of these years we have no record, nor even faint tradition. Who could foresee his future and the part he was to play in the history of his country and of the world, and note for future generations the incidents of his childhood and his youth? In fact, but few events are recorded of his life until his appointment by King Manuel as the commander of the Indian expedition—and even some of these are of doubtful authenticity.

Some facts can be assumed for a certainty. His education and experience as a navigator were such as to bring him while still a young man to the attention of the government. No man who was not well versed in the nautical knowledge of his day would have been entrusted with the command of a fleet for the Indian adventure.[2] In addition to his reputation as a careful, resourceful navigator, Gama must have shown himself a master of men. The crews of those days were tough, hardy, lawless fellows, held in check only by one uniting shrewd knowledge of human nature and the iron hand of severe discipline. Many voyages had been rendered futile by insubordination and mutiny on the high seas, and Dias himself would probably have proceeded much farther, perhaps even to the coast of India itself, had it not been for the rebellion of his men and their refusal to follow him at a crucial time. The leader of the expedition, moreover, would meet foreigners both barbarous and civilized, and must have knowledge of the ways and the wiles of the alien. Then, too, tact and skill in dealing with the king, his counselors, and his court would be no small part of his equipment, for conspiracy and a constant undercurrent of spying and intrigue seem to have been part of the very life of those gathered around Portugal's throne.

That the choice fell on Gama would indicate that Dom Manuel and his shrewd advisers believed that in this man from Sines they had found exactly the intrepid, indomitable, and diplomatic person for the mission. The men of the Gama family had a reputation not only for bravery, but also for being very quarrelsome and unruly. Evidently Vasco had been in trouble more than once, for tradition tells of his being stopped by the night watch in the narrow dark streets of Setúbal. He was closely muffled in his cloak—in itself a suspicious circumstance in the eyes of the authorities. Ordered to stand and identify himself, he haughtily refused to reveal his face. The watch crowded around him, lanterns in hand, and summoned the alcaide. When the officer demanded his name and that he show his face, Gama's only answer was, "I am no criminal." With that he stalked haughtily away, and the alcaide did not dare arrest him. And men spoke of him as "bold, daring, patient, determined in adversity" but quick to anger, even more so than his brothers.

The only time that Gama's name appears definitely [3] in the chronicles (until his connection with the Indian command) is in a chapter in which Garcia de Resende tells of a clash between Dom John II and the King of France in the year 1492. It is worth quot-

ing, as it indicates how high Vasco da Gama stood in the estimation
of the king, and, moreover, gives an enlightening glimpse of Dom
John's character and his direct methods of handling matters that
threatened international complications:

At this time, when the king was in Lisbon, the French seized a
caravel [returning] from Mina with much gold, though there was
peace with France.

As soon as he learned this, he [the king] took counsel with the leading men at court, and all advised him to send someone to the King of
France to take up the matter. He answered: "I have the exactly opposite impression from all of you, for I do not wish anyone whom I
might send on the mission to be badly received, or put off with delays,
which would weigh upon me more heavily than the loss of the gold."
Whereupon he left the council without announcing what he was going
to do.

There happened to be lying in Lisbon [harbor] ten great French
ships with fine merchandise. He ordered that they all be seized at once
and the merchandise stored with great care in the customs warehouse.
Moreover, the yards and tillers were to be removed from the ships, men
were to be placed aboard to guard them, and the Frenchmen were to
be ejected from them. And he sent in great haste to Setúbal and to the
kingdom of the Algarve Vasco da Gama, with full powers and authority (that Vasco da Gama who was later Count of Vidigueira and
Admiral of the Indies, a man in whom he had confidence, and one
who had seen service in the fleets and in maritime affairs) to do any
and all things that were necessary, which he did with great speed. And
in like manner he sent another such to the city of Oporto and to
Aveiro. And all the owners [of the ships] presented themselves to the
King of France to make complaint and to petition that he see to it that
each could regain his ship. And the King of France forthwith applied
such diligence and ordered such things to be done in the matter that
it was accomplished at once, and he sent the king his caravel with all
his gold, without a doubloon missing. And so it came about without
discussion of the matter, and the King of France sent his apologies,
and he [Dom John] ordered that everything be returned without delay
to the shipowners in the manner in which it had been taken away,
that is, with nothing missing.[4]

And so Gama reached manhood, with the endowment of a fine,
sturdy physique, well fitted to bear the hardships of a mariner of his
day, and trained and experienced in the navigation of ships and the
control of men. He had worked his way upward in a hard age,

among tough, ruthless men, and had, in ways entirely unknown to us, won a high place in the confidence and respect of his king, as well as having acquired a remarkable reputation for expert seamanship among a people where well qualified mariners experienced in knowledge of the African coast and its waters swarmed in every port.

No two records of the manner in which Gama received his royal appointment are alike, and the statements of the various chroniclers of the period are so entangled, contradictory, and obscure that no clear and definite statement can be made. Two of the narratives state that the father, Estevão da Gama, had been given the command by King John, and that, since he had died, King Manuel had offered and the son accepted the command as of right. Castanheda avers, on the other hand, that the oldest brother Paulo was proffered the position, but that he declined it because of ill health. He did, however, volunteer to accompany the fleet "as a captain of one of the ships to advise and assist"—an offer which the king later accepted.

Correa (whose narrative of Gama's first voyage was written later than the others, and who appears therein to have drawn very often on hearsay or on his own imagination) tells an odd, though interesting, tale of the appointment. According to his *Lendas da Índia*, when the grandees of the kingdom submitted the names of a number of persons whom they deemed eminently fitted for the position of capitão-mór of the fleet, King Manuel put them off and, though he made no announcement, informed them that he had already made his choice. Some time passed. Then:

One day as the king sat in his council chamber examining documents, he by chance raised his eyes as Vasco da Gama happened to pass through the room. He [Gama] was a gentleman of the household and of noble lineage, son of Estevão da Gama, who was Comptroller of the Household of King Dom Affonso [V], for at that time a man was more honored by nobility of blood than by the titles of "dons," which [titles] were not then customary among those who were noble by direct lineage. The king felt his heart go into transports as his eyes rested upon Gama. He called him, and he knelt before the king, who said to him: "It would give me great happiness if you would take upon yourself a commission for which I have need of you, [one] in which you will find much travail!" He [Gama] kissed his hand, saying, "Sire, I am already rewarded for any labor that may be, since you ask that I serve, and I shall perform [that service] as long as my life endures."

Whereupon the king arose and seated himself at a table which was set out with a repast in the chamber. As he dined he told Vasco da Gama what his desire was, and that he was to go in those ships where he [the king] commanded him [and] that it was an affair on which he was very much set, and that he should make himself ready. To this Vasco da Gama replied that his soul was in readiness, and that he had nothing which would prevent him from embarking at once.

The king finished his meal and retired to his robing room. He asked if Vasco da Gama had any brother. He answered that he had three * . . . and that all were truly men [fit] to serve in any capacity wherein they might be charged. The king said: "Summon him [that is, whichever brother you may choose] to go with you in one of the two ships. Do you select the ship which pleases you best, in which to fly my standard, for you shall be the capitão-mór of the others." Vasco da Gama kissed his hand and said, "Sire, it would not be right for me to fly your standard, for my brother is older than I am; but he shall fly it, and I shall go under his command, which is right, and Your Highness should have it so for your service."

After further conversation the king insisted on Vasco taking the command and was well pleased at his show of humility. He dismissed him with the assurance:

"My heart tells me that my wishes will be carried out by you, therefore make arrangements as you see fit, for to you alone I give the command and the whole charge. . . . Do you meanwhile see to the preparations and the equipment that the ships should have, and take the sailors who please you most, and so with all other things, because if it be pleasing to God, you will discover India and its navigation. And I pray our Lord that He may so will it for His Holy Service, and I commend you to Him, and your labors for me will be well rewarded." For which Vasco da Gama kissed his hand.

The story, whether true or not, is a pretty one, and probably expresses the desires and prayers of Dom Manuel. One may choose the tale that pleases most. This much is certainly clear: Gama had been favorably known to Dom John and had been employed by him in the French ship affair of 1492, five years before his selection. King Manuel, then Duke of Beja, was constantly near Dom John and

* All other narratives state clearly that there were three brothers in all

was well acquainted with his agents, their actions, and their capabilities. It would appear that, whatever form the tale has taken, Manuel considered Vasco da Gama the man to head the Indian venture, and so chose him.

Upon receiving his commission, Gama proceeded to the first of the duties imposed upon him by his sovereign—the supervision of the final preparation of the ships, their equipment and stores, and the selection of officers and crews.

Dom Manuel had granted him permission to take one of his brothers with him. He selected Paulo, for whom he had a deep attachment. In fact their relationship, together with his grief at Paulo's death, has given us the only glimpse we shall have of lovable traits in Vasco's nature.

Before Paulo could accept a commission, Vasco was forced to take a humiliating but important step on his behalf—no less than the securing of a royal pardon for him. Paulo had attacked and wounded the judge of the town of Setúbal in a quarrel and at this time was a fugitive outlaw.* The king is reported to have granted the request with the words: "For love of you I pardon him my justice, for the services which I expect from you and from him, provided that, having received his pardon, he satisfy the parties [to the complaint], and let him come, at once, and not delay." The way was thus cleared, a message was dispatched to Paulo, and Vasco proceeded with his preparations.

* Vasco (according to Correa) pleaded for the pardon for him at the same interview during which he received his orders from Dom Manuel.

NOTES

[1] The date of Gama's birth is very questionable. No official records of the event have survived, and the dates given by various authors range from 1460 to 1469. The former date seems the most acceptable.

[2] It has been conjectured that he acquired much of his seamanship on voyages to the Guinea Coast, but there is no sure proof of this

[3] There is in existence in the archives of Spain a safe-conduct for travel to Tangiers granted by Ferdinand and Isabella in 1478 to two Portuguese, Vasco da Gama and one Lemos. Some historians hold that this was the Vasco da Gama of the Indian adventure, others that it refers to his grandfather, who bore the same name. It may well have been the latter, who lived until late in the year 1496.

[4] Resende does not give the date of this occurrence, but the preceding and following chapters of his narrative refer to events of 1492, so it is safe to assume that the seizure of the ships and the employment of Gama by the king took place in that year

CHAPTER VIII

THE SHIPS' COMPANIES

For all the sons of Mars and Neptune
Are prepared to follow me everywhere.
—CAMÕES, *Os Lusíadas,* IV, lxxxiv

AMA chose the *São Gabriel* as his flagship and appointed as its captain Gonçalo Álvares. He was a thoroughly competent mariner who later held the important position of pilot-major of India.

Pero D'Alenquer, who had accompanied Bartholomeu Dias on the cape voyage, was selected as the *São Gabriel's* pilot. The pilot on vessels of the period was really the most important person of the ship's company. Since ships' captains often received their appointments because of family, social position, or as a reward for services rendered, rather than for their proficiency as mariners, the pilot bore the heavy responsibility of the navigation of the ship —in D'Alenquer's case, for the entire fleet. As D'Alenquer had also sailed to the Congo in 1490 with Gonçalo da Sousa (who was sent as an ambassador to the King of Manicongo), the selection by Gama was an eminently wise one.

The *São Rafael* was captained by Paulo da Gama. Her pilot was João de Coimbra, who took a negro slave abroad with him. Nicolau Coelho was appointed commander of the *Berrio.* He was evidently a very competent officer, for he was later chosen to sail to India in 1500 with Cabral, and again in 1503 with the fleet of Affonso d'Albuquerque. In 1500 Dom Manuel granted him a handsome pension for his services, together with a coat of arms. The pilot of the *Berrio* was Pero Escolar. He, too, was deemed worthy of a royal pension, granted him on February 18, 1500, "for the service which Pero Escolar our pilot has performed for us both in the regions of Guinea and in the discovery of the Indies, where we sent him." Later in 1500 he returned to India as a pilot in Cabral's fleet. Gama appointed Gonçalo Nunes, one of his own retainers, as captain of the storeship. No other officers of this vessel are listed. Besides the navigators the rolls of the expedition bore the names of other administrative officers, all of whom had interesting adventures. The clerk (*escrivão*) of the *São Gabriel* was Diogo Dias, a brother of Bartholomeu Dias. João de Sá served in the same capacity on the *São Rafael*. He worked rapidly upward in government service, was sent back to India with Cabral, and later became government treasurer there. The clerk of the *Berrio* was one Alvaro de Braga. Gama later appointed him Portuguese factor in Calicut. In a decree of February 1, 1501, Dom Manuel referred to him as "Alvaro de Braga, esquire of our household."

The plans for the voyage would take the fleet to many unknown ports, where it was assumed (with good reason) that Portuguese was not spoken or understood. Three men were therefore shipped as interpreters. One was Martin Affonso, who had lived for a considerable period in the region of the Congo and had learned several dialects of the Bantu tribes. The second was Fernão Martins, chosen for his ability to speak Arabic, which he had acquired during a long imprisonment among the Moors. He proved of great value to Gama and is mentioned several times in the narratives of the voyage. The third interpreter was João Nunes, who spoke Arabic and some Hebrew. Correa adds that "he was a man of keen intellect, who could understand the language of the Moors [natives of Calicut] but could not speak it."

The fleet also had on its muster rolls a strange group of men—convicts adjudged guilty of serious crime and condemned to banishment or death. They were to be put ashore in various places, most often where danger threatened or treachery was suspected, to gather information, find food or water, locate native villages, act as messengers, and so forth. Goes, a chronicler of the reign of Dom Manuel, informs us that "of these he [Gama] took with him ten or twelve, who were seized for mortal crimes and whose misdeeds the king pardoned so that they might serve on this voyage, and he granted them grace and mercy, giving them a chance as persons who might [thus] prolong their lives, no matter in what manner." The other writers of the time refer to the custom just as unconcernedly. Correa notes that Gama had requested a number of criminals, "to adventure them or leave them behind in desolate lands, where, if they survived, they might prove of value to him when he returned and found them again. This seemed good to the king, and he sent him ten men who were condemned to death, and he [Gama] possessed them [just] as though they had been banished to desolate lands." The poet Camões, in his poetic narrative of the voyage, speaks of the criminals as "men condemned for crimes and shameful deeds, that they might be risked in dubious circumstances." The names of some of these convicts are known. One, João Machado, spoke a little Arabic and therefore was very useful. It is supposed that he was left by Gama at Moçambique but later found his way to India. There his crimes were evidently not held against him, for he held several responsible government posts and finally was appointed alcaide mór of Goa by Affonso d'Albuquerque. He was killed in fighting the Indians at Ponda in 1517. The story of another convict has been preserved by Correa, who doubtless heard it later in India. He was Damião Rodrigues, a friend of João Machado. The two had murdered a man on the *Rocio* (Promenade) of Lisbon and were condemned to be hanged. They were lying in the Limoeiro Prison of Lisbon when Gama made his request for convicts, and were placed in his custody. Rodrigues was assigned as a seaman on the *São Gabriel*. When Machado was put ashore at Moçambique by Gama, Rodrigues dived from the ship during the night and swam ashore to join his friend. When the fleet sailed away shortly thereafter without them, they presented themselves before the local sheik, who welcomed them and took both into his service. Here Machado's knowledge of Arabic was of value to him, and he increased his proficiency in it. Within a short time after their arrival Rodrigues fell ill and died. His friend buried him outside the town and set up a cross on the grave, together with a board on which he carved the inscription: "In this grave lies Damião Rodrigues, whom Vasco da Gama left behind in this land. He who came with him as a banished man and a seaman of the *São Gabriel*." [1] Thereafter Machado wandered about the coast, telling tales of the great power of Dom Manuel, and thus persuading the chiefs to come to terms with the Portuguese. These services, together with his improved knowledge of Arabic, probably account for his later pardon and advancement in India. João Nunes, listed among the interpreters, was also a banished convict. The names, stories, and ultimate fate of the remaining convicts are uncertain or unknown.

The members of the crew were all carefully selected. Because of the frequent voyages to Africa, a large pool of seafarers was available from which to choose. Wherever possible, Gama enrolled men who had made the cape voyage with Bartholomeu Dias, that he might utilize their knowledge and experience.[2] In most cases his selections were justified by the crew's conduct both on land and at sea.

The contemporary authorities disagree on the number of men who sailed with Gama. Probably the wide discrepancies arise from the various methods of counting, some considering only the members of the crew, others including officers and/or servants, slaves, and gentlemen volunteers—if there were any. It would probably be safe to accept the number who embarked as somewhere between 140 and 170. Besides the navigators and able-bodied and ordinary seamen there were soldiers, gunners, trumpeters, a surgeon, ropemakers and sailmakers, carpenters, armorers, cooks, and cabin boys. Of the four ships' companies, thirty-one members are mentioned by name in the various narratives (though a few may be variants or repetitions) ; we know nothing of the identity of the others.[3]

After the selection of his men one more important task remained to be performed by Vasco da Gama before reporting to the king that all was ready: the securing of the most up-to-date data and nautical instruments that might be of value on the voyage. There was available a large accumulation of maps and charts, rutters and other reports brought to Lisbon by the navigators who had sailed for Dom Manuel's predecessors to the countries of the East. Among the documents, according to the chronicler Barros, was information brought to Lisbon by an Abyssinian priest, one Lucas Marcos, in 1490. And it may well be that Covilhan's letters sent to King John, containing much invaluable data on India, the Indian Ocean, and the coast of Africa, were in the collection.

The compass was the most useful nautical instrument available in Gama's day. As Samuel Purchas in his *Pilgrimes* quaintly remarks, "The Load-stone was the Lead-stone, the very Seed and ingendring stone of Discoverie, whose soever Joviall Braine first conceived that Minerva." The first reference to the compass in Europe was made early in the twelfth century by Alexander Neckam, an English churchman, and his casual mention of it indicates that he assumed that his readers were quite familiar with its properties and uses.[4] Most of the early writers believed that it was invented in Italy—

indeed the writer of the *Roteiro* of Gama's first voyage calls it the *agulha genoisca* (the Genoese needle). It had been improved much since its introduction into Europe. As early as 1380, Da Buti, a commentator on Dante, speaks of sailors who use a compass with the needle fastened to a pivoted card on which the points of the compass were painted. The compass cards were not marked with letters and numbers as are those of today. The illiteracy of most of the sailors would have rendered that futile, so the points were drawn or painted in different shapes, lengths, and colors, all radiating out from the pivot point or center.[5] The north was indicated, as today, by a fleur-de-lis, the other points by their varying shape or color. The card, set on a pivot in a round bowl, was lighted by a tiny lamp, and the whole was mounted on a stand in a hooded box, so as to be seen easily by the steersman. The masters of vessels always carried with them a piece of "adamant" or lodestone * with which to remagnetize the needle if necessary. Extra compasses and needles were also carried.

Though portable timepieces were first made in Germany toward the end of the fifteenth century, it is very doubtful if Gama took any with him. They were still clumsy and inaccurate, and in no way adapted to use at sea. Time was measured by large hourglasses, and smaller ones (in which the sand ran for thirty minutes) were used to check off the crew's watches. Each time the ship's boy turned the glass, a bell was struck, and eight bells—four hours—constituted a watch. The present system of ringing a ship's bell each half-hour is a survival of this custom. The best hourglasses were imported from Venice, and each ship carried an ample supply, to use in case of breakage.†

Improved navigating instruments had been devised and more accurate astronomical and other mathematical tables and data had been compiled during the reign of King John II. Master Purchas, in his *Pilgrimes,* puts the matter thus:

Yet doth Navigation owe as much to this Prince as to any, who imployed Roderigo and Joseph [Vizinho], his Jewish Physicians, cunning Mathematicians of that time, with Martin Bohemus [Martin Behaim] the Scholler of John Monte Regius, to devise what helpes they

---

* Magnetite: a magnetic oxide of iron.

† Lines for roughly computing dead reckoning and lead lines for taking soundings were also part of the equipment.

could for the Mariners in their saylings thorow unknowne Seas, where neyther Starres (as unknowne) nor Land (being out of kenne) could guide them. These first, after long study, applyed the Astrolabe, before used onely by Astronomers, to Marine use, and devised the Tables of Declinations, to find out the Latitude of Places . . . whereby the Mariners Art first began to free it selfe from the rudenesse of former times, and . . . to prepare a Way to open our Eyes in these parts, to see a new World.

These instruments were very crude and inaccurate in comparison with those of today, or even with those of a short generation after the Portuguese pioneer voyages. Barros, in his narrative of Gama's first voyage, admits that the wooden astrolabes * in use were very unsatisfactory, because the ships were small and their rolling and pitching prevented accurate readings, though wooden tripods were devised to steady the instruments. Other smaller astrolabes of metal or wood were also taken for use in calm weather and for checking purposes.

For solar observations great reliance was placed in the *Almanach Perpetuum* of Abraham ben Zacuto.[6] Zacuto, who had been professor of mathematics in Salamanca, Spain, came to Portugal in 1492, when life was becoming impossible for Spanish Jews. As one of the most famous mathematicians of his age, he was made Astronomer Royal. In 1484 King John had appointed a Council of Mathematicians to aid and advise in matters of mathematics and navigation. This council consisted of Bishop Diogo Ortiz, Master Rodrigo, and Master Joseph Vizinho—the latter two Jews, Vizinho being the pupil of Zacuto. Vizinho developed and improved an astrolabe adapted to nautical use and translated the *Almanach* of Zacuto.† Perhaps Gama also took with him a copy of the *Ephemerides* of Regio Montanus.‡ Besides the almanacs the fleet possessed tables of

* Astrolabe (Arabic, *asthar-lab;* Greek, ἀστρολάβον—to take a star), basically a flat brass ring, graduated along its rim in degrees and minutes, and with two sights for reading. The log line was not invented until the 17th century.

† According to two entries in the *Notas* of Columbus, Vizinho was sent by King John in 1485 to establish the latitude of various places on the west coast of Africa.

‡ Johann Müller, who took the name Regio Montanus from his birthplace, Königsberg, was the leading fifteenth century German mathematician. He had calculated a set of tables, which he called *Ephemerides,* similar to that of Zacuto. His tables, however, were based on astronomical observations at Nuremberg, whereas Zacuto's were calculated on those taken at Salamanca.

traverses (*toleta de marteloia*) which were used when the ships sailed on a zigzag course. Quadrants may have been used by the navigators of the expedition; of this there is no record.

In keeping with the procedure followed in previous expeditions, the king ordered three stone padrões [7] to be prepared and placed on board. These were similar to the pillars erected by Cão and Bartholomeu Dias on their African voyages and, in obedience to Dom Manuel's command, were named São Rafael, São Gabriel, and Santa Maria.

NOTES

[1] Of course the statement that Gama left him behind was not true. Rodrigues was a deserter. When Pedro Álvares Cabral visited the place en route to India in 1500, the sheik showed him the grave and the board with the inscription.

[2] Correa states that before the departure Gama urged his men to learn to be ropemakers, blacksmiths, etc., and "gave them an increase of two cruzados a month beyond the sailors' pay which they had, which was of five cruzados a month; so that all rejoiced at learning, so as to draw more pay. And Vasco da Gama bought for them all the tools which befitted their crafts."

[3] One Pedro de Covilhan, a priest of the order of the Holy Trinity, is named by a few of the chroniclers as the chaplain and confessor of the expedition, but most of the narratives do not even mention him. Later writers claimed that his was the first Mass held in India since those of St. Thomas, and that he died a martyr in India in July, 1498. As Gama was still in India at that time, this is very questionable.

Another priest, João Figueiro, is mentioned several times in Correa's narrative of the voyage. In fact he claimed (Chap. XXI) that he obtained a copy of portions of a diary of the expedition kept by the priest and used them in preparing his book. No other authors refer to Figueiro. It is interesting to note that this priest was one of the three councillors who advised against Portugal's backing of Columbus's enterprise.

[4] "In 1258 the famous Brunetto Latini, afterwards tutor of Dante, paid a visit to Roger Bacon, of which he gives a description in a letter to his friend the poet Guido Cavalcanti: The Parliament being summoned to assemble at Oxford, I did not fail to see Friar Bacon as soon as I arrived, and (among other things) he showed me a black ugly stone called a magnet, which has the surprising property of drawing iron to it; and upon which, if a needle be rubbed, and afterwards fastened to a straw so that it shall swim upon water, the needle will instantly turn toward the Pole-star; therefore, be the night ever so dark, so that neither moon nor star be visible, yet shall the mariner be able, by the help of this needle, to steer his vessel aright. This discovery, which appears useful in so great a degree to all who travel by sea, must remain concealed until other times, because no master mariner dares to use it, lest he fall under the imputation of being a magician; nor would the sailors venture themselves out to sea under his command, if he took with him an instrument which carries so

)

great an appearance of being constructed under the influence of some infernal spirit. A time may arrive when these prejudices, which are of such great hindrance to researches into the secrets of nature, will be overcome; and it will be then that mankind shall reap the benefit of the labours of such learned men as Friar Bacon, and do justice to that industry and intelligence for which he and they now meet with no other return than obloquy and reproach."—John Fiske, *The Discovery of America*, I, 314

[5] From the design on the card, the compass has been called "the rose of the winds" (Portuguese *a rosa dos ventos*) in many languages of Europe.

[6] Zacuto's book was entitled *Ha-Jibbur Ha-Godol: Compositio Magna.* Seven copies of the original Hebrew text are known, two being in the United States.

[7] See pp. 30, 36.

CHAPTER IX

THE DEPARTURE

There increased in my heart a great flame of desire to attempt some notable thing.
—Sebastian Cabot, speaking to certaine Gentlemen of Venice: HAKLUYT, *Voyages* (ed. 1598–1600), III, 6

LL was at last ready. The expedition of which Dom John II had dreamed and for which he had planned and labored for so many years was poised for its venture into unknown seas. Last-minute touches had been given to vessels and equipment, stores and fresh water were on board, the crew was waiting and eager to depart. All that remained for Gama and his officers was to present themselves to King Manuel to receive their formal sailing orders and his royal farewell.

It is strange and unaccountable that no official reports or other records were kept of the various steps in the preparations for this momentous expedition, or of the voyage itself. That a journey of such tremendous import in its aims and its accomplishments received scant attention from contemporaneous chroniclers, that but few and inaccurate notes of any of the events were preserved, that even the most important dates—such as those of the departure of the fleet and Gama's return to Lisbon—are uncertain, is well nigh unbelievable. We are left with an incomplete narrative of the voyage, some fragmentary documents and letters of foreigners—and later some of King Manuel's—as our sole sources for this story.*

The chronicles differ as to where Dom Manuel bade Gama and his officers farewell. One asserts that the meeting took place in Évora, another in Montemór o Novo, and Correa (the least reliable in matters dealing with Gama's first and second voyages) relates, with much circumstance and flowery description, that Lisbon was

* It is well within the range of probability that many of the records were destroyed before or during the great Lisbon earthquake of 1755, but that no official records remain is surprising.

the meeting place. The weight of authority, however, places the historic farewell at Montemór o Novo.

Montemór o Novo, eighteen miles west of Lisbon, was one of Portugal's oldest settlements. Its ancient, grim Moorish castle dominates the town at the south. Though now falling into ruin, its high towers and turrets and dilapidated walls are still imposing as they look out over the town to a bleak and melancholy countryside, through which wind the dark waters of the river Almansor, which finally ends its weary journey in the Tagus. There Dom Manuel was holding court, and there Gama and his captains were summoned to appear.

It was a solemn occasion, and to it the court brought the becoming restraint and gravity. No pomp or ceremony was omitted by the king. He had assembled about him the most important personages of his court, and in attendance were the highest dignitaries of the Church. All were arrayed in their ceremonial robes, and the audience chamber was a mass of color and magnificence.* Gama, his brother Paulo, and the other principal officers of the ships were announced and led before the king, who, when they were grouped about him, delivered an address from the throne.

In reading Manuel's discourse one should remember the famous warning of Thucydides,[1] for Barros, who described the occasion and has preserved the speeches of the king and Gama, wrote his *Décadas* about sixty years after the event he describes:

"Since," began the king, "it pleased Our Lord that I should assume the scepter of this royal heritage of Portugal, by favor of His Grace, and to receive the blessings of my ancestors from whom I have inherited it—they who by glorious deeds won victories over their enemies, victories made so much greater through the support of such loyal vassals and knights as were they from whom you are descended . . . the principal objective which I have borne in mind—next to the care of ruling over you and governing in peace and justice—is [to decide] how I might increase the patrimony of this my kingdom, so that I might the more liberally allot to each one the reward of his services.

"And I, pondering much on what might be the most profitable and

---

* For the reader interested in social customs of the times, it is significant to note that a list of the officials and servants employed in the palace of the Infante Dom Louis, Manuel's son, embraces 633—213 pages, 48 squires, 80 knights, 47 chaplains and altar boys, 26 grooms, 36 horse boys—and but 1 laundress for the whole palace!

honorable enterprise, and one [that might be] worthy of much glory [and one], in which I might undertake to carry out this my intention— since, God be praised, we have, by the power of the sword, expelled the Moors from these regions of Europe and of Africa, capturing the principal ports of the Kingdom of Fez, which is our conquest—I have come to the decision that no other is more proper for this my kingdom —as I have debated with you often—than the search for India and the lands of the East. In those places, even though they be situated far distant from the Church of Rome, I hope in the mercy of God that not only may the faith of Our Lord Jesus Christ His son be proclaimed and received through our efforts, and that we may obtain the reward thereof—fame and praise among men—but in addition kingdoms and new states with much riches, wrested by force of arms from the hands of the barbarians. . . .

"Since if this my kingdom has acquired new titles, new profits, and revenues from the coast of Ethiopia [Africa], of which practically the whole route has been searched out, how much more can be hoped for [by] going ahead further with this quest, if we can obtain those Oriental riches so celebrated by the ancient authors, a part of which riches have, through commercial transactions, aggrandized such power- ful states as are Venice, Genoa, Florence, and other very great com- munities of Italy!

"So having taken into consideration all these affairs in which we have had experience, and also because it would be an [act of] ingrati- tude to God to reject what He so propitiously offers us, and an insult to those princes of lauded memory from whom I have inherited this quest, and an offense to you who have shared in it, if I neglected it for [too] long, I ordered to be prepared four sailing vessels which— as you know—are in Lisbon provided with all things to pursue this voyage with its great expectations.

"And I have in my mind how Vasco da Gama, who is here present, has given a good account of himself in all matters which were en- trusted to him, or with which he was charged. I have chosen him for this journey, as a loyal cavalier, worthy of such an honorable enter- prise. I hope that Our Lord may grant he may perform such services for himself and for me that his recompense may be as a memorial both for him and for those who may aid him in the work [to be] performed in this voyage, because with this confidence and with the knowledge which I have had of all [of them] I have chosen them as his co- workers, with the intention that they obey him in all things which pertain to my service.

"And, Vasco da Gama, I commend you to them, and them to you, and on all of you together [I enjoin] peace and concord, the which is so powerful that it overcomes and transcends all dangers and travail, and makes the greatest [burdens] of life easy to bear—how much the more those of this journey, which I trust in God will be fewer than those that have been suffered. And that through you this my kingdom may share the benefactions."

As Manuel ceased speaking all present, including Gama, knelt and kissed the royal hand [2] in thanks for the boon that had been granted to him [Gama], as well as to the kingdom, in ordering the [continuation of the] quest which had been carried on for so many years and which had been made his [the king's] heritage. When silence had come upon the assembly after it had received this act of grace, Vasco da Gama knelt before the king, who presented to him a silken banner with the cross of the Order of Christ [3] in the center—the Order of which the king was the head and the perpetual administrator. As the monarch's private secretary held the flag clasped in his arms, Vasco da Gama spoke in a clear tone and gave his oath of allegiance in these words:

"I, Vasco da Gama, who now have been commanded by you, most high and most powerful king, my liege lord, to set out to discover the seas and the lands of India and the Orient, do swear on the symbol of this cross, on which I lay my hands, that in the service of God and for you I shall uphold it and not surrender it in the sight of Moor, pagan, or any race of people that I may encounter, and in the face of every peril of water, fire, or sword, always to defend and protect it, even unto death. And I further swear that, in the pursuit and the labors of this quest which you, my king and lord, have ordered me to undertake, I shall serve with all fidelity, loyalty, watchfulness, and diligence, observing and enforcing the orders which have just been entrusted to me, until such time as I return to this place where I now stand, in the presence of your Royal Highness, with the help of the grace of God, in whose service you are sending me."

When this pledge had been given, the banner was placed in his keeping and in his hands were placed orders in which were set forth what duties he was to perform during the voyage, together with letters to the several princes and kings to whom it was proper that they should be addressed. There was one also for Prester John of the Indies (so called in this kingdom) and to the King of Calicut, according to the fuller information and data which King Dom John had received from those parts.* . . . When these documents had been delivered the king bade him [Gama] farewell.

* This would seem to imply receipt of Covilhan's reports.

This concluded the ceremony. The king retired to his apartments. Standing at attention until the monarch passed through the great doors and until they had closed behind him, Vasco da Gama and his captains, followed by his officers bearing the white silken banner with its great red cross, turned and left the audience chamber. The next day Ortiz de Vilhagas celebrated a solemn Mass for the court and the mariners, and shortly thereafter Gama and his men took horse to the capital, where their ships and crews awaited them.

NOTES

[1] "I have put into the mouth of each speaker the sentiments proper to the occasion, expressed as I thought he would be likely to express them, while I at the same time endeavored, as nearly as I could, to give the general purport of what was actually said."—Thucydides, *Peloponnesian War*, I, 22 (Jowett transl.).

[2] "In that court [of Portugal] exists a strange custom, of kissing the hands of the king. . . . We do not kiss the emperor's hand."—Nicholas of Popelau.

[3] The Order of Christ was founded in 1319 by King Dom Diniz to take over the property of the Knights Templars when that order was suppressed by Pope Clement V. Prince Henry the Navigator used the order in his development of Portugal's maritime power. The order became in his hands (he being the Grand Master) an instrument to further his exploring and colonizing enterprises, and its income was devoted largely to the furthering of his ambitious plans.

CHAPTER X

THE SAILING OF THE FLEET

Little by little now receding sight
Parts from our country's mountains which remained;
Dear Tagus, too, remained and Cintra's height,
Which for long time our longing eyes retained;
There also in the home of our delight
The heart was left behind, by grief constrained,
And then, when all was hidden from the eye,
At last we nothing saw but sea and sky.
—CAMÕES, *Os Lusíadas,* V, iii.
Translated by J. J. Aubertin.

HE great adventure was at hand. All difficulties had been surmounted, all delays were at an end, the day of sailing had been determined, and all that remained were the last farewells of the mariners to their families and the commending of themselves to God's care during the hazardous voyage.

About four miles west of the Arsenal of Lisbon the river Tagus widened for a space, providing ample anchorage for a fleet in midstream. There was located the suburb of Restello,[1] on the right bank of the river, where the blue waters gently lapped a beach of golden sand. On the long slope between shore and hills lay broad orchards and green gardens, and here and there on the heights the dark sails of windmills turned merrily in the brisk ocean breezes. The south bank of the river was steep and wooded, and deep ravines came down to the water's edge.

Here the ships of Gama's fleet, new, shining, and freshly painted, with flags and pennons flying bravely in the wind, had dropped anchor opposite a little chapel on the shore. It had been built many years before by Prince Henry the Navigator and was dedicated by him to St. Mary of Bethlehem.* There the crews of departing ships were wont to offer up their prayers and petitions for a prosperous

* In Portuguese, Belém.

[121]

voyage and a safe return. On the evening of July 7, 1497, Vasco
da Gama rode down from Lisbon to the little church and there kept
vigil the whole night long with his brother Paulo, his other officers,
and the priests of the near-by monastery of Santo Thomar, making
confession of his sins and praying for strength and success.

Soon after sunrise on July 8, men and women began to gather
about the chapel, until the shore was crowded. The sailors were
there from the fleet, sun-bronzed, barefooted, in loose trousers, tight
cotton shirts, and red caps. With them were the men-at-arms in
gorget, breastplate, and helmet. All were surrounded by their
families and friends. Many of the womenfolk, even though in
bright-colored garments, wore black mantles over their heads and
shoulders and appeared more like mourners at a funeral than those
come to bid a cheering farewell to a ship's company of young and
lusty men bound for high adventure. Presently (according to the
quaint account of the chronicler Osorio), as though by a common
impulse, they gave vent to their emotions in loud cries and lamentations. They burst into tears, crying:

"Ah miserable mortals! See to what a fate such ambition and greed
are rushing you headlong! What more dreadful punishments could
be visited upon you if you had committed the most heinous of crimes?
What far distant and measureless seas you must penetrate, what
merciless and mountainous waves you must brave, and what dangers
threaten your very lives in those faraway lands! Would it not be wiser
for you to face death in whatsoever fashion [it may come] here at
home than to launch forth into hidden places far from your fatherland, and to find graves in the salt depths of the sea?"

Whether or not this opera-chorus lament was really heard on Tagus's
banks that day we shall never know, but we can be sure that similar
sentiments filled the hearts of many at that moment. We are told
that Gama himself shed tears, austere and severely self-disciplined
as he was. He brushed them aside hastily, however, and gathering
together his officers and crew, led the way into the chapel for the
final Mass.[2]

The building was too small to admit all who desired to partici-
pate, and many of the crew with their families and friends were
forced to stand outside in the sun, bareheaded, throughout the
solemn ceremony. The scene within was a vivid and colorful one.

The small windows admitted but little of the sunlight, and in the gloom the candles and tapers gleamed on gold and silver and steel and jewels, accenting helmet and sword hilt and breastplate, and glowed dully on the velvet of cloaks and the silk of consecrated flags. When the closing words of the Mass had been intoned, the bells of the chapel and the monastery were rung. Immediately a procession was formed from the church to the shoreline, where the ship's boats had been drawn up on the sand. The vicar of the chapel led the way, followed by the priests and friars with folded hands and bowed heads, walking slowly and solemnly, chanting a litany as they went. They were followed by acolytes swinging smoking censers, and behind came the cross-bearer and more chanting priests in their long robes. Next came Gama, alone, head erect, severe and unsmiling, looking neither to the right nor to the left, and bearing a lighted candle. Behind him the officers and crew of the fleet fell into line two by two, each man likewise carrying a lighted candle. And so, with blue clouds of incense, the measured chanting of the litany, and the murmur of the responses from the multitude, the long procession reached the foreshore. The vicar turned, and at a sign all present knelt with bowed heads. The priest held a general confession and granted plenary absolution [3] for their sins to all who might lose their lives in the venture. The multitude arose as the religious service ended, and at an order from the captains the officers and men entered their boats and rowed off to their vessels.

The river Tagus presented a brave sight that far-off July day, crowded as it was with boats filled with men in shining armor, or clad in crimson and green, yellow and white, blue and purple. Flags and pennons of every shape, size, and color fluttered in the breeze, the motley livery of servingmen and the crowds on shore in their bright garments, together with the silvery flash of rising and falling oars added to the brilliant tapestry of the scene. It was a sight to stir one's heart, for, as one old chronicler has it, "It appeared in no way like the sea, but like unto a field of flowers."

Marshaled on deck, the assembled men-at-arms blew a loud fanfare on their trumpets. As the royal standard was hoisted to the masthead of the *São Gabriel,* the musicians beat out a great bass ruffle on their kettledrums; and the pipes and timbrels, flutes and tambours added to the din, drowning out the groans and cries and lamentations of those left behind on shore or in the small boats in which many had rowed out to catch a last glimpse of their dear ones aboard the ships.

And now it was afternoon, and, as usual at that season, as the shadows grew longer a keen wind arose and blew down the river toward the sea. The admiral had planned to take advantage of this wind and he gave the order to weigh anchor. The men jumped to the task with a will, in an effort to forget the trying hours behind them, when they had torn themselves away from grieving parents, families, or sweethearts. The anchors slowly and grudgingly rose dripping from the river's mud to the rousing rhythm of an old sea chantey. The next order was to set the sails. As the crew heaved and hauled, the wind caught the canvas and bellied it out, revealing on each sail the great painted red cross of the Order of Christ, the same cross as that emblazoned on the flag that Manuel had entrusted to Gama a few days previously at Montemór o Novo. The ships felt the first strength of the wind—that wind which was to be their servant (but too often a raging, rebellious, and sullen servant) for many, many thousands of weary miles—and, obedient to the helm, heeled slightly over and slowly gained headway down the river.

People still lined the shore, straining their eyes to catch hoped-for recognitions. Hands were waved, scarfs were shaken in the wind, and cries and shouts came faintly over the water to the ships as they dropped down toward the sea on tide and wind. The men crowded to the bulwarks and swarmed up the rigging, while officers leaned on the poop rail and out the sterncastle windows, all eager for one last sight of the crowds, of their beloved city of Lisbon with its hills and valleys, palaces and churches, now gradually dropping astern. The long rays of the setting sun gleamed on spearhead and cannon, ship's gear and helmet, and on shore it touched with flaming red-gold the stone and scaffolding of the half-completed Cathedral of the Sea. They gleamed once more on the waters of the Tagus, now turned a burnished steel-gray. Then twilight descended.

With the coming of the dusk the crowds on shore gradually dispersed and returned in small groups to their homes. The wind freshened as the fleet drew nearer the open sea. In the dim twilight a few fishing boats with rust-colored sails hastily scudded out of the path of the high ships bearing down on them. Flags were hauled down and stowed in their lockers, the night watches were set, lanterns were hauled aloft, and night fell on land and ships and river. The greatest adventure of the Portuguese nation had begun, the final realization of the dreams of Prince Henry and the plans and labors of King John II. It had taken the best part of a century to bring these dreams and plans to fruition—years of travail and disappointment, of trial and error, of success and failure. It had cost the lives of many brave men and also much gold. But Manuel, called by history the Fortunate, was to become the richest monarch in Europe; while Portugal was for a time to rule over many far-off lands and seas and peoples never before under European dominion, and for the greater part unknown, except for the tales of Marco Polo and a few other daring souls.

Few aboard the ships slept that night. Hearts were too full and excitement burned too high. But with the coming of a new day, all were early astir and active. They had crossed the bar, no land was in sight, and they were alone with sea and sky and God, their only company that of the squawking, quarreling white and gray gulls that followed the ships on their voyage far out into the western ocean.

As the crew of the *São Gabriel* went about their usual tasks, they had their first opportunity of seeing their commander at close range. They beheld, above them on the poop deck, a man in a beretlike velvet cap. He was medium of stature, in the full manhood of his thirty-odd years, rather thick-set, with face and neck the dark brick-red of one long exposed to tempest and hot sun and the salt of the sea. His features were partially covered by a black mustache and a full spade beard; but these rather accentuated than hid the strength of square jaw, the full and sensual, yet firm, even hard, mouth. His eyes were quick, keen, and wary, surrounded by the tiny network of wrinkles of one who had faced sun and wind and the glare of the sea for long years. At times there was revealed in the quickly veiled eyes and compressed lips a latent cruelty, seemingly an innate part of his nature. He was not a man to be loved, or one who courted affection. But the hard-bitten sailors, who had sailed the African seas with such men before, saw in him a man of iron will and inflexibility of purpose. They recognized in his voice, his quick, decisive orders, his whole appearance and bearing, a competent mariner, a stern disciplinarian, and a man not to be crossed or challenged. They knew he had the full confidence of the king, and that, come what might, he would execute his sovereign's will to the letter. Withal, they knew him from reputation as a brave man, and one who would never hesitate to lead wherever he ordered others to go. Those who were fortunate enough to return with Gama to Lisbon, and who fared forth with him again to the Indies, were to see all that was written on their admiral's face translated often into swift action—the determination, the intelligence, the stubbornness, the unreasoning, terrible anger, and the cold-blooded cruelty that was nothing short of sadistic. He was to bring victory and undreamed-of riches to King Manuel, and he was to lay the seas and lands of the Indies at his feet; but he was also to bring unnecessary suffering and horrible torture and death in almost unbelievably fiendish forms to untold numbers of unhappy folk, whose only sin was that they were not of Gama's faith, and whose only crime was that they had unwittingly crossed his path as he relentlessly pursued his star.

And so the fateful expedition set sail; and in the words of the author of the *Roteiro* of Vasco da Gama's first voyage to India, "we departed from Restello on a Saturday, which was the eighth day of July of the said year 1497, on our voyage, [and] may God Our Lord grant that we accomplish it in his service. Amen."

NOTES

[1] *Restello:* a machine or place for carding or combing flax or hemp.

[2] Tradition has it that the Mass was celebrated on a stone altar, which was preserved until 1872 at the foot of the oratorio of the Senhor Jesus dos Navegantes, located in the barracks which were built in front of the church. The account given of the Mass was taken from an unpublished MS in the monastery library, called Chronica de S. Jeronymos and recounted by the abbot to Sr. Teixeira d'Aragão, a noted historian of the end of the 19th century. He was also shown by the abbot three stones on a rubbish heap which he was told were the veritable stones of the altar. *Sic transit!*

[3] The right thus to grant plenary absolution to departing mariners was granted by a bull of Pope Martin V (1417-1431) at the solicitation of Prince Henry the Navigator. No copy of this bull has been found.

Barros says that there was so much weeping at the departure that the shore in front of the chapel might be called "the shore of tears."

CHAPTER XI

AFRICA

Thus we went forth those unknown seas to explore,
Which by no people yet explored had been.
     —CAMÕES, *Os Lusiadas,* V, iv.
     Translated by J. J. Aubertin.

HE voyage began quietly, with no unusual or note-worthy incidents. After a run of a week to the south-west, the Canaries were sighted, and thence the ships continued on their way close to the African coast. The men cast their lines here and caught fish for their messes. Proceeding farther, the fleet ran into a dense fog on the night of the 16th, off the inlet known as the Río de Oro (River of Gold). When the sun rose on July 17, the ships had become separated in the fog and in a wind which had arisen in the night. Gama had foreseen such a contingency, and, following his orders, the ships set their course for the Cape Verde Islands. On the morn-ing of July 22 the lookout of the *São Rafael* sighted three ships off Ilha do Sal, the northeastern part of the Cape Verde groups. They were the *Berrio,* the storeship, and the vessel commanded by Bar-tholomeu Dias, discoverer of the Cape of Good Hope.* The four vessels joined company and on the evening of July 26 finally over-took the *São Gabriel.* The following day the entire fleet dropped anchor in Porto da Praia, the harbor of Santiago, largest of the Cape Verde Islands. There the men were granted shore leave; and while repairs were being made to the yards of the ships, stores of fresh meat, water, and wood were taken aboard.

From the Cape Verdes a course was set to the eastward along the Guinea Coast and Sierra Leone. After further repairs were made on the yards of Gama's ship (probably the damage was the result of

* A fort had been built by Diogo d'Azambua in 1482 at São Jorge da Mina, one of the strategic outposts of the Portuguese on the Gold Coast. Dias had been awarded its captaincy for his services to the crown and had been ordered to accompany Gama's fleet on the first part of his voyage.

a storm), the course was changed. Instead of keeping close to the land in order to cover the 3,370 miles to the Cape of Good Hope, Gama struck boldly out from the Sierra Leone coast toward the west and south, making a great circular swing toward the hitherto undiscovered coast of Brazil.* Several explanations are given for his action. One is that he had obtained information as to the prevailing winds (and perhaps as to land to the west) from earlier navigators; the second is that the admiral took counsel with his officers and pilots, with the resultant consensus that they would avoid contrary and dangerous coastal winds by striking west. The third explanation is that Vasco da Gama took the action on his own initiative and that "it was," in the words of one commentator, "an act of super-lative audacity." It may well be that all three explanations are correct—that he had some information from earlier mariners, that his officers contributed ideas and theories, and that he himself decided to make the trial. Another possibility is that the whole route was planned and the details were worked out before the ships had crossed the Tagus bar.

The fact remains that in this first voyage to the East Vasco da Gama not only opened the sea road to the Indies for his royal master, but that he either found by chance or plotted the best sailing route from Europe to the Cape of Good Hope, the route still used by sailing vessels and the one advised in both the latest sailing directions of the British Admiralty and those of the United States Hydrographic Office. The great circular course by which he turned southwestward from Africa to a point about 5° N. latitude, sailed to within a short (undetermined) distance of the Brazilian coast, and swung east by southeast again at a point approximately 20° S. latitude, gave him the advantage of the most favorable winds and currents.[1]

It was a long, wearisome voyage, one beset with tempests interspersed with calms, and which revealed no island or coast where ships could take on fresh water or renew their provisions and supplies of wood.

After many days of sailing toward the southeast, whales and seals were seen on October 27, and coastal seaweed and other indications of the proximity of land were observed. Soundings were taken at

* See Samuel Eliot Morison, *Early Portuguese Voyages to America,* pp. 105 ff.

intervals, and on the morning of November 1 land was sighted. The ships were signaled to draw closer together, salutes were fired, and the ships were decked out with flags to celebrate a safe arrival at the African coast after more than three months of storm and calm in mid-Atlantic. The landfall could not be identified by D'Alenquer, who, it will be remembered, had sailed along this coast with Bartholomeu Dias, so the order was given to stand out to sea and proceed farther southward. Three days later the ships again approached land and entered a broad bay where Gama sent men in a small boat to make soundings and to search for a safe anchorage. On receiving a favorable report, he sailed in with his ships and dropped anchor. The inlet was forthwith christened Santa Helena Bay, and preparations were made to clean the ships both inside and outside, to mend the sails, and in general to repair the damages suffered at sea. The supply of drinking water had run very low, and what remained was stale and foul. Men were sent out to search for fresh water and located a stream flowing into the bay four leagues from the anchorage. Following the usual custom, the stream was named the Santiago.*

Gama was not satisfied with the shipboard readings of the sun's altitude, for with the imperfect instruments at his command the findings made on tossing, pitching vessels could not be trusted. So, while the crews were busy with repairs, wood gathering, and the filling of the water casks, he landed to make more accurate calculations. A tripod was set up on shore, the instruments were landed, and new observations were made. As he was thus engaged, some of the crew who had wandered away from the shore and back of the sand dunes came to report that they had seen two negroes near by, little fellows who appeared to be gathering something from the ground. This pleased Gama, for he was most anxious to obtain information about the unknown coast to which they had come. He ordered his men to surround the natives silently, close in, and seize them. The natives were clothed only in sheaths of wood or leather, with which they covered their nakedness, and carried fish spears of wood tipped with horn hardened in the fire. They were searching for honey in the bushes and, intent on driving away the bees with a smoking torch, did not hear the Portuguese until they were upon them. The poor Bushmen—for such they were—were terrified at

* Now the Berg River.

the apparition of the white men, for they had never seen such strange beings before and did not know whether they were gods or devils. One managed to elude the sailors, but the other frightened little fellow was taken down to the shore. Gama called for his interpreters, but none of them could understand the Bushman, who, when he spoke, "seemed to sob." Nor could the native in turn make himself understood, and he was too terrified to understand even the gestures made by the Portuguese. The impatient Gama realized that no progress was being made by this method, and he ordered a cabin boy and a negro sailor to take the prisoner aboard his ship and feed him well. The food and the absence of a crowd of bearded gesticulating strangers gradually quieted the man's fears, and when the commander returned after finishing his calculations he found that he could learn at least a little through the use of signs. The Bushman pointed to some mountains about two leagues distant and indicated that his village was at their base. Gama, shrewd judge of men that he was, decided that the native would be a better messenger to his village than would any of his own men. So he fed him once again, dressed him in clothes from the ship's slop chest, gave him some bells and glass beads, and sent him off. He had judged his man well, for the next morning about fifteen natives appeared. They accepted the presents offered them readily enough, but displayed absolute ignorance and indifference when shown spices, pearls, gold, and silver. They quickly vanished with the gifts, but two days later (November 12) half a hundred appeared. The crew at once started to bargain with them for souvenirs, which were as popular with seamen then as now. The writer of the only extant journal of the voyage tells us that for copper coins worth about one-tenth of a cent he obtained shell ear ornaments, foxtail fans, and a sheath.

One of the men-at-arms, Fernand Veloso, a loud and boastful fellow, decided that he would like to go to the native village to see what the Bushmen ate and how they lived. Gama hesitated, for he knew his men, and feared that the visit might lead to trouble. In this he was proven right. He yielded to Veloso's pleading, however, especially as his own brother Paulo urged him to allow the man to go. So, when the commander went aboard his ship to eat his dinner, Veloso departed with the crowd of laughing, chattering negroes. A number of the crew were still ashore under the direction of Nicolau

Coelho, collecting wood and gathering lobsters, of which there were large quantities in the inlet. On the way along the coast to their village the Bushmen caught and killed a seal, which they carried with them to cook as a feast for Veloso. With Vasco on his ship and the sailors on shore fully occupied, Paulo da Gama decided to enjoy himself. Calling some of his men, he entered a small boat with two of them and ordered the rest to follow in another. He had seen some young whales coming inshore for food and decided it would be good sport to catch one of them. He took two harpoons with him and foolishly attached the ends of the lines to the bows of the boat. Approaching one of the whales stealthily, a sailor flung his harpoon and sank it deep in the creature's side. The whale thrashed about in the water, dived, and started to swim seaward. In a few moments the coiled line had run out and drawn taut, until the boat was racing through the water in the bloody, foaming wake of the wounded whale. The men clung to the gunwales, for the boat threatened to capsize at any moment, and there was no knife or ax at hand with which to cut the rope. Just when they were despairing of escaping with their lives, the whale veered sharply from its course and headed back for the shore. There it soon struck bottom and, as it lay quiet for a bit, gave Paulo and his men an opportunity to disengage the rope and row to their anchorage. It was a narrow escape.

While all this was going on, Veloso's black friends had become hungry and they decided to stop where they were to roast the seal. The afternoon wore on, and Coelho and his men, having finished their tasks, had entered their boats and were rowing back to their ships. Meanwhile Gama, worried at Veloso's long absence, was anxiously pacing up and down the deck. Suddenly he heard a shout and, looking landward, saw Veloso running down a hill toward the ships, calling and gesticulating as he came. Gama shouted to Coelho and his men to turn about and pick him up. The men, however, believing that it was another of Veloso's pranks, rowed slowly. What Veloso did to offend his hosts none knew, but, as the men in the boats drew near the shore, two of the Bushmen raced down from behind the hill to head him off, while a number of others ran down to the landing place with bows, arrows, and stones. The two foremost Bushmen tried to seize Veloso, but he evidently knew how to use his fists to good effect, for they both ran back with bloodied faces, while he climbed into one of the boats. Gama was watching all this from his ship. When he saw the natives gathering in force and threatening the boats, which were still close inshore, he jumped into a skiff and was rowed speedily to his men. He arrived none too soon, for stones and arrows were raining down on the boats and their occupants. One arrow struck Gonçalo Álvares, master of the *São Gabriel,* and two other sailors were wounded. As Gama stood up in his boat and tried to pacify the enraged Bushmen, they turned on him and wounded him in the leg with an arrow. Since none of the Portuguese was armed—for they believed that they were dealing with feeble, docile folk—Gama ordered the boats to row with all speed back to the ships. Arrived there, he sent several of his crossbowmen back in the boats with full loads of arrows and with instructions to give the natives a salutary lesson.

Of course this unfortunate clash made it impossible to remain longer in the bay, and Gama, disappointed at learning nothing of the land where he was, ordered sail set two days later, on November 14. Luckily, the ship's repairs had been completed and ample stores of wood and fresh water were aboard. It was an inexcusable conflict between natives and Europeans, this time caused by the folly of one man.

Gama was now in a quandary. He believed that he was in the proximity of the Cape of Good Hope but was not sure how far away he was. He looked to D'Alenquer, who had sailed these seas with Dias, but he could not help much, though his guess was within three leagues of the correct distance. So Gama made the decision himself —for indecision was never one of his faults. The course was set south-southwest. At the end of the second day the lookout shouted, "Land in sight on the port bow"; and there, in view of all, rose the welcome sight of the Cape itself, the landmark toward which Gama and his ships had been striving for almost five months. Though the Cape was before them, adverse winds prevented them from doubling it until noon of November 22, when the ships rounded the point and sailed farther along the coast, passing close to False Bay on their way.

This part of the voyage had been a severe test of Vasco da Gama's abilities as a master mariner dealing with unknown winds and currents and in weathering the sudden violent storms of the South Atlantic. He stood the test well and won the respect, admiration, and confidence of his officers and crew not only as a seaman but also as a leader of infinite resourcefulness in the handling of ships and men.

Three days more of coastal sailing brought the adventurers to a bay which they named São Brás—the present Mossel Bay. This was without doubt the Herdsmen's Bay, where Bartholomeu Dias had shot the negro with his crossbow ten years before. As the four ships sailed into the bay, several score of the natives flocked down to the shore to greet them. Some, seemingly timid, held back on the hills, but others came to the water's edge. The boats were launched and filled with men, this time, however, armed against a surprise attack. Gama led the way and, as the boat drew near the shore, he threw little tinkling bells to the negroes, who danced with joy as they caught them. After locating an open spot where there was no danger of ambush, the captains of the vessels, led. as usual by Gama and guarded by men with crossbows, landed. There were many elephants in the hinterland, and the Hottentots who had come to meet the ships gladly gave ivory bracelets to the Portuguese in exchange for red caps and more bells.

Two days later about two hundred more savages appeared, driving before them oxen, cows, and sheep. The boats again left the ships for the shore, and the officers saw visions of a plenty of fresh meat to replenish their greatly depleted stores. The natives were in a festive mood—they were always a lighthearted people—and several had brought with them their *goras* (native pipes), upon which they forthwith began to play. Soon the Hottentots formed a circle and dancing began. Gama enjoyed the outlandish Hottentot dancing and relaxed sufficiently to command his trumpets to be sounded on shipboard. He returned to the *São Gabriel* shortly afterward and, observing that his men were also in a holiday mood, ordered the musicians to strike up a dance step. The crew all joined in and, to their astonishment, Vasco da Gama himself entered into the dance with them.[2] All rank was forgotten for the moment in the rejoicing at having braved and conquered the wild Atlantic and at having doubled the Cape with all its storied terrors. When the dancing on land and on shipboard ceased, the officers returned to the shore and for three bracelets bought a fat black ox. "This ox we dined off on Sunday. He was very fat, and his flesh was as toothsome as that of Portuguese beef."

The friendly relations between the natives and the Portuguese did not last long, and the ships sailed away after a padrão had been erected, together with a great cross made from one of the spare masts. To his chagrin Gama saw negroes come down and destroy the padrão and the cross even as the ships got under way. The Portuguese were not leaving behind them a tradition of friendship in Africa.

The voyage continued along the coast, severe storms alternating with fine weather. On December 16 the fleet passed the last pillar erected by Dias and reached waters never before seen by Portuguese eyes. After some difficulty in beating against the Agulhas Current, the fleet proceeded once more, and by Christmas Day of 1497 had discovered seventy leagues of coast beyond the point where Dias's men had forced him to turn back. This was the land now called Natal—the Portuguese word for Christmas. The ships had been at sea continuously since December 8, and water was running so low that the men were each receiving less than a pint a day for drinking, and all cooking was being done with sea water. Gama gave the order to approach the coast, and on January 11 the vessels dropped anchor at the mouth of a small river. As the ships' boats were rowed toward shore, a large number of negroes—men and women—gathered on the beach to greet them. These were tall, well built people of the Bantu tribes, far different from the small Bushmen and Hottentots whom the Portuguese had encountered heretofore. Gama ordered Martin Affonso, who had lived in the Congo region, to land with another sailor and to try to communicate with one who seemed to be the chief. Affonso found that he and the negro could understand each other fairly well. As the natives seemed friendly, Gama sent the chief a jacket, a pair of red trousers (the natives did not wear much more than loincloths), a cap, and a bracelet. Affonso and his companion were invited to the village. On his return the next morning he told of his adventures. The chief had donned the red trousers and cap and paraded before his subjects, who clapped their hands in salute of the strangers. The men had been lodged in the chief's hut and were given a meal of millet porridge and chicken, and all through the night men and women had come to stare at them in their hut. In the morning they were accompanied back to the ships by two natives with gifts of fowls for their commander, but by the time they arrived at the shore they were surrounded by several hundred natives. Affonso reported that the country was densely populated; that the people were farmers and lived in straw huts; that they used long bows and iron-tipped arrows and spears; that they wore copper armlets and anklets and had copper ornaments in their hair, and that some of the men carried daggers in ivory sheaths. Affonso also told of how the natives carried sea water in pots to their villages and evaporated it in pits to obtain salt.

Because of the friendliness of the natives, Gama called the country Terra da Boa Gente (Land of the Good People), and because of the copper used by the people the little river was named the River of Copper. The natives remained friendly and even carried the water casks out to the ships. Before all the casks were filled, however, a favorable wind sprang up and Gama, taking advantage of it, left his friendly hosts.

On January 25 the ships entered the mouth of the Quelimane River. Here they found more natives who gave a pleasant reception to the Portuguese. They were also Bantus, like those at the River of Copper, and, like them, both sexes wore only loincloths. The writer of the *Roteiro* found the young women *parecem bem* (good-looking) even though they had their lips pierced in three places and wore pieces of twisted tin inserted in the openings. The kindly folk brought the produce of their tilled patches to the ships in their dugout canoes and helped the crew take on fresh water.

A few days after the fleet had come to anchor, two chiefs paddled down the river from the interior to see the newcomers, the news of whose arrival had traveled quickly by means of the jungle "grapevine." Though these chiefs held aloof and looked with disdain on the presents offered them, their coming was very important to Gama. He noticed that one of them wore a cap with a silk-embroidered fringe and that the other had a headpiece of green satin. Moreover, one of their attendants made the Portuguese understand, largely by signs, that he had come from a faraway country and that he had seen large ships like those of the Portuguese before. Both the presence of silk and the remarks of the chief's attendant brought great joy to the commander in chief, because here, for the first time since doubling the Cape of Good Hope, were definite indications that at last he was approaching India and that traders from the East had visited the African coast where he was now anchored.

The chiefs ordered grass huts set up on the riverbank, very near
the anchorage, and remained for about a week trying to sell the
Portuguese cloth with a red design on it. Then they vanished up the
river again in their dugout canoes. The fleet remained at the river
mouth for thirty-two days, repairing a broken mast on the *São
Rafael,* taking on water, and careening their ships, for the bottoms
had grown foul and the hulls had sprung leaks during the long
Atlantic calms and gales.

Each ship was run up and towed into shallow water. When
everything below decks had been shifted to one side so that it heeled
over, tackle was erected by which the crew were able, by hauling
on ropes, to lay the side of the vessel bare to the keel. Then scaffoldings were built over the exposed side, and the sailors went to work,
scraping off the accumulation of weeds and barnacles. A boiler for
pitch was set going and the seams were recaulked with fresh
oakum, pitch, and oil. Then the hulls were repainted. After this was
done on one side, the ship was careened again and the operation
was repeated on the other side. The vessel was then hauled back to
an even keel, relaunched, and thoroughly scrubbed inside and out;
after which it was reloaded and fitted with the necessary equipment,
the worn-out and damaged spars and rigging being replaced
from the extra sets that had been brought from Lisbon for the purpose.

While they were at work on the ships, scurvy broke out among
the crew, brought on—as we now know—by a lack of certain
vitamins in their food.[3] Evidently they had not been able to obtain
sufficient fresh fruits or vegetables from the natives whom they had
met thus far during their landings in Africa. The dread disease had
been known and described by physicians and mariners from very
early times. Probably the most vivid account of the disease and the
strange remedy used is that of Jean Mocquet, who voyaged to
Africa and the East and West Indies in 1601:

I had that troublesome and dangerous malady "lovende," which the
Portuguese call "berber" and the Dutch "scorbut." It rotted all my
gums, which gave out a black and putrid blood. My knee joints were
so swollen that I could not extend my muscles. My thighs and lower
legs were black and gangrenous, and I was forced to use my knife each
day to cut into the flesh in order to release this black and foul blood. I
also used my knife on my gums, which were livid and growing over

my teeth. I went on deck each day, and over to the bulwarks, clinging
to the ropes, and holding a little mirror before me in my hand to see
where it was necessary to cut. Then, when I had cut away this dead
flesh and caused much black blood to flow, I rinsed my mouth and
teeth with my urine, rubbing them very hard. But even with such
treatment there was as much [swelling of the gums] again each day,
and sometimes even more. And the unfortunate thing was that I could
not eat, desiring more to swallow than to chew, because of my great
suffering in this trying malady. Many of our people died of it every
day, and we saw bodies being thrown into the sea constantly, three or
four at a time. For the most part they died with no aid given them,
expiring behind some case or chest, their eyes and the soles of their
feet gnawed away by the rats. Others were found dead in their bunks
after having been bled. Moving their arms [in their racking pain] they
thus caused the [cut] vein to open again, and, their blood flowing out
again, they passed into an intensely feverish stupor, dying with no one
to help them. All that could be heard were cries of intense thirst and
dryness. For very often, after having received their ration of water,
which might be about a half-pint to a quart, they would place it close
at hand to drink when thirst seized them, whereupon their companions,
either those close at hand or those farther away, would come and
snatch the poor dole of water from the miserable sick wretches when
they were asleep or had their backs turned. And also, in the 'tween
decks and in other dark places they struck at each other and fought
without seeing their opponents, when they caught them stealing. And
so, very often, thus deprived of water, they died miserably for the lack
of a few drops. There was no one willing to give a little water to save
a life, no, not a father his son nor a brother his brother, so great did
the desire to cling to life by drinking drive each to think of himself
alone. Often did I find myself thus cheated and deprived of my
[water] ration, but I consoled myself with many another in the same
evil case as myself. This was also why I dared not sleep too soundly,
and why I put my ration of water in a place where none could seize
it easily without touching me. Among us was the greatest confusion and
chaos imaginable, because of the great number of men of every class
who were there, vomiting, some here, some there, relieving themselves
on each other. On every side were heard only the cries of those
assailed by thirst, hunger, and pain, cursing the hour when they had
come aboard, and calling down maledictions even on their fathers and
mothers, so that they all appeared bereft of reason.

The same symptoms are described in the narratives of Vasco da
Gama's expedition, and one writer tells us that the commander

ordered his men to use the same remedy as that mentioned by Mocquet.[4]

In connection with this visitation of scurvy, we have a second demonstration of the kindly and sympathetic nature of Vasco's brother Paulo. The first was when we were told that he interceded for Affonso Veloso when the latter asked permission to visit the Bushman village. A very early account of the voyage remarks that the sickness and mortality

would have been far greater had it not been for the kindliness of Paulo da Gama. He visited the sick both night and day, and comforted them and ministered to them. Moreover he shared generously [with his men] those things for the relief of illness which he had brought with him for his own use.

Evidently some fresh and health-giving foods were obtained by barter from the natives, for the scurvy finally disappeared. While the ships lay at Quelimane—which the Portuguese called the River of Good Signs, because of the promise it gave that they were at last nearing their destination—Vasco da Gama had a misadventure which nearly cost him his life. Having occasion to discuss some matter with his brother, he was rowed to the *São Rafael*. The conversation was carried on by Gama in his boat, with his sailors and himself holding on to the main chains, while his brother Paulo leaned over the bulwarks of his ship. "Suddenly the water beneath their boat sank so suddenly that it swept the boat away from under them, and he [Vasco] and his sailors were saved only by clinging and hanging to the chains until they [the crew] came to their rescue."

The work of repairing, refitting, and of taking on wood, water, and fresh provisions was completed at last, and a padrão was erected, named São Rafael, after the ship which had carried it from Portugal.[5] On February 24, 1498, when the repairs were finished to Gama's satisfaction, anchors were weighed and sail was set. There was a delay of several hours, for Paulo da Gama's vessel grounded on a sand bank and was held fast until the rising tide refloated it. Then all four ships sailed out of the harbor.

Vasco da Gama, intent on obeying the royal command to find the sea road to the Indies, never dreamed that when he thus left the waters of South Africa he (together with his sovereign) was casting away a golden opportunity, that of claiming and occupying a land with a climate perfectly suited to European colonization, one rich in agricultural lands and minerals, and one marked by destiny to become a center of European civilization and culture.

On the ships sailed to the northeast for over three hundred miles, through the Moçambique Channel (between Africa and Madagascar) holding offshore and lying to at night to avoid islands and shoals on the uncharted coast. On Friday morning, March 2, the island of Moçambique at the north end of the channel was sighted, and the fleet slowly entered the harbor. Nicolau Coelho's vessel led, as usual, but struck a shoal and broke the tiller. Luckily, he was able to extricate his ship, get her into deeper water, and let go his anchor, together with the other three vessels, close to the town. As they took their positions, a number of small boats surrounded them. Other boats put out from the shore with men in them playing a tune of welcome on their *anafils*,* for they believed the new arrivals to be Mohammedans like themselves—and the Portuguese did not undeceive them.

With their arrival at the island of Moçambique, Gama had passed from the section of the East African coast inhabited by savage tribes and had entered that portion of the littoral controlled by the Moslems—full-blooded Arabs, Arab-African half-castes, and converted natives. Heretofore they had been touching at shores peopled by a simple negro society which consisted of tribes of limited size and political organization, federated but loosely, if at all, and absolutely incapable of offering a united resistance to the superior discipline and armed force of the Europeans. But now they had entered an area with a far different political and social organization, an area permeated to a certain degree with Moslem culture, which was not inferior to that of the Portuguese of the period. The Arabs had been invading the coasts and infiltrating into the interior for centuries. The northeast monsoon blew steadily each year from December to February and was reversed from April to September by that from the south-southwest. This constant succession of winds made the visits of vessels from Arabia, Persia, and India inevitable. Merchants knew that in the winter they could sail to the east coast of Africa and that in the spring favorable winds would take them

* *Anafil* (Arabic, *El nafir*), a kind of Arab trumpet.

home again. It is probable that this traffic, at least as far as India is concerned, dated as far back as the sixth century B.C.; and it is believed that Indian travelers took the coconut palm * to Africa at that early date.

The exchange of products—including African slaves—had developed a flourishing commerce, and for centuries before Gama's ships made their appearance in East African waters, the Arabs had controlled this carrying trade and were the undisputed masters of the Indian Ocean. Not only did they convey merchandise between India, Persia, Malaya, and the East Indies, China, Arabia, and Africa, but Europe depended on them for the transport of the products of the East to Alexandria and the other emporia whence the ships of the Italian cities carried them to their ultimate destinations. As business developed and expanded, factories and trading stations were established and towns sprang up around them. They were peopled partly by traders or their agents and partly by the natives of the coast who, either as slaves or as servants, formed the lower class and performed the manual labor of the settlements. Though many of the Arabs did not plan to make the East African towns their permanent homes, numbers of them settled there and took native wives or concubines. From these unions sprang the half-caste group called "tawny," "red-skinned," or "ruddy" by the early Portuguese travelers. To this mixed population were gradually added fugitives from African and Asiatic wars, feuds, and conquests. The Arabs brought with them the customs, language, and religion of their homeland, and these, though often in a diluted or perverted form, were absorbed and became those of the trading settlements.

These settlements were not politically subject to the mother countries but were independent city-states. There was no political unity, nor was there ever a single state exercising empire over the others. At times, for varying periods, some one city dominated a few others, but there was never any such close-knit federation as might resist invasion or conquest. It was this fatal political weakness that facilitated the conquest and domination of the East African coast by the Portuguese during the sixteenth century.

The entry of the Moslems into the East African trade and the

* "Coconut" is derived from the Spanish and Portuguese *coco* (goblin), because of the fancied resemblance to a goblin's face made by the three "eyes" of the coconut.

growth of their towns was in no sense a military conquest. The natives, unwarlike and broken up as they were into small tribes, were easily controlled. In fact, they appear to have acquiesced without any recorded resistance to the occupation by the Arabs. Penetration of the coast and the back country was gradually extended with the appearance of a generation of half-breeds. They naturally found it no difficult task to move about among the negroes of the coast and farther inland. The simple concepts of Islam were congenial to the tribes with which they came in contact, and the religion of the Prophet penetrated far and wide into the Dark Continent, until today it is the predominant nonpagan religion of the black man. Except for the upper classes and among new arrivals, the half-castes found that it was simpler and easier to use Swahili, the language of the East African mainland. Though Arabic words and phrases crept in, this hybrid Swahili is today the lingua franca of the land. As trade was the sole motive of the Arab residents and visitors in the East African towns, the interior of the country did not interest them, and comparatively few trading posts were established there, except along the slave routes.

The institution of slavery * had existed for ages in East Africa and was developed further and systematized by the Arabs at a very early date after their arrival. They recruited their slaves from the interior, and the most heartless and vicious of the slave traders were the half-castes and the natives themselves. They hesitated at no cruelty in the collection of slaves into caravans which finally ended their tragic and hideous journeys at the Arab coastal towns. It is impossible even to estimate the number of native Africans shipped out from the settlements. Most of them were transported to Arabia, Turkey, and Persia. As late as the year 1853, one-third of the inhabitants of the Arab state of Oman were slaves, and those of us who have visited the states of southern Arabia can attest to the marked negroid features and characteristics of many of their inhabitants. The Moslem King of Gaur, in India (1459–1474), possessed eight thousand negro slaves. In addition to the trade in ordinary slaves, the barbarous practice of making and selling eunuchs became very widespread. For centuries a constant stream of these helpless, cruelly mutilated creatures flowed across the sea to supply the courts and harems of the Moslem world of North Africa, Egypt,

* See Hart, *Venetian Adventurer*, 3rd ed., p. 17.

and Asia—and to fill the coffers of the traders with gold. In fact, in spite of the loss of prodigious numbers of handsome slaves as a result of the crude operation, the trade was the most lucrative that passed along the east coast of Africa and over the Eastern seas.[6]

Most of the Arab dwellers on the coast were merely middlemen. There was practically no manufacturing done, except of woven cloth and iron implements. Nor were there commercial crops except, in some places, coconuts and coconut oil. The African commodities in demand were slaves, ivory, gold, and ambergris. In exchange the Arab merchants imported cloth, metalwork, beads, and other manufactured goods suitable for the native trade from India, Persia, and Arabia. The Arabs appear never to have ventured in their poorly constructed vessels farther southward along the coast than Sofala. It is believed that they feared the swift currents of the region. For this reason Gama found no Arab traders or ships along the coast as the fleet worked its way up from the Cape of Good Hope.

It is important to note that in spite of the impotence of the scattered Arab settlements before the superior force of the Portuguese, they were representatives of a rival creed, one as fanatical in its hostility to the Christians of the era as were the Portuguese in their hatred and contempt of all those professing the faith of Islam. The struggles of Gama against the malevolent forces of the sea and the ignorant savages of the southern coasts were now temporarily at an end. The new and more dangerous challenge was that of the civilized and semicivilized peoples of the east coast. And in meeting this challenge, Gama began to display some of his weaknesses: a quick, violent temper, a lack of tact and judgment, and an insensate cruelty. These were destined to affect the fortunes of his country in both Africa and Asia, and they laid the foundation of suspicion, mistrust, and fear which dogged the footsteps of his successors for centuries.

The people of Moçambique were far different from the naked savages whom the Portuguese had met on their previous landings. They were much lighter in color than the negroes, and their language was a bastard Arabic. The usual costumes consisted of flowing robes of white or striped linen and cotton, with head coverings of cotton and silk. Moçambique was a busy emporium, doing business with India, Persia, and Arabia, as well as with other East

African towns. Many foreign ships were in port, loading and discharging cloves, pepper, and ginger, gold, silver, pearls, and precious stones. Gama summoned Fernão Martins, who spoke Arabic, and through him was able to obtain much valuable information as to the source of the traffic, for Moçambique produced none of these things on display in the town. Of course he was told—and repeated —"tall" stories of the wares about which he inquired, such as: "All the precious stones, pearls, and spices were in such great quantity that it was not necessary to buy them, but to gather them in baskets." They learned, too, of the people of the mainland across from the island. They were "heathen who are like beasts, savages, naked except for a strip of cotton cloth around their loins, and with bodies smeared with red clay." These tribes wore lip ornaments of cowrie shells, bones, and little stones. Some of the aborigines, too, were to be seen in their dugouts or in and about the town.

Gama and his men examined with much interest four Arab dhows of fair size which were lying in the harbor. They were decked over and had sails of palm matting. To the Portuguese the strangest feature of their construction was that no nails were used on them,[7] the planks being sewed together with coir.* The officers of the dhows were expert navigators and possessed compasses, quadrants, and charts, all of which were probably more accurate than those possessed by the Portuguese. It may be that it was from the Moçambique Arabs that Gama learned to construct wooden tanks below decks for his water supply.

The Portuguese of the expedition saw their first coconut palms in Moçambique. The author of the *Roteiro* noted: "The palms of this land produce a fruit as large as melons, and they eat the kernel, which has the flavor of hazelnuts; they also have cucumbers and melons in great quantities, which they brought to barter with us."

On the day the fleet entered the port, the local sheik came aboard Coelho's ship. Correa relates:

He arrived in two canoes lashed together, and upon them poles and planks, covered over with mats which gave shade. Ten Moors came thus seated [on the canoes], and the sheik sitting on a low round stool covered with a silk cloth and a cushion. He was dark, well built, and of goodly appearance, and was attired in a pleated Arab jacket of

* For a description of these vessels see Hart, *Venetian Adventurer,* 3rd ed., pp. 101 ff.

velvet. He was wrapped in a knee-length blue cloak, ornamented with braid and gold thread. His trousers were of white cloth reaching to his ankles. His body was otherwise naked. Around his waist, over his cloak, he wore a silk sash, into which was thrust a silver-mounted dagger, and in his hand he carried a silver-mounted sword. On his head was a dark tight-fitting cap of Mecca velvet, over which he wore a many-colored silk turban, embroidered with braid and fringes of gold thread.

Though Correa was not present, the description of the attire of the place and period is correct.

To this gorgeously appareled chief Coelho made the gift of a red hood! The dignified sheik, under the impression that the strangers were Moslems like himself, gravely presented his black rosary to Coelho to be used in saying his prayers, and asked to be rowed back in the ship's boat. He invited the Portuguese who accompanied him ashore to his dwelling, where he offered them refreshments, and on their departure sent to Nicolau Coelho a jar of dates made into preserves with cloves and cumin seed. Thereafter the sheik visited the vessel several times and dined with the commander. In his turn Gama made the same mistake as had Coelho, and offered the sheik such trash as hats, garments, and strings of coral. Perhaps Gama had nothing of any value to give him, for, as noted above,* the selection of goods in the ships' storerooms was good enough for ignorant savages but not suitable for the exchange of gifts with civilized officials. Be that as it may, the sheik "was so proud that he treated whatever we offered him with contempt, and asked for scarlet cloth. We carried none with us but gave him of whatever we had."

Meanwhile the officers were obtaining all the information possible about India and the land of Prester John. The facts they gathered were for the most part inaccurate or false. They were informed that Prester John's land was near by, "that he owned many cities on the seacoast, and that their inhabitants were great merchants and possessed large ships." The Portuguese also met two native Christians, brought as captives from India, who were taken out to visit the *São Gabriel*. As soon as they saw the painted figurehead of the Angel Gabriel, they fell on their knees and worshiped. When the Moslems saw that Gama took pleasure in talking with the despised captives, they realized that the Portuguese were also

* See p. 89.

Christians, and precipitously hastened ashore. They dragged their captives away with them, and neither Gama nor his men were ever permitted to come in contact with them again.

The time was now approaching for the fleet to continue its voyage. Gama invited the ruler of the island to dine on board. The sheik gave no intimation that he now knew that the Portuguese were hated and despised Christians, but accepted the invitation. After a fine dinner had been served, Gama, who had told the sheik previously that he was seeking the route to India, asked if he could be furnished with two pilots to assist him. The sheik consented with alacrity, with the simple proviso that the terms should be satisfactory to the two men hired. When the pilots appeared, Gama offered them each thirty gold *matikals* * and two *marlotas* † in advance, but stipulated that from the day they received their payment, if they wished to go ashore, one of them would always remain on board the ship. "They consented, but insisted on receiving their wages and the *marlotas* at once, as otherwise they could not go, inasmuch as they would have to leave them [the wages] with their wives for their support." The money and gifts were handed over at once, but by laying down such conditions Gama indicated clearly that he did not put much faith in the men with whom he was dealing.

With the passing days the tension, which had begun to manifest itself after the knowledge leaked out that the fleet was really a Christian expedition, grew greater, until frequent open clashes occurred between the townspeople and the crew members landing for wood and water. Gama avoided these conflicts as much as possible, but as he had wilfully taken advantage of the belief of the people of Moçambique that he and his men were Mohammedans, he was only reaping the fruits of his own misrepresentation. Since the number of able-bodied men had shrunk greatly by reason of deaths from scurvy and other diseases, and because he had many sick men on board, the commander decided to take no chance of a mass attack.

On Saturday evening, March 10, the fleet was ordered to draw off from the town to a small island (São Jorge Island) which lay about a league out in the bay. Here, on March 11, Mass was said and confession and Communion were offered to those who wished to avail themselves of the opportunity. Immediately after the reli-

* Approximately $90.
† Short silk or wool garments worn in India.

gious services the crews were ordered to return to their ships. One of the pilots had sneaked ashore during a fracas between some of the crew and the sheik's men and had not returned. With two boatloads of men Gama set out to find him, the second boat being under the command of Coelho. As the boats were rowed toward the town, five or six Arab craft darted out from the shore, each crowded with men armed with bows and very long arrows and shields. Gama immediately seized the remaining native pilot, whom he had taken in the boat with him, and, holding him fast, ordered his men to fire with their bombards at the approaching Arabs. Paulo da Gama had remained on the *Berrio* to give aid if another clash occurred. As soon as he heard the sound of firing, he bore down on the Arabs in his ship, whose sails had been spread. When they saw him coming, the Arabs, who were beginning to give way before Gama's attack, now fled in confusion and beached their boats before Paulo's ship could get within range. Disgusted, Gama and his men rowed back to their vessels, the *Berrio* swung about, and the whole fleet set its course up the coast. It had taken on a goodly supply of wood, vegetables, fowl, goats, and pigeons, all at the cost of a few strings of yellow glass beads. A supply of water had also been taken aboard, but not sufficient to last very long. The commander heaved a sigh of relief at escaping from a position which, with his reduced crew and prevalent sickness, was rapidly becoming untenable. But he was congratulating himself too soon.

By Tuesday, March 13, the fleet had proceeded but twenty leagues when the wind dropped and the fleet lay becalmed for two days. At sundown on March 14 Gama ordered the vessels to stand farther off shore, in an endeavor to catch a favorable wind. Instead they were caught by an adverse current and by morning had been carried some distance below their former anchorage off Moçambique. They hastily dropped anchor close to the little island where Mass had been held and lay there for eight days, waiting for a propitious wind. Upon their reappearance the sheik, for his own ends, sent an Arab (reputedly a sherif, a descendant of Mohammed, but evidently far from orthodox, as it is particularly noted that "he was a great drunkard") to announce that he wished for peace with the Europeans and to be their friend, though he made no move to assist them.

Because of the long delays, the fleet's supply of water began to run low and become foul. Since there was none on the island, it became necessary to land once more near the town to obtain it. The pilot who had been detained on board promised to guide the Portuguese to a place where the water could be obtained without danger. Gama and Coelho led the ships' boats to the shore; but the pilot, who probably was only trying to escape without fulfilling his contract, whether purposely or through his own ignorance, led them here and there in the dark without coming upon water, and when the sun rose the boats returned to the ships with empty casks. The next evening the same group returned to the search with the pilot. When a watering place was at last located, a score of the sheik's men armed with assagais ran down to the beach and ordered the sailors off, threatening them with their weapons at the same time. Gama with no hesitation—for it was imperative to have water—ordered three of his men to fire their bombards, whereupon the men on shore took to the woods and Gama and his crew landed and filled their casks. On the return to the ships, João de Coimbra, pilot of the *São Rafael,* discovered that a negro slave whom he had brought with him from Portugal had escaped.

So matters rested until Sunday, March 24. Early in the morning a boat put out from shore and rowed to Gama's ship, its occupants shouting menacingly that if the Portuguese tried to get more water they would meet with a reception that would be little to their liking. This was just the kind of threat needed to rouse Vasco da Gama's insensate anger, and he resolved to show the Arabs forthwith that he would do just as he pleased and would stand no nonsense from them. All the boats were ordered lowered, each loaded with armed men carrying bombards. The crew bent to their oars and soon drew near the shore. There they found that the Arabs had erected crude palisades of planks, before which were gathered many men armed with assagais, swords, bows, and slings. As the boats approached, stones began to rain down on them from the slings; but a few shots from the bombards put the Arabs to rout, and they sought refuge behind their wooden fort. This was no protection from the stone balls hurled by the bombards, which kept up their fusillade for three hours, during which one native was killed on the beach and another behind the palisades. "Then," adds the author of the *Roteiro,* "when we tired of this we went off to dine on our ships." When dinner was over, Gama decided to provide a bit of diversion by trying to take a few prisoners whom he might hold as hostages for the surrender to him of the two Indian Christian captives and Coimbra's escaped negro slave. As his men sallied forth, they saw boats and dugouts loaded with people and their possessions fleeing to the mainland, for they feared a raid on the town by the terrible white men. Paulo da Gama captured one dugout manned by four negroes, and two others, one of them laden with goods belonging to the sherif. These were seized when they were run ashore and abandoned. The negroes were taken on board Gama's ship. Of the booty Gama retained copies of the Koran to show King Manuel on the return to Portugal, and all the remainder—fine cloth, baskets, perfumes, and so forth—he distributed as spoils of war to his officers and men.*

The following day more water casks were filled and taken aboard without interference, for the inhabitants feared to leave their houses. After taking on all the water the fleet required, Gama, for good measure, ordered that a few more bombards be discharged at the town before departing. On Tuesday, March 27, the ships again drew off to the island of São Jorge, where they lay for three days "in the hope that God would grant a favorable wind." [8] The wind— a light one—came up on March 28, but dropped again on the 31st after the ships had advanced but twenty leagues up the coast. After being again overcome and carried back by the currents, the ships were able to proceed slowly on their way. The Arab pilot was a most difficult person, and Gama wasted no time on him. When he misrepresented some small islands off the low-lying coast as the mainland, Gama had him triced up and "flogged most cruelly," naming one of the islands Ilha do Açoutado (Island of the Flogged One), by which name it is entered on the maps of the early sixteenth century. While sailing along the coast of Moçambique, Gama picked up a small native *zambuk* † containing an old Arab and two negroes. In order to get information about the coast towns and India, Gama "at once put the Arab to the torture to answer his questions." It is not to be wondered that with the treatment thus accorded innocent persons who crossed his path Vasco da Gama laid the foundation of the traditional hatred of the African for the

---

* In the melee the pilot who had "jumped ship" was evidently retaken, for he is mentioned as escaping again at Mombasa.

† A small coastal sailing vessel.

Portuguese. No scruples of conscience or of fair play ever interfered with his dogged—even truculent and savage—determination to gain his ends.

On Saturday, April 7, 1498, the fleet arrived off Mombasa, the finest harbor on the East African coast. The view of the city from the ships was a nostalgic one for the weary Portuguese mariners. It was built on the slope of a rocky peninsula rising out of the sea.

Its whitewashed stone houses had windows and terraces like those of the Peninsula [Portugal and Spain]—and it was so beautiful that our men felt as though they were entering some part of this kingdom [Portugal]. And although everyone was enamored of the vista, Vasco da Gama would not permit the pilot to take the vessels inside as he desired, for he was already suspicious of him and anchored outside.

The ruler of Mombasa had doubtless been informed of the unfortunate incidents along the coast either by swift runners ashore or by boat, for as soon as the Portuguese ships hove into sight a *zavra* (dhow) went out to meet them. Several Arabs climbed the ladder to the deck of the *São Gabriel* and inquired of Gama whence he came, who he was, and what he was seeking. Gama answered them through Affonso Martins, telling them that he wished to obtain provisions. Suspecting treachery, he had ordered all the sick men below decks, and all those in good health were drawn up fully armed.[9] When his visitors departed with all sorts of extravagant protestations of friendship and promises of assistance, the commander feared treachery more than ever, and set a large all-night guard on each vessel. At midnight a *zavra* crept up to the *São Gabriel,* with a hundred armed men on board. As they began to swarm over the side, Gama stopped them short and allowed only a few to come aboard, and these left after a time. It was evident that the Mombasans were reconnoitering to learn if the Portuguese were on the alert.

The sheik of the port continued in his duplicity and sent presents to Gama: "a sheep, large quantities of oranges, lemons, and sugar cane, together with a ring as a pledge of security, and informed him that if he wished to enter the port he would furnish them with everything which he required." Again Gama committed a serious error in dealing with the coastal Arabs. His gift in exchange for the provisions was nothing but a paltry string of coral beads. Instead of sending some of his officers as the bearers of the miserable present, he sent two of the convicts whom he had with him. In spite of this great breach of courtesy the men were well received, hospitably entertained, and shown all over the city; and when they were about to return to the ships they were given specimens of cloves, pepper, and corn to show to their commander as samples of the cargo with which the sheik could furnish him.

As the ships sailed slowly into the harbor the next morning, the confusion caused by a slight collision between two of the vessels gave the opportunity to some Arabs who were on the ships to jump overboard into a *zavra* hovering close by; and the two rascally pilots hired at Moçambique dived overboard at the same moment, swam to the *zavra,* and escaped. Gama flew into a towering rage and that night had two of the four men (whether Arabs or negroes is not known) whom Paulo da Gama had seized in a dugout at Moçambique dragged before him. He demanded that they tell him what they knew of any plot of the Mombasans against him. The poor devils protested that they knew nothing. Gama repeated his demand with tightened lips and narrowing eyes. They insisted that they knew nothing. Gama turned to an officer and pronounced the words "O pingo" (the drops). A fire was brought, an open basin placed over it, and into the basin were poured oil and resin. Soon the mixture was bubbling and boiling, giving off an odor of pitch. The two wretches were stripped, their hands tied and so held that they could not move. One of the crew took a ladle of the boiling mixture and stood at Gama's side. After a third denial of the prisoners Gama nodded. The sailor stepped forward and slowly and deliberately poured the boiling oil, drop by drop, on the smooth bare skin of first one man, then the other. They writhed and shrieked and moaned. The ladle was empty, the skins covered with horrible blisters and corroding burns. Gama waited in stony silence. Then one and the other confessed. They had heard from the sheik's men who had boarded the vessel that he planned to entice the vessels into the harbor and "then to attack the Portuguese when they were off their guard, and avenge the evil that Gama and his men had done in Moçambique." This information, gasped out between the moans of the tortured men, was not enough for Gama. Again he nodded, and again the ladle was dipped in the pot, and again, drop by drop, the scalding mixture fell on the tormented men. One could stand the agony no longer, but, convulsed with pain, wrenched himself with a supreme effort from the grip of his torturers, ran to the rail, and, though his hands were tied, leaped overboard into the waters of the harbor. Gama, seeing that nothing more could be extorted from the second man, ordered him to be taken away. He, too, contrived to escape and swim ashore after dark.

Night drew on, and Vasco da Gama again alerted his ships against a surprise attack. About midnight two dugouts filled with natives drew noiselessly near the fleet. Men slipped from the boats into the dark waters, some swimming toward the *São Rafael,* others in the direction of the *Berrio.* The watchers on the ships heard splashing but at first thought that tunny fish were playing about the ship. The swimmers who reached the *Berrio* began to hack at her anchor cables. Others climbed the sides and commenced chopping away the rigging of the mizzenmast. The sailors of the *Berrio,* finally realizing their peril, attacked them and at the same time shouted a warning to the other vessels. The Mombasans, when they saw that they were discovered, slipped back into the water and swam to their boats, which they then rowed hastily back to shore. The writer of the *Roteiro,* who had witnessed Gama's treatment of the natives all along the coast, piously enters in his log at this point:

These dogs tried many another knavery on us, but our Lord did not will them to succeed, because they did not believe in Him. . . . It pleased God in His mercy that while we lay to off this city, of a sudden all the sick whom we had with us recovered, because this place possessed very good air.*

In spite of the "malice and treachery which these dogs connived against us, and which he had laid bare," the ships remained off Mombasa two more days, then set sail on the morning of April 13. While crossing the bar, Gama had another mishap. One of the anchors could not be raised; and in the strenuous efforts to disengage it, the cable broke and the anchor was lost.†

---

* He gave no credit to the generous supply of citrus fruits sent on board by the sheik's order, but probably did not recognize their value as antiscorbutics.

† It may be that the cable was one of those partly severed during the night attack. The Arabs raised the anchor and placed it as a trophy before the sheik's gate, where it was found later by Francisco d'Almeida when he captured Mombasa in August, 1505.

Vasco da Gama, still persisting in the hope of finding a pilot who could take his ships across the unknown Indian Ocean, anchored offshore about eight leagues from Mombasa, and the next morning captured a small vessel with seventeen men in it, besides gold, silver, and provisions, and two of its passengers, an old Arab and his young wife. They then set sail and at sunset on Saturday, April 14, the fleet dropped anchor off Malindi, thirty leagues north of Mombasa.

Malindi . . . is a fair town on the mainland, lying along a strand. . . . [It] has many fair stone and mortar houses of many stories, with great plenty of windows and flat roofs after our fashion. The place is well laid out in streets. The folk are both black and white; they go naked, covering only their private parts with cotton and silk cloths. Others of them wear cloths folded like cloaks and waistbands, and turbans of many rich stuffs on their heads.
They are great barterers, and deal in cloth, gold, ivory and divers other wares . . . and to their haven come every year many ships with cargoes . . . of gold, ivory and wax. . . . There is great plenty of food in this city and . . . abundance of fruit, gardens, and orchards. Here are plenty of fat-tailed [Ethiopian] sheep, cows, and other cattle, and great store of oranges, also of hens.

Thus wrote Duarte Barbosa, who visited the town (probably in 1500 with Cabral's fleet), and who has left an account of the countries bordering on the Indian Ocean.[10]
On his arrival at Malindi, Vasco da Gama at last found an ally. Doubtless the news of the progress of the Europeans along the coast had come to the ears of the ruler of the city. He was, fortunately for the Portuguese, a rival of Mombasa, and welcomed allies as powerful as he believed the Portuguese to be. The Arab captives informed Gama that there were usually Indian ships at Malindi and that he could doubtless find competent pilots to guide him across the Indian Ocean. Since hostility and truculence had been the attitudes of the Arab chiefs up to this time, Gama resolved to use milder tactics, and, if possible, to placate the inhabitants of Malindi. He certainly must have learned by this time that cruelty and abuse and highhandedness were of no avail. If the feud between Mombasa and Malindi had not been so open and intense, he would probably have fared no better at Malindi than at Moçambique or Mombasa.

On April 15, Easter Sunday, the tiny fleet dropped anchor in the roadstead off Malindi. No signs of recognition were visible on the shore, and no boats came out to greet the strangers. Fear and suspicion had preceded the four vessels. On Monday morning the commander had a talk with the old Arab whom he had captured with his wife a few days before, and later in the afternoon landed him on a sandbank near the town, with a request that he act as his ambassador to the sheik, to explain his reasons for coming to Malindi and to tell of his need of a pilot. As Gama watched from his deck, he saw a dugout put out from the town to the sandbank. It took off the old Arab and returned with him to the shore. In the evening the Arab returned to Gama's ship in a *zavra,* accompanied by one of the local sheik's officers bearing a gift of three sheep and a message from his master, offering friendship, provisions, and a pilot. Thereupon Gama waxed most generous and sent the sheik an ecclesiastic's cloak, two strings of coral, three basins for washing the hands, a hat, little bells, and two pieces of striped trade cloth! Truly a regal gift to the ruler of a rich, independent city! In return the sheik sent the commander on the following day generous gifts of "six sheep and much cloves, cumin, ginger, nutmegs, and pepper," and also a message that if the commander wished to visit with him he would come out in his *zavra* and the commander could remain in his own boat.

The sheik was an old man, and his son, who was acting as regent, took his place at the interview. After dinner on Wednesday, the 18th, Gama, whose royal orders forbade his landing (a statement of the chroniclers rather difficult to understand, as Gama had already landed several times on the coast) awaited the sheik's arrival on the deck of the *São Gabriel.*

Soon after dinner the *zavra* came out and Gama climbed down into one of his boats which had been suitably decorated for the occasion. The boats drew alongside each other and the commander of the fleet met the regent. He wore a robe of damask lined with green satin, and a very rich head covering, and his cushioned chair was of bronze. Over his head was held a long-handled round parasol of crimson satin. At his side was his page, an old man, who carried his master's short sword in a silver scabbard. The sheik was attended by musicians who played on *anafils* and *siwas*—great trumpets of ivory and wood (or copper), beautifully carved, and "which made sweet harmony with the *anafils*." The meeting was most amicable and successful, and the following week was spent in festivities and the exchange of friendly visits. Gama was wary, however, and never allowed his men to go ashore except in heavily armed boats.

In the harbor of Malindi lay four merchant ships from India, whose owners called on the captains of the fleet. It is an idea difficult for us to comprehend that the Portuguese, while on the East African coast (and for some time in India), really believed that many of the Indians they met were Christians. When the Hindus saw the religious pictures and images on the ships, they believed them to be the Western way of depicting their own deities, and made offerings to them. In like manner the Portuguese, evidently ignorant of the Hindu religion, thought that the gods and goddesses whose images they saw in the temples were part of their own pantheon. The Indians of Malindi were constant objects of curiosity to the sailors, who had evidently never seen any before arriving in East Africa. "These Indians are swarthy men and wear but few clothes; they have great beards and the hair of their heads is very long, and they wear it plaited. According to what they said, they eat no beef." A native entertainment was given to the Europeans, including the setting off of fireworks.

After a week had passed, Gama's short stock of patience was exhausted by the aimless round of festivities and he again resorted to arbitrary action. When a servant of the sheik came out to his ship on a peaceful errand, he seized and held him as a hostage and sent a peremptory message demanding that the pilot who had been promised for the Indian voyage be sent on board at once. The sheik, who did not wish to lose his newly found allies, complied forthwith, and the pilot who was to guide them across the Indian Ocean to Calicut came on board the *São Gabriel,* whereupon the hostage was released by the commander.

Vasco da Gama was most fortunate in the choice of the pilot thus sent him by the sheik of Malindi—a pilot described as "the highest exponent of Moslem nautical science." He is referred to by the author of the *Roteiro* as "a Christian of Gujerat" and by contemporary chroniclers as "Malémo Caná." Neither of these statements is correct. It has been conclusively established that the pilot was an Arab of Julfar, named Ahmad ibn Majid.[11] "Malémo

Caná" was the Portuguese transliteration of his Arabic title. "Mu'allim" means "the instructor, pilot, or sailing-master." "Caná" is a corruption of the Tamil "Kanagan," "an arithmetician, or a master of astronomical navigation." The son and grandson of pilots, he was a hadji, that is, a man who had made the pilgrimage to Mecca, and he had the right to wear the green turban. In *Al Muhit* (all-embracing), a book of the period treating of the navigation and nautical lore of the Indian Ocean by Sidi Ali bin Husayn, the author, a Turkish admiral, refers to Ahmad as "the most trustworthy of the many pilots and mariners of the west coast of India in the fifteenth and sixteenth centuries—may Allah grant him mercy!" Not only was Ahmad a successful practical pilot, but he was the author of many rutters, or logbooks. Of these the manuscripts of nineteen are still in existence.* They were written between 1460 and 1495 and are remarkably full and accurate in their descriptions, especially of the monsoons and other winds of the regions traversed. Ahmad was no longer a young man when he entered Gama's employ. Born somewhere between 1430 and 1435, he was well in his sixties when Vasco da Gama arrived at Malindi.[12]

As soon as Ahmad ibn Majid arrived on board the *São Gabriel,* the commander in chief invited him, together with the interpreter, to his cabin to become acquainted and to estimate his abilities. Ahmad unrolled his maps of the west coast of India, accurately drawn with bearings, parallels, and meridians laid down in the Arab fashion, and explained them to the commander. During the discussion the latter brought out the great wooden astrolabe which the *São Gabriel* carried, as well as the smaller brass ones which he used for taking readings of the sun. The Arab showed a perfect familiarity with these, and indicated that they and similar instruments were used by Red Sea pilots for solar and sidereal readings. He then explained the way he and other pilots of the Indian seas took their readings by *taboas,* or plates with perforations for sighting, and also elucidated the mysteries of the cross-staff. As a result of the interview Gama was convinced that he had obtained a master navigator. The outcome proved that his confidence was not misplaced.

Nothing now remained to detain Gama and his fleet any longer in Malindi. Thanks to the friendship of the sheik, the water butts

* MSS in the Bibliothèque Nationale, Paris.

were filled, the provision rooms stacked high, and a plentiful supply of wood laid in, and the generous gifts of fresh fruit and vegetables had restored the surviving members of the crew to health. The long-hoped-for pilot was aboard. The monsoon had set in. Gama gave the order to weigh anchor and set sail. On April 24 the steersman swung the prows of the ships to the northeast, the monsoon caught the sails with their great red crosses and bellied them out, and the fleet of Dom Manuel was off on the last stage of its momentous voyage to the coast of India.

The voyage from Malindi across the Indian Ocean was uneventful. Five days after leaving the coast city the Portuguese "rejoiced at seeing once more the Great and Little Bear, Orion, and the other stars about the Northern Pole." For twenty-three days the ships held steadily on their way, with the favoring monsoon ever carrying them nearer their goal. Land was sighted dimly through the haze on the twenty-third day, whereupon the pilot changed the course away from the coast. Heavy rain and a thunderstorm prevented Ahmad from identifying his position until May 20, when high land was sighted—Kotta Point. The pilot made his way to Gama, who, with his men, stood looking anxiously from the prow out over the blue waters of South India. "We have arrived; we are just north of Calicut! Here is the land where you desired to go."

The long outward voyage was over. The thousands of weary miles of ocean, the eleven months of storm and calm, of stale food and foul water, of unfriendly savages and still more hostile Arabs lay behind them. Many of their companions, victims of scurvy and storm, of infection and fever, lay in the deep waters of the Atlantic or were in scattered graves along the African coast. But they, the survivors, had successfully won their way to the golden lands of the east, the lands of which Prince Henry and King John had dreamed, and which Bartholomeu Dias had almost reached. The sea road to India was no longer a vision of the future—it was a reality, traversed and duly charted by the indomitable commander Vasco da Gama.

He had won an enviable place in history. But the adventure of Vasco da Gama had hardly begun. He was yet to experience much on land and on sea, at home and in India. It is a pity that his fame was to be marred and besmirched by his constant lack of diplomacy, his ungovernable temper, his ruthless determination and his callous cruelty. Too many ugly pages were to be written in his story, pages which were to obscure and tarnish the glory of the great achievement, brought to a climax that hot sunny day in May, 1498, when Gama anchored off the coast of Malabar, a few miles from the famous city of Calicut.

NOTES

[1] There are varying and often contradictory accounts of the voyage and of the route followed. It is not the intention of this book to follow these divergences. It will be wiser to accept the judgment of such authorities as Hümmerich and Teixeira de Aragão and follow the author of the *Roteiro* until his narrative breaks off, and from that point to follow a synthesis of the reliable contemporary, or nearly contemporary, sources.

[2] In dancing with his men, Gama had the precedent of the Portuguese kings. "In the old times of the King Dom Pedro the fiestas were shared by them. When the trumpets were sounded for the people to dance in the street, the king danced with the girls."—Oliveira Martins, *História*, I, 198.

[3] Barros asserted that the outbreak was brought on by the diet of salt meat and fish and by the sea biscuit, which had become moldy and decayed.

[4] Scurvy is described vividly in a letter of Filippo Sassetti (1540–1588), a Florentine who died in Goa, Portuguese India. He wrote that 160 men fell ill in one day, their gums and their legs swelling to a monstrous size. They cut their gums with razors "in order to be able to open their mouths." Men died within a few days of their seizure, "expiring like a lamp when the oil has been exhausted."

[5] No trace of this padrão has ever been discovered. São Rafael was the patron of travelers (cf. his journey in the apocryphal Book of Tobit).

[6] This Arab slave trade lasted for two thousand years and was suppressed (perhaps not entirely) in the last part of the 19th century. As the Portuguese were the first to take slaves from West Africa to Europe, so they were the first Westerners to ship them from East Africa, purchasing them from the Arabs and transporting them to European (and later American) markets.

[7] Hümmerich asserts that the Arabs avoided the use of iron nails in the construction of their vessels because of the age-old Asiatic superstitious belief in the magnetic mountain which would draw to itself a vessel built with nails.

[8] It was in Moçambique that, according to Correa (I, XII), Gama left the convict João Machado. See p. 110.

[9] The author of the *Roteiro* notes at this point that the ships were very short of men "for even the small number we had were very ill."

[10] Duarte Barbosa accompanied Magellan on his great voyage of circumnavigation and was murdered by the natives of Cebu, in the Philippines, on May 1, 1521, a few days after the death of Magellan.

[11] His full name was Sihab ad-din Ahmad ibn Majid bin Muhamad bin Amr bin Fadl bin Duwik bin Ali ar Rakaib an Nadji.

[12] Sir Richard Burton, in his *First Steps in East Africa*, states that Ahmad ibn Majid is now revered as a Syrian saint to whom Allah gave power to see into the interior of the earth. To him is ascribed the invention of the compass, and prayers in his honor are recited by Red Sea mariners before setting sail on their voyages.

CHAPTER XII

MALABAR AND CALICUT

Give me a map. . . .
Lo, here, my sons, are all the golden mines,
Inestimable drugs and precious stones.
—MARLOWE, *Tamburlaine the Great*, Act V, Scene iii

Melibar is a great kingdom lying towards the west. The people
are Idolaters; they have a language of their own, and a King of their
own, and pay tribute to nobody
—MARCO POLO, Book III, Chap. 25

The whole Malabar coast is green, full of high trees, a very
greene and pleasant lande to behold.
—JAN HUYGHEN VAN LINSCHOTEN, *Voyage to the East Indies*, I, 67

And Ffurst ye shal understande that the city of Calicout is large
and of grete trate and stondeth in the mayne lond hard upon the see
side but it hath never a port nerer than almost a lege unto hit.
—ROGER BARLOW, *A Brief Summe of Geographie*, p. 139

N 1498 the city of Calicut was the most important of
the busy commercial ports on the Malabar coast of
India.[1] A narrow strip of territory, it extends from
Mount Deli (latitude N. 12° 2′) at the north for
about 150 miles to Cape Cormorin at the south. It is
separated from the remainder of the Indian peninsula by a range of
hills—the Western Ghats. Malabar constituted a distinct geographical and ethnical unit, which even today preserves many of its
peculiarities of customs and social organization.

In spite of its limited area the Malabar coast was split into many
petty political states, each vying with the others for a share in a very
important and lucrative export and import trade. Well served by
the monsoons and strategically situated as way stations for the trade
of India, Malacca, Ceylon, China, and the East Indies on the one
hand, and for that of Africa, Persia, Arabia, and the lands of the
Red Sea on the other, the coast cities had for centuries been the
chief entrepôts for the sea-borne traffic of Asia.

[158]

Of all the ports, Calicut was the most prominent and the richest; and Gama, well provided with letters and reports concerning the city and its trade, made it his goal after leaving Malindi. The city was not, and even today is not, especially well favored by nature as a seaport. Its coast line is unbroken by any harbor; it is open to the full force of the southwest monsoon; it is not near any navigable river. In 1498 the sea beat almost against the walls of its houses, which crowded down to the water's edge. Ships were forced to anchor in an open roadstead near the many mouths of a river which approached the sea about a mile south of the town and thence flowed in many shallow streams and canals through the city to the beach. Its ill smelling, oozy, muddy banks were the habitat of swarms of little red crabs, which scurried about everywhere underfoot. In the mud wallowed crocodiles,[2] an ever present menace to boatmen, longshoremen, and swimmers, while about the banks of the creeks and along the beach were great flocks of kingfishers and snowy egrets in long lines, seeking their food in the shallow waters. Only seagoing craft of the shallowest draft and the small native boats and dugout canoes could approach the beach.

The town itself was not imposing to a newcomer. The houses were crowded close together for a mile, then straggled for about six miles along the beach and back for some distance. The walls were "as high as a man on horseback"—in the words of an Italian traveler at the time of Gama's visit—"and the houses were mostly thatched with palm leaves. Only a few had more than one story, for one cannot dig down four or five spans without striking water" —so no solid foundations for larger structures could be laid. Some of the homes of the better class were of adobe and a few were of stone, but all showed good carpentry, were well made, and attested to the prosperity of the inhabitants.

The streets of Calicut were narrow and often winding, following the banks of the watercourses. Monkeys swung from the tall coconut palms and pepper vines that grew everywhere, and parakeets strutted solemnly on rooftop and tree branch with raucous screeches, while peafowl and pigeons scratched for their food unconcernedly and undisturbed in the dust of the road. At night foxes and other small animals raided the gardens for fruits and vegetables. Though all of these depredations caused much loss to the inhabitants, their religious beliefs forbade the taking of life, so that even the most poisonous of serpents were never killed—and took (and still take) a heavy toll of human life.

Down near the sea front stood great warehouses, built to resist the damp, and bursting with boxes and bales and bags: silk from China, fine local cotton weaves famous throughout the East and Europe,* cloves, nutmegs, mace, camphor from the Indies, cinnamon from Ceylon, pepper from the Malabar coast, Sunda, and Borneo; medicinal plants, ivory from the interior of India and Africa, bundles of cassia, sacks of cardamom, heaps of copra, coils of coir, piles of sandalwood, both red and yellow—all gathered here for sale or transfer to the vessels that would take their rich cargoes west and north and south to the lands of the Arab, the black, the Egyptian, the Persian, and the Frank.

Inside the city, their shops protected by awnings from the hot sun, were the markets. Here, as in the narrow streets, great crowds jostled, shoved, and surged from daybreak until nightfall, when the air was a trifle cooler. Hindus, Nairs, Arabs, Persians, Syrians, Turks, tall, slim black Somalis in white, their hair plaited in thin, greasy braids, slant-eyed Chinese and men of Annam and Cochin China, Malays from Malacca and the farther Indies, hadjis from Mecca in flowing robes and green turbans, wild men from the hills, haughty Brahmins wearing their triple cord, native Christians and Jews of the coast, negroes, slave and free, and now and then a swarthy Italian—all these rubbed shoulders in the bazaars and streets of Calicut. A score of languages and a hundred dialects were heard on every side—yet peace and order always reigned in the city streets.

The trays and baskets and bundles of the merchants were full to overflowing, for Calicut was rich and her people were prodigal with their coin. In the fruit market were great heaps of hog plums and red brindas, yellow carambola the size of hens' eggs, carandels green and large as a filbert, cucumbers, bulging bags of rice and nuts and baskets of cardamom seeds flavored with betel pods, tempting hearts of palms for cooling salads, cinnamon, both in sticks and powdered, and the dark-red mangosteens, sweetest of all fruits. Trays were stacked high with pyramids of lemons, oranges, and mangoes, together with great bunches of bananas of every size and color. Cakes of palm sugar were ranged neatly on counters along-

---

* The fame of Calicut weaves has given us our word "calico."

side brown and white heaps of cane sugar and long bundles of the sweet cane. Arrack—toddy distilled from the sap of the palm—was plentiful in great jars for those who would drink strong liquor. Breadfruit and odoriferous rose-apples were there too, and the fingerlike pods of the tamarind, preserved in sugar or in salt. Ginger, both green and in wet or dry sugary preserve, was on sale, and coconuts, both those young and full of milk, and the more mature nuts with more fleshy pulp for grating and slicing.

Next to the market for fruits were the stalls of the fishmongers, heaped high with the catch brought daily from within a few miles of the city, and hard by them were ranged the shops of the druggists. One could buy the olivelike fruit of the graceful neem, whose oil was pressed for anointing. Dogbane was there, to cure the flux, and aloes from Socotra. In tiny packages one could buy powdered rhinoceros horn, a sovereign remedy. Dried and green galanga were there, to sooth the nerves, and poultices of powdered cloves, guaranteed to cure the headache. Fingerlike slices of rhubarb from China were to be had for the ailing, and asafetida, a favorite remedy and a much sought-after flavoring. There, too, were ever replenished yet ever depleted heaps of areca nuts and betel leaves, with lime of burnt oyster shells—that combination of leaf-wrapped nut and lime which is chewed everywhere throughout southern Asia. The apothecaries offered, too, aniline leaves, dried in the sun and ready for the dyer's vat. Spikenard was to be had, the valerian root brought from Nepal, at the foot of the far Himalayas, and the fragrant putchock incense root from the storied Vale of Kashmir, with myrobalan and myrrh and gum arabic. On the counters were offered trays of yellow turmeric for flavoring and coloring curries. Sandalwood could be found, too, pounded on stones and mixed with oil to anoint and make lithe young bodies satiny and fragrant, for the dwellers in sweltering Calicut loved perfumes and sweet odors on their bodies and all about them. Street peddlers offered great armfuls of the flower of the champak and the rose, whose petals were strewn thick on the floors of the houses. Indeed, the Arab Abd-er-Razzak writes at this time: "These people could not live without roses, and they look on them as quite as necessary as food." *

Another blossom which was eagerly sought for its lingering,

* It is said that in the great rose gardens of Ghazipur "the sound of the opening of the countless buds is distinctly heard in the stillness of the night."

haunting fragrance was that of the hursinghar *—"the flowers of sadness." The old folk of Calicut never wearied of telling the tale of why it bloomed only after dark: Many, many years ago there lived a lord whose daughter was the most beautiful in all the countryside, one whose ravishing loveliness drew suitors from all the lands of Ind. But she turned away from her earthly lovers and lavished all her affection on the proud and distant god of the sun. He finally deigned to hearken to her oft-repeated, far-off prayer, and cast his glance down upon her face. She was so altogether lovely in body and spirit that he was drawn to her by the irresistible force of her dazzling beauty. That night he descended to earth and lay with her, and took from her that which a maiden can give but once, and which in her great love she gladly gave. But in the dawn he departed, and, disdaining his easy conquest, came not back again. And she, abandoned and distraught, in shame and desperation took her own life. Her superb and matchless beauty, now cold in death, was laid upon the pyre and the funeral torch soon enveloped her in the greedy flames. But a short time and naught remained of the wondrous maiden but a handful of white ashes. From these, when the parched and thirsty earth drank eagerly of the first gentle rains, sprang a graceful tree, bearing clusters of great white and orange blossoms—delicately tinted flowers—that ever, when the rainy season draws near to its close, scent the air and the breezes far and wide with their exquisite fragrance. But the flowers open their white hearts only at the hour of dusk, when the hated god has descended into the sea, and swiftly close their petals with the first coming of the dawn.

The apothecaries of Calicut had other wares to offer, small sinister packages, bought in the shadows and quickly hidden in the garments of the furtive buyer—bhang,† crushed leaves and seeds, drunk with nutmeg, cloves, or opium, long called by the Vedas one of the five "liberators of sin"—bhang, that arouses the passions to fever pitch, or stupefies, according to the dose; datura,‡ which if administered to an unsuspecting victim brings on temporary loss of mind and understanding, so that he who administers it may work

* *Nyctanthes arbortristis* (night jasmine).
† Bhang: hashish. (Indian hemp—*Cannabis sativa*).
‡ Datura: *Datura alba.*

his will for seduction, thievery, or even murder. On trays were heaped poppy pods, exuding their tears of forgetfulness, bought and eaten by those who would feed and increase their lusts. Many nostrums were there, too many to recount; but the most pathetic sight was that of feeble old men who paid unbelievably high prices for pills of powdered magnetic iron, guaranteed to drive out old age and bring back their long-lost youth.

Live animals were for sale—peacocks for the houses of the great, pet monkeys and mongooses, sought then as now to rid the flimsy houses of the rats that infested them. In other streets were the shops of workers in ivory and tortoise shell and the shell of the chank, all cut and quaintly wrought into armlets and bangles and anklets. There was a constant demand for bracelets in Calicut, for women commonly wore twenty to thirty from wrist to shoulder, and it was the custom to break every one at the death of a relative—and then to buy new ones to replace them!

The dealers in precious stones had no need to shout their wares. The rich came to them as they sat on their mats with their scales and tiny packets of stones before them. At a word the jewelers would spread out diamonds and the sapphires and star sapphires of Ceylon, the rubies and spinel rubies of distant Burma, emeralds, amethysts, garnets, jasper, beryl, and turquoise. One of the most sought-for stones was the cat's-eye, for it was believed to be not only potent to bring wealth to the wearer but also to increase it for him, and to protect it from all theft and diminution.

The sovereign lord of Calicut was the samorin,* a Hindu of the Nair group (see pp. 166 ff). Because of his prestige, wealth, and power he was the most powerful ruler of Malabar—and the object of the hatred and jealousy of all the other rulers of the land. By protecting and making their Nair brethren their special charges by granting special privileges to the Moslems, and by developing a strong navy of sorts the succeeding samorins of Calicut had made their city the greatest export and transshipment center of the Malabar coast, and the profits and wealth that flowed into their coffers were tremendous.

* Samorin: a Malayalam word from the Sanskrit—*samundra* (lord of the sea). The etymology has been questioned; the local title was samudrin raja, corrupted by the Portuguese to zamorin.

Royal descent passed through the female line, and "the first son born to the king's eldest sister is heir to the throne, and thus all the brothers inherit one after the other, and where there are no brothers, nephews." If the sisters had no sons, a family council elected a near relative as samorin. This strange custom usually resulted in the sovereign's being an old man—a state of affairs still obtaining in Calicut.*

Because of the peculiar laws of succession, the samorin did not marry, nor was he bound by any marriage laws. It was the custom for him to select a young Nair girl as a concubine and to instal her in a house near the palace and support her comfortably, to dismiss her when he wearied of her—and then to select another at his pleasure.

Though the palace of the samorin contained many rooms, it was not an imposing building. It was surrounded by palisades whose gates were guarded by soldiers day and night. Outside the gates men were stationed under the trees. They had before them tables on which stood "large vessels in the form of pitchers, with a tube or pipe a span and a half long and made of gilded copper. Those who are athirst approach these men without entering the enclosure and offer their mouths without touching the vessel in any way; the water is then poured into their mouths from above, and all the while the pipe or vessel must be more than a span from contact with them. But before they give them to drink, they give them one or two pieces of coconut to eat, instead of bread. This custom has been ordained by the king, by reason of the fierce and oppressive heat of that country, and the great multitude of people that throng to the palace every day." As is usual in India, cows wandered at will through the streets of the city, and into the palace enclosure as well.

In the palace were rooms set aside for the scribes and clerks of the samorin. They entered their records (as is still done today) on long stiff palm leaves (ollas), writing with a pointed stylus without ink. Each clerk carried a bundle of leaves and a stylus as the badge of his office. They began the day's work with an odd little ceremony.

* A variation of the succession was effected by the custom of holding a royal festival every twelve years, at which time if a member of certain families could succeeded in killing the reigning samorin, he became the ruler in his place. See J. G. Frazer, *The Golden Bough*, 3rd ed., IV, 47 ff.

A bit of a leaf was cut off, the name of the god whom they worshiped was inscribed on it, they offered up a prayer, tore up the leaf, and set to work.

The palace was kept clean by a corps of women of high caste, the cleansing being ritual. After sweeping and sprinkling, the women, each carrying a brass basin of moist cow dung, spread a thin coating of the mixture on the floors and paths to be trodden by the samorin.* The surface was then smoothed and polished by hand, and it lasted about a week. After the coating (held to be most sanitary in India) had dried, the flowers of the champak and the rose were scattered everywhere, scenting the whole palace with their perfume.

The samorin's ordinary dress consisted of a silk garment clothing him from the waist down; the upper part of his body was naked, but he wore heavy golden armlets and anklets and was loaded with jewels. Like his subjects, he was a habitual chewer of betel. "This was handed him in a gold basin or in a gold or silver box, and a page stood always beside him to receive the royal blood-red saliva in a jeweled cup. When eating, the samorin dined off a silver tray and silver dishes, drinking water from the spout of a silver ewer held high above his head. His staple diet was of dry boiled rice and highly seasoned vegetables." When the ruler went out into the city, he was borne in a silken litter swung on a jeweled pole "as thick as the arm of a fat man, and they [two men] carry him with certain steps to which they are trained from birth. Nair warriors walk before him; he is preceded by musicians and on either side [of the litter] walks a man, one carrying a large round fan, the other a white yak fly-whisk, fixed to a gold staff."

The ruling classes were two, the Brahmin autocracy, which was practically beyond the law, and the warrior Nair group. The samorin's justice was severely administered and the punishments were harsh. For violations of religious law the penalties were deodands —forfeitures of property to the temples. The punishment for murder and theft was impaling and beheading. There were two punishments for adultery—one, the throwing of the guilty woman from a roof in a piece of matting swung by women; the other, the locking up of the accused woman in a room swarming with cobras, from

---

* This is still the common floor covering of countless Indian houses. The Portuguese adopted it in the houses of Goa.

which, if she escaped unharmed, she was adjudged innocent. No mention is made of the punishment of the man in the case.

The civil law was liberal. No tax was collected on land; and contrary to the custom obtaining in the other ports of Malabar, ships which were wrecked off Calicut were not seized by the samorin's treasury. This liberality was one of the attractions of Calicut for merchants and mariners. Customs duties were low, too, 2½ per cent ad valorem being charged on imports, the duties payable after sale by the importer.

When a man owed money and refused to pay, if

the creditor finds the debtor he takes a handful of green grass and stands before him with the grass in his hand, and the debtor cannot depart until he has satisfied him or sees that he leaves him contented. Also in the said place there is a custom that when two men have a difference between them and neither has proof, by common accord they go before the lord who causes to be brought from the temple a certain oil—and places it over the fire and causes it to boil and takes him who denies the debt and makes him dip his fingers in the boiling oil, and being guilty he is burned, and being innocent he is not injured and remains whole.

Aside from the Brahmins, who dominated the religious life of Calicut, the most powerful group was that of the Nairs, or warrior class. Much has been written about the Nairs; it will suffice to indicate here some of their characteristics and customs, many of the latter of which survive today. The Nairs constituted a community more than a caste. Their social system was matriarchal, the matrilinear relationship being exclusively counted on the mother's side. The family group was called the *tharawad*.

Marriage was performed when the pair reached puberty. The boy tied a *tali* (puberty string) around the girl's neck, gave her presents, and departed. The consummation of the marriage took place much later. Virginity was considered a nuisance among the Nairs, and it was customary for a girl's parents to hire an outsider (a non-Nair from another part of India) to take their daughter's virginity when she reached the age of ten years. Thereafter a great feast was given, "and they hung a jewel about her neck, which brings her during her whole life into great esteem, as a token of the liberty which has been granted her to do whatever she pleases, because without that ceremony they cannot lie with a man." The

women made a free choice of their husbands. The wedding gift of
the husband was usually a simple one—a piece of cloth. Divorce
was easy, and was accomplished by the woman's returning the cloth
to the husband.

Polyandry was the common practice of the Nairs.

Each young girl lies with three or four men by a sort of an arrangement . . . by which each one has to lie with her from noon to noon
and then give place to another. . . . These girls must be Nairs, for
the men cannot lie with other women. Since the men are so many in
proportion to the women they do not have [claim] for their children
those who are born from them [their common wives] even if they
resemble them. The children of their sisters are their heirs. . . . The
kings made this law . . . in order that, not having wives or children
whom to love, they could devote themselves to warfare. . . . If one
of them kills another, or a cow . . . or lies with a low-class woman
or eats in the house of an outsider or speaks evil of the king, and if
the king learns of it he issues an order that he be put to death by the
other Nairs . . . and this they do by stabbing wherever they find him,
and after his death they place on his corpse the writ of the king, in
order that all may know why they killed him.

An exchange of wives was quite commonly practiced by the
Nairs. The following quaint description of such an exchange has
been preserved by a contemporary of Gama:

The gentilmen and marchantes of Calicut acustometh often tymes
in token of grete love among them, and to encrese more love betwene
them to chaunge ther wifes one with another, and in ther language
thei speke one to another and on this maner, My frende and brother,
many yeres we have had company together and I thinke more conversation and love ther can not be amonge frendes, wherfore I wil,
if it be your pleasure, in ernest token of the amitie betwene us to
chaunge wifes, you to take plesaure w^t myne and I w^t yours. Unto the
wh^{ch} the other aunswereth that it is of trouth and that he is content
to do as he wil have him. And so he goeth home to his hous and calleth
his wife onto him and saith to her, Hit is so as you knowe this our
frende of long contynuance we have ben frendes, and now in token
of more amitie I am content that you shal go with him and to fulfylle
his wylle, and he is content that his wyfe shal come to me to perfourme
the same. Then she answereth and saithe Sir, I thinke you do but
jeste, then he swereth by his deores [dears?] that he jesteth not, but
that he speketh ernest, then she saith if it be so let us go, and so she

departes w^t his frende, and when he cometh to his house incontynent he sendeth him his wyfe. And this chaunge of wyves is a comon custome amonges them, and the children of either goeth with the mothers in chaunge.

The Nairs were easily recognized by their dress on the street. The men wore dhotis (a short skirt like a towel, wrapped about the middle and draped in various ways) and were naked from the waist up. They wore rings in their ears and on their fingers, and bracelets as well. Their hairdress was peculiar and was surmounted by a *kudunu,* or tuft. The women went unveiled and wore white skirts, the upper part of the body being naked, as the wearing of garments above the waist denoted immodesty or low caste. The ear lobes were pierced, and from childhood larger and larger rolls of leaves were stuffed into the openings so that they were distended until the lobes often hung lower than the breast. They were then ornamented with gold rings. The richer women were heavily loaded with gold and silver ornaments—necklaces, bangles, finger and nose rings— and wore elaborate sashes.* The hair was worn long, or with a knob caught up on the left side of the head in front.

The Nair males were trained in warfare from the age of seven, especially in the use of the sword, which was worn in a red-leather sheath—though in fighting the sword was carried naked, and a small buckler or shield was worn on the left arm. The swords were of iron, of various shapes, some short, but they were never used for stabbing. The handles had no hand guards but were hung with brass rings that rattled in swordplay. Fighting was carried on in ritualistic fashion, both sides mingling and chewing betel together until the drum called to battle. The feet were often used to draw the bow. Fighting was done in close columns, the swordsmen in front, while archers behind fired from the ground to hit the enemies' feet, as did the throwers of heavy blackwood clubs and ironlike quoits with sharp edges. Scribes accompanied the armies to note the play-by-play movements of the battle, which usually consisted of an attack on, and the defense of, a camp. At a signal from a drum the foes again ceased fighting and mingled anew in a friendly fashion. The samorin's war trumpet was so heavy that four men were needed to lift it when it was used. There were no ambuscades and

* The custom of loading children with jewels was responsible for much child murder on the Malabar coast.

no night fighting. One old chronicler remarks that "the Hindus fight more with their tongues than with their hands, and with rigid elaborate rules, violations of which brought dishonor worse than death." These peculiar fighting methods of the Malabar warriors explain why they were not able to resist the Portuguese, even though the latter were always far inferior in numbers.

The Nairs were a people of cleanly habits, and "they would rather die of hunger and thirst than eat before washing. . . . They shave their beards, leave their mustaches grow long like the Turks." The upper-class Nairs often kept their fingernails filed to long points the better to remove the veins from the betel leaves before chewing them.

Many of the Nairs and Brahmins were well educated, and one Italian contemporary of Gama noted: "I see that in mathematics there are great men among them, and in the principles of astronomy there is no difference between them and us, and the Arabs have taught them. They know Aristotle and Galen and Avicenna."

Other Indian groups prominent in the business life of Calicut were the Gujaratis (who still play a large part in western Indian commercial life) and the Chetties, who are today the money-changers and money-lenders throughout the East as far as Siam, Indo-China, and Island India. The Gujaratis were easily distinguishable by their lighter color, their large hats or turbans, long beards, and scarfs. The Chetties wore round hats with their hair done up in chignons woven with horsehair, "and engage in the business of precious stones and in witchcraft. For the rest their women are the most libidinous that can be found under the sun."

Among the many castes that lived in Calicut, perhaps the strangest was that called Inseni, "who are those who climb the trees to gather pepper, nuts, and other fruits. These, because they expose their lives to dangers are abhorred by the others, and cannot converse with them, as though they were contaminated. . . . They do not bury or burn their dead. They go naked, men as well as women, with their shameful parts exposed."

The most important and influential group of foreigners in Calicut were the Arabs (called "Moors" by the Portuguese). All the foreign and the greater part of the Indian sea-borne trade were concentrated in their hands, both as merchants and as carriers, since caste taboos prevented many of the Hindus from crossing salt water. The commercial movement of the Arabs began in the eighth century, the trade of the conquered countries passing into Moslem hands as the Arab Empire expanded. Long before the arrival of the Portuguese, the Arabs had swarmed everywhere along the Malabar coast and controlled practically all its maritime commerce. This lucrative trade brought them into close touch with their fellow countrymen in Tunis and the whole North African littoral, Cairo, and the Arabian and Persian ports. In fact Basra was founded by the Caliph Omar to foster and develop the Indian trade. This wide range of commercial interests had brought the Arabs of Malabar into many relations with Europeans, and the Portuguese were probably known to them by hearsay, if not by personal contacts.

The Arabs of Malabar, like their fellows in Africa, were motivated in their enterprises both by self-interest and by bigoted religious zeal. They had not only appropriated the carrying trade of the Indies, but then, as now, acted as shrewd middlemen, buying cheaply from the ignorant (and often wild) natives of the interior and selling dearly to the coast and foreign merchants. Their trade passed largely from India to Hormuz and to Basra, whence caravans set out for Trebizond, Aleppo, and Damascus. At those points the Venetians and Genoese became the distributors of the products of India throughout Europe. Jidda, on the Red Sea, was also an important terminus, whence small boats took the merchandise to Suez and across the desert on camels to Cairo. From Cairo, boats conveyed the goods down the Nile to Alexandria, where again the Italian merchants purchased them and sold them to Europe.

The discovery of the succession of the monsoons probably was made in the first century after Christ, and this newly found natural aid to navigation enabled ships to cross and recross the Indian Ocean even long before the Moslem hordes forced their way into Asia, and it gave the early Arabs a monopoly of the trade.* The Moslems were also the distributors of the merchandise brought to the Malabar coast from abroad, and even controlled the trade in grain.

Thus the Arabs were welcome sojourners in Calicut, for they supplied the lifeblood of the city's commerce. They occupied their own quarter, as well as warehouses and shops throughout the city,

* As there was little wood suitable for shipbuilding available on the coasts of Arabia, the ships were constructed of Indian materials but manned by the Arabs

and had their own *kadis* (judges) and religious leaders. They wore their national dress, which varied but little from Morocco to Malacca, and to all intents and purposes were the equals of their Hindu hosts. In fact they were allowed to make converts to Islam without interference, and by many of the natives, even of the highest castes, it was deemed a great honor if an Arab asked for the hand of a Hindu girl in marriage.

Dwelling in the Arab quarter were also the Moplahs, descendants of Arab fathers and native Indian mothers. Living in the faith of Mohammed and engaged with the immigrant Moslems in shipping and business, they were a turbulent group and often caused dissension and disturbances in the city. It could be foreseen that the Arabs would be the immediate and most active enemies of the Portuguese in India from the outset.

The Hindus were divided into many castes, and ignorant superstition held the minds of the great majority in terrifying slavery. But the samorins ever insisted on absolute religious freedom for all the dwellers in their domain, and quarrels over religion were punished by severe beatings, regardless of the nationality, race, or beliefs of the participants. Then, as now, ascetics roamed the streets and dwelled in the forests. Sassetti, who visited India in 1585, saw many. "Some stand in the ashes or in the hottest sun. Others have deflowered two thousand to three thousand girls, traveling everywhere to do it, and there is there [in Calicut] a temple set aside for the purpose of deflowering virgins."

As in all busy seaports throughout the world, prostitution was rife. An Italian visitor of the period wrote: "Public women are everywhere easy to be had for whomsoever desires them, residing in private houses of their own in all parts of the city, who attract the men by sweet perfumes and ointments, by their blandishments, beauty, and youth. And indeed the Indians are much inclined to licentiousness."

This, then, was Calicut, richest city on the Malabar coast, before which the fleet of Vasco da Gama dropped anchor on the evening of May 20, 1498.

NOTES

[1] Malabar: from Dravidian *mala*, "a hill," and Arabic *barr* (or Persian, *bar*), "a country or continent."

[2] The early Europeans were much puzzled by the crocodile. Barlow says of them in his *A Brief Summe of Geographie* (*ca.* 1518): "In the river . . . be cocodrilles, the wy[ch] be fysshes that hathe the shape of man and woman, and in the daie thei be in the waters and at nyght come in lande, these be those that we call marmaydes."

CHAPTER XIII

THE PORTUGUESE IN CALICUT

Oh strangers, who are ye?
Whence came ye, sailing o'er the watery ways?
Come ye on some lawful enterprise,
Or wander ye haphazardly o'er the seas,
Like unto pirates who rove,
Risking their lives, and bringing woe
Down on the men of other lands?
—*Odyssey*, IX, 252 ff

ARDLY had Gama's fleet come to anchor two leagues from Calicut and about a league and a half from shore, when four small boats (*almadias*) came out from the land, inquired briefly whence the foreigners had come and to what nation they belonged, and departed again. The sailors leaned on the bulwarks and watched them row back to shore, the phosphorescent water dripping like diamonds from the oars as they rose and dipped. Fishing boats were all about the fleet, too, and the Portuguese saw a new and strange way of fishing. The fish, attracted by torches and lanterns held by the fishermen, leaped into the low-gunwaled boats, thus saving all effort except that of taking the catch to market.

The night passed without incident, though the whole fleet's company was chafing to set foot ashore after the long confinement of twenty-one days spent in crossing from Malindi. The crew were already anticipating the joys of shore leave in the town, and sang in groups on the hatches until far into the night. Their favorite was a "Cantiga" of Gil Vicente, who wrote in both Spanish and Portuguese:

Muy graciosa es la doncella
Como es bella y hermosa,
Digas tu, el marinero,
Que en las naves vivias,
Si la nave ó la vela ó la estrella
Es tan bella.

[173]

> (How winsome is my beloved!
> How lovely and how fair!
> Tell me, if thou canst, O sailor,
> Thou who hast roamed ·
> The oceans wide,
> If there be ship at sea
> Or sail, or star in heaven
> As lovely as is she!)   ˎ

The next morning's sun was still low in the east when the same boats that had come out the previous evening appeared at the ladder of the commander's vessel. Gama lost no time in putting his plans into execution. One of the convicts, João Nunes, a converted Jew who had some knowledge of Arabic and Hebrew, was summoned to Gama's quarters and given instructions to land in one of the *almadias* and bring back a report of all he might see and hear.[1]

A crowd gathered at the waterside to see the stranger from the great ships land, and Nunes and the men who had rowed him ashore had difficulty in forcing their way through to the city. He was taken at once to the house of two Arabs from Tunis (or Oran), men "who could speak Castilian and Genoese." Their greeting was rude—their very first words a forecast of the conflict that was to be waged in India between Christian and Moslem. "The devil take you! What brought you here?" * They then asked him what he was seeking so far from his home, and he answered, "We come in search of Christians and spices." When asked why the government of Castile, France, or Venice had not sent ships, he boldly lied, "Because the King of Portugal will not permit it."

After further conversation with the two Moslems, Nunes was given wheaten bread and honey to eat, and then he returned to the ship with one of his hosts. The latter, called Monçaide † by the Portuguese,[2] was evidently more concerned with profits than with the political and economic threat to his group—if he gave the matter a thought or understood its import, which is most unlikely. His first words to the group about the commander were: "A lucky venture, a lucky venture! Plenty of rubies, plenty of emeralds! You

---

* "Al diabro que te doo: quem te traxo aquà?"

† Monçaide: probably a corruption of the Arabic El Masud (the happy one).

owe great thanks to God for having brought you to a country possessing such riches!"

When Gama learned that the samorin was absent in Panane, a
coast town twenty-eight miles south of Calicut, he sent the interpreter Fernão Martins and another Portuguese, accompanied by
Monçaide, to Panane with a message to the effect that an ambassador from the King of Portugal had arrived off Calicut with letters
for His Majesty, and that, if he so desired, the letters would be forwarded to him where he was. The samorin received the two Portuguese in most friendly fashion, sent a message of welcome to Gama,
in which he stated that he was about to return to the city, and
returned the two men to their ships with a present "of much fine
cloth."

There is little doubt that the samorin was absolutely honest and
sincere in his welcome and offer of friendship to Gama. The prosperity of his realm depended on commerce, and it was surely to his
advantage to open up as many channels as possible for trade between India and Europe. It was largely the intrigues of the Moslem
merchants (together with the tactlessness and arrogance of Gama)
which caused him to change his attitude and his tactics.

Meanwhile Gama unwisely caused a report to be circulated in the
city that not only was he King Manuel's ambassador, but that he
had been separated by storms from another and far larger fleet,
and that, moreover, the voyage had lasted two years. Though he did
not realize it, Gama had made a serious error. Without doubt
swifter vessels than his had brought the news of his clashes on the
East African coast to Calicut, and his misrepresentations branded
him as a liar from the outset. In fact he and his men were looked
upon as nothing short of freebooting corsairs. In all his dealings with
the Indians—in their way as civilized as the Portuguese of the era—
Gama conducted himself as highhandedly toward them as he did
toward the naked ignorant savages of the African coast. His conduct laid a foundation of ill will that lasted as long as did the Portuguese conquest and control of the Eastern seas—and it was all inexcusable as well as undiplomatic.

When Nunes, his companion, and Monçaide had concluded their
interview with the samorin, Nunes ordered a pilot to accompany
them back to the ships, with instructions to direct the fleet to a safer
anchorage at Pandarani, a little north of Calicut. On the same day,

under the pilot's guidance the fleet moved to the new location, which offered far better protection than the first against dragging anchors in case of a storm.

The ships had hardly arrived in their new berth when a messenger arrived on board announcing that the samorin was already back in his palace in Calicut. With him came a wali (chief of police), accompanied by two hundred swordsmen to conduct Gama to meet the sovereign. As it was almost nightfall, the commander asked for a postponement of the interview until the morrow.

On the following morning, Monday, May 28, 1498, Gama set out to visit the king, taking with him thirteen men. Fortunately the author of the *Roteiro* was one of the group, so we have an eyewitness account (though from the Portuguese viewpoint) of the interview between the ruler of Calicut and King Manuel's envoy. As Gama and his men entered the boats, the fleet's guns fired an impressive salute and flags and banners were broken out on mast head and yard-arm. Officers and crew were attired in their best, and trumpets and flags accompanied the little cortege, while, for safety's sake, bombards were placed in the boats. Gama's brother Paulo was left in command of the ships, and Nicolau Coelho, captain of the *Berrio,* was instructed to stand by with the boats to await the commander's return. Before leaving his ship Gama gave orders that if any serious untoward incident should happen to prevent his return, the ships were to set sail immediately for Portugal and give an account of the voyage and its outcome.

At the shore a large reception committee was drawn up, many of whom were armed. Gama entered a waiting palanquin borne by relays of six men, and, followed by his men, set out along the road to Capua (called by some authors Capocate). There the Portuguese were served a meal of buttered rice and fish. At Capua, seven miles from Calicut, the party entered boats and were rowed on the river Elatur for about two miles. On landing, Gama again entered his palanquin and the group, together with its escorts and native interpreters, proceeded to Calicut along a road crowded with men, women, and children, all curious and eager to see the newcomers.

On entering the city, the first place visited was a temple. The Portuguese were so ignorant of the religion of the Hindus that they appear to have believed, throughout the entire duration of their stay in Calicut, that the people were Christians and that the temples were churches.* They were taken to a chapel with a sanctuary in which stood an image which they mistook for that of the Virgin Mary. In fact, according to one chronicler, the Hindus crowded around the foreigners and pointed to the statue, crying, "Maria, Maria." † The Portuguese were not allowed to enter the sanctuary, where the Brahmin priests officiated, but they were given "white earth, which the Christians of this country are in the habit of putting on their foreheads, breasts, around the neck, and on the forearms." This Gama refused to smear on himself ‡ but said he would do it later. "Many other saints were painted on the walls of the church, wearing crowns. They were painted variously with teeth protruding an inch from the mouth, and four or five arms." At least one of those present, João da Sá, clerk of the *São Rafael*, doubted that these paintings were of Christian saints, for as he knelt in prayer by the side of Vasco da Gama, he whispered, "If these be devils I worship the true God," upon hearing which, Gama gave one of his rare smiles.

On leaving the temple, Gama and his men were accompanied the rest of the way by a large escort "beating drums, blowing *anafils* and bagpipes and firing off matchlocks. In conducting the captain they showed us much respect, more than is shown in Spain to a king." The crowds thronged the streets and people leaned out of windows and swarmed up onto the roofs to watch the colorful procession pass. Finally the multitude became so great that when the palace gate was reached, the escort had to force its way through the tightly packed mass, knives were drawn, and several Indians were stabbed before an entrance could be effected.

The entire day had been consumed on the journey from the ships, and when the company entered the palace it was an hour before sunset. The samorin received Gama and his men in a small court, reclining on a couch covered with green velvet, holding in his left hand a golden betel cuspidor, at his side a golden basin heaped high

* This belief appears in the official letters in which King Manuel described the results of the voyage to the Spanish sovereigns and to Cardinal Dom Jorge da Costa at Rome.

† The image may have been one of several—Krishna and his mother Devaki Gauri, "the white goddess," or more likely Mari (or Mariamma—"Mother Mari"), the greatly feared and venerated goddess of smallpox.

‡ The "white earth" was a mixture of dust, cow dung, ashes, sandalwood, etc., mixed with rice water. It is still in common use in religious ritual throughout Hindu India.

with the prepared betel. Gama entered the court and gravely saluted the sovereign with raised joined hands, in the manner which he had observed the Indians employed. The Portuguese were seated before the king on a stone bench, water was poured over their hands, and they were served with slices of jack fruit and bananas—fruits not known to them before. After the fruit had been eaten, the samorin asked through an interpreter that Gama tell him and his entourage about his voyage and its purpose. Gama demurred, stating that, as the ambassador of the King of Portugal, he could only deliver his message personally. Whereupon the samorin good-naturedly acquiesced and withdrew with a few trusted councilors to another room, where Gama presently joined them, leaving the other Portuguese in the court.

The commander of the fleet told the story of the various expeditions sent out by Prince Henry and King John, and of the present fleet sent out by Manuel, "who had ordered him [Gama] not to return to Portugal until he should have discovered this King of the Christians, on pain of having his head cut off." The chronicler Osório has preserved what he believed to be the last words of the address :

Manuel, a prince of vast dignity and aspiring soul and great curiosity, having heard much of India, particularly of the empire of Calicut, was struck with admiration at the ingenuity of the people as well as the dignity and grandeur of their sovereign, and was extremely solicitous to enter into a league of friendship with so renowned a monarch. For this purpose he, Gama, had been sent into these parts, nor did he doubt but such a league would greatly tend to the mutual advantage of both princes.

In conclusion Gama stated that he would deliver two letters sent by his king to the samorin on the following day. The sovereign's reply was most gracious. He welcomed the Portuguese envoy, telling him "he held him as a friend and brother, and would send ambassadors with him to Portugal." *

Meanwhile the hours had passed swiftly, and it was already ten o'clock. The samorin ordered that the foreigners be given suitable

* The author of the *Roteiro* states brazenly at this point that the samorin promised to send ambassadors at Gama's request, "the captain pretending that he would not dare to present himself before his king and master unless he was able to present, at the same time, some men of this country."

lodging and went personally into the court to bid his guests farewell. Gama left in his palanquin, followed by his men and a great crowd of Indians. They had gone but a short distance when a heavy rainstorm overtook them. They were conducted to the house of a Moslem, and there they sat on "a veranda roofed in with tiles" until the rain was over. Thereafter proceeding to the house assigned them, they found Gama's own bed which had been brought from his ship and set up by his own men, together with the gifts to be presented to the ruler of Calicut.

On the following morning the commander summoned the samorin's officers to inspect the gifts. They stared with astonishment at the paltry, miserable things set out, goods fit for a petty Zulu or Hottentot chief, but an insult to the lord of Calicut: "twelve pieces of striped cloth, four scarlet hoods, six hats, four strings of coral, a case containing six basins for washing the hands, a case of sugar, two casks of oil, and two of honey." The Arab officer laughed contemptuously at the proffered gifts and refused to forward them to the samorin, "saying that it was not a thing to offer to a king, that the poorest merchant from Mecca or any part of India gave more, and that if he wanted to make a present it should be in gold, as the king would not accept such things." Whereupon Gama again lied, saying that the gifts were his own private property and that if the King of Portugal ordered him to return, he would intrust him with far richer presents. "But the samorin's officers flatly refused to forward the gifts or to allow Gama to send them, and when they had gone there came certain Moorish merchants, and they all depreciated the present which the captain desired to be sent to the king."

After the refusal of his gifts, Gama demanded a second audience with the samorin. The officers promised to return shortly and take him to the palace. Though he waited all day, first with impatience, then with a growing but impotent wrath, the officers did not return. Finally he determined to go unaccompanied to the palace, but thought better of it and decided to wait. Evidently his men did not take the affair very seriously but wandered here and there in the city. Many strange sights met their eyes, but perhaps none stranger than the elephants at work along the shore. They were employed to haul loads, for riding, for dragging logs, and for lifting and moving them with trunk and tusks. They even saw three elephants bring in a ship from the sea. The vessel was beached sideways to the shore. Rollers were placed under the keel, then the elephants were driven by their mahouts to the sea side of the hull, made to kneel and to push the ship with their heads onto the dry land. Indeed, the elephants performed so many tasks that one early Italian visitor, after recounting their accomplishments, remarked, "In conclusion I say that I have seen some elephants which have more understanding and more discretion and intelligence than any kind of people I have met with." The crew, never having seen the beggars of India, could not understand why children and adults crowded about them pleading for food and money. Finally, returning to quarters, and entirely untroubled by Gama's anger and frustration, the author of the *Roteiro* wrote, "As for us others, we diverted ourselves, singing and dancing to the sound of trumpets, and enjoyed ourselves much."

And now the morning of May 30 had come, and with it the Moslem officers, who conducted the commander and his men again to the palace. But this time Gama was kept waiting, fuming and fretting, "for four long hours outside a door," which was finally opened to admit him attended by two men only. He chose Fernão Martins, his interpreter, together with his secretary. At this audience the samorin was less gracious and more curt than before and came to the point at once. It was evident that some influence adverse to the Portuguese had been brought to bear. In the light of our knowledge of what was transpiring, it is easy to understand his change of attitude and tone.

In the first place, the exchange of gifts on such occasions was so customary that the failure of the Portuguese to provide proper presents thoroughly angered the samorin. Moreover, the leading Moslems of Calicut, intelligent and quick-witted, were not slow to grasp the import of Vasco da Gama's feat of navigation and to perceive the dire threat to their monopoly of the commerce of the Indian coast. They at once set about devising schemes to thwart Manuel's envoy. They represented Gama to the samorin as a "cruel, bloody-minded pyrate." The supposed Moslem address to the samorin has been recorded:

Most renowned Prince, we have ever been such dutiful and useful subjects in your state that, methinks we have a particular claim to your friendship. The increase of your revenues from our trade is apparently so considerable that we shall but just mention it. Ask the commissioner of the customs; examine your public accounts; they will inform you whether the Saracens have been unprofitable members of the community. We ourselves have always had a particular attachment to this country as well as our ancestors, who regarded it as their native soil, and were ever dutiful and loyal to the kings of Calicut. We hope then your Majesty will not allow this agreeable harmony, this ancient friendship to be dissolved by a set of abandoned wretches lately arrived in these parts. . . . Besides, you have had no occasions of being acquainted with the nature of these men. But we have known numberless instances of their perfidy and villainy. They have destroyed nations; they have ravaged countries—and all this without provocation, merely to soothe their ambition and gratify their lust of power. Can you then suppose that men of such a stamp would come from regions so remote and encounter such horrid dangers only to engage in commerce with your people? No, it is incredible. They are either pirates who want to abuse your lenity and turn it to the public detriment or they are sent by their ambitious prince, not to make a league of friendship, but as spies to examine the situation of the city. Have not the Portuguese by artifices made themselves masters of most of the towns of Africa? . . . They have fallen upon Mozambique with their hostile arms; they have made great slaughter at Mombasa . . . and if with so small a force they dare show the ferocity of their disposition, what will they not perpetrate when they have greater strength? If you have then any regard for the welfare of your kingdom, destroy these pernicious wretches that, if pirates they may suffer the punishments due their crimes, or if the wicked instruments of ambition that the destruction of those whom you have in your power may put an end to this dangerous navigation and prevent the rest of the Portuguese from coming into these parts. . . . Did their king whom they so much extol imagine he had to do with some petty Ethiopian prince whose poverty and folly would make him an easy prey? . . . But perhaps it may be said that these are groundless aspersions, proceeding from a hatred which the Arabs bear to the Christians. We own we have an utter aversion to a people who have always been our implacable enemies. But though our interest may be somewhat affected in the present case, yet I think I may venture to say your all is at stake. If you enter into a league with these Christians we can remove into other countries where we shall meet with a kinder reception and settle more advantageously. . . . Wherever we go we shall be enabled to carry on our trade with equal gain and advantage, but as for you, if you do not immediately exert yourself with spirit I am afraid—which Heaven avert—that in a few years not only your crown but your life will be in the greatest jeopardy from a people so covetous, so ambitious, so warlike.

Whether or not the exact words of the Arab spokesman were reported correctly, the arguments in the address were cogent reasons for the samorin's altered attitude toward the Portuguese. He did not know them, rumors of their violence had preceded them, and he was well aware of the value of the Moslem group to himself and his people. The sovereign was placed in a dilemma by the arrival of the Portuguese ships. He chose—and who would not have so chosen under the circumstances?—to throw in his lot and that of his city with the Arabs who had built up their prosperity. He lost his gamble, and from that time Calicut steadily declined in wealth and importance. Nevertheless the ruler, from the reports of the Portuguese themselves, acted with fairness and dignity in his dealings with the exacting and arrogant Gama.

When the fleet's commander was finally admitted, the samorin remarked that he had expected him two days before. Gama replied that the long road had tired him and that for this reason he had not come to see him. The samorin told him bluntly that the failure to bring presents was very displeasing and that the letters which Gama had said he would deliver had never been received. The Portuguese apologized and said the letters would be delivered at once. Then the samorin suggested that he be given "the golden image of a Santa Maria from his ship." Gama replied that she was not of gold "and that even if she were he would not part with her, as she had guided him across the ocean and would guide him back to his own country." The letters (one in Portuguese and one in Arabic) were then produced by Gama, but the latter again offended by declaring that he did not trust the Moslem interpreter to translate the Arabic, and as he could not read it himself he desired that some Christian who knew Arabic be summoned. When one appeared it was found that he could speak but not read Arabic, and in the end Arabs were called in. However, the contents of the letter were innocuous and everyone was satisfied.

A desultory conversation followed about the products of Portugal, of which Gama stated that he had samples. He suggested that he return to the ships for them while several of his men remained behind in the lodgings assigned them in Calicut. This brought forth a flat refusal from the samorin, who curtly told him to take all his men back with him, "securely moor his ships, land his merchandise, and sell it to the best advantage." Thereupon the second audience with the samorin was abruptly terminated. As the hour was late, the Portuguese group remained for the night in their quarters in the city.

The next morning, May 31, Gama, riding in a palanquin and followed by crowds of idle curious people, started back to the anchorage at Pandarani. The palanquin soon outstripped the crew members, who were walking. The latter lost their way and were finally found and brought back by an officer of the samorin to the rest house where Gama was awaiting them. Upon the reunion of the party at Pandarani, Gama demanded a boat to take him and his men off to the ship. Because darkness had come on and a gusty wind had come up, the wali (the samorin's officer in charge of the escort) refused. This immediately caused the impetuous Gama to suspect treachery. He sent his men along in different directions to warn Coelho and Paulo da Gama, but the men did not find them or the Portuguese boats, and one of them lost his way. The commander and his men were lodged in the house of a Moslem trader, and they sent out for fowls and rice for the evening meal. The next morning he "again asked for boats to take him to his ships," and was told he could have them if he would order his vessels to anchor closer to shore. On his refusal, followed by a threat to appeal personally to the samorin, all the doors of the house were closed and an armed guard was thrown around it, nor were any Portuguese allowed to go out except under close guard. Next a demand was made that he order his ships' sails and rudders given up (and thus render the vessels useless). Gama flatly refused. The Portuguese "felt very downhearted, though outwardly [they] pretended not to notice what they did." Gama then requested that if he was not to be released, his men be permitted to go, "as at the place they were in they would die of hunger. But they said that [they] must remain where [they] were, and that if [they] died of hunger [they] must bear it, as they cared nothing for that." Meanwhile, the man who had been sent to find Coelho and the boats the night before and who had not returned put in an appearance and reported that Coelho had awaited his commander all night. Gama hastily sent the sailor back with a message to return to the ships and see that they were well guarded. As Coelho proceeded to obey the order, he was pursued in his boats by Arab *almadias,* but managed to get his men safely out to the fleet; and though later even greater pressure was brought on Gama to order his ships inshore, he steadfastly refused.

Another day passed, and that night Gama and his men were more closely guarded than ever "by over a hundred men, all armed with swords, two-edged battle-axes, shields and bows and arrows." * On Saturday morning, June 2, the wali returned and demanded that Gama order his merchandise landed, together with the crews of the ships, who would not be allowed back on their vessels (according to the local custom, as the wali said) until all the goods had been sold. Gama thereupon sent a letter to his brother Paulo to land certain goods; as soon as these were brought on shore, Gama and his men were permitted to go to the ships, leaving behind, in charge of the goods, Diogo Dias as factor and Alvaro de Braga as his assistant. No sooner was the commander on board ship than "he ordered that no more merchandise should be sent ashore."

Five days passed with no action on either side, whereupon Gama sent a message to the samorin, complaining of his detention on leaving the audience, and saying that "the Moors only came to criticize, not to buy" his merchandise. The ruler, still friendly, deprecated the actions of the Moslems and sent several other merchants to inspect the goods and to purchase some "if they felt inclined." He even went so far as to send "a man of quality to remain with the factor . . . and authorized them [the Portuguese] to kill any Moor who might go there, without fear of punishment."

The merchants remained several days, but they, too, scorned the merchandise and would have none of it. The Moslems, having been warned, kept away from the storehouse but insulted Gama's men at every turn, and "when one of them landed they spat on the ground, saying 'Portugal, Portugal.' Indeed, from the very first they had sought means to take and kill us."

The days thus dragged on from June 2 to June 23, and Gama had made no progress with the Moslems or Hindus in either buying

---

* Though the suspicions and conclusions of the Portuguese can be easily understood, the guards were probably stationed to protect the foreigners from molestation by the Moslems, who saw in them a dangerous threat to their prosperity—a threat that soon became a reality.

or selling. On June 23 he applied again to the samorin for permission to move his merchandise from Pandarani to Calicut itself. The sovereign again showed his good will by not only ordering that Gama's request be granted, but by ordering the wali to have porters "carry the whole on their backs to Calicut, this to be done at his expense, as nothing belonging to the King of Portugal was to be burdened with expenses while in his country."

On June 24 the goods were sent to Calicut for sale. Gama then issued orders that a man from each ship should visit Calicut by turns, to have shore leave and buy such things as they desired. These men were well treated by the Hindus ashore, were received hospitably everywhere, and freely given both food and lodging. The natives in turn were allowed to come on board to sell fish in exchange for bread, and they and the children who often accompanied them were well fed at the captain's orders. So many came that at nightfall it became difficult to get them all off the ships, and some even snatched the sailors' food from their hands as they sat at mess.

The sailors landed in "two's and three's, taking with them bracelets, clothes, new shirts, and other articles which they desired to sell." Though the author of the *Roteiro* complained of the small prices obtained, and averred that the sales were made by the crew "in order to take some things away from this country, if only for samples," in the next sentence he states: "Those who visited the city bought there cloves, cinnamon, and precious stones." The men were never molested at any time on shore or as they wandered the city at will, making the most of their shore leave.

After nearly two months had passed uneventfully, Gama decided that it was useless to remain on the coast any longer. On August 9 he sent Diogo Dias to the samorin with a gift "of amber, coral, and many other things," and a message informing him that the Portuguese desired to sail for home. He asked for some representative of Calicut's ruler to be sent to accompany the fleet to Portugal, begged the gift of a bahar (204 kilograms) each of cinnamon and cloves for his king, as well as of samples of other spices, offering, however, to pay for the samples. Dias was compelled to wait four days before an audience was granted, and then was received with scant ceremony. The samorin showed no interest in the gifts sent him, but demanded that Gama be instructed to pay him immediately the sum of 600 xerafins (about $900) if he desired to leave the country, as those were the custom charges on the merchandise. When Dias left the palace, he was followed by the samorin's officers, who entered the warehouse where the unsold Portuguese goods lay, to prevent their removal. Moreover, a proclamation was issued prohibiting all boats from visiting the ships. Dias managed to send a negro crew member out to Gama in a fisherman's boat after dark with his report.

The news was most disturbing to the commander of the little fleet. Some of his men were now virtually prisoners of the samorin, and the departure of the ships appeared to be indefinitely delayed Monçaide informed him, moreover, that the Moslems had offered large bribes to the samorin to destroy both fleet and men and advised that neither Gama nor any of his officers go ashore again. Friendly Hindus also cheered them by telling them "that if the captains went ashore their heads would be cut off."

On the next day (August 14) no boats appeared, but thereafter many *almadias* came out. Their occupants were well received and fed by order of the wily Gama, who was biding his time. On Sunday, August 19, some twenty-five men came out to Gama's ship, "among them six persons of quality." Suddenly Gama ordered the six and twelve others to be seized. All others were put ashore in a ship's boat with a message to the samorin's Moslem factor, declaring that the hostages would be returned when the men on shore and the Portuguese goods in the warehouse at Calicut were sent him.*

After waiting in vain for four days, on Thursday, August 23, Gama ordered anchors weighed and sail set, sending word on shore that he was returning to Portugal and would return soon to teach the people of Calicut whether or not the Portuguese were thieves. They had proceeded but four leagues from Calicut when a strong headwind forced them to anchor once more. On the following day the fleet returned and anchored again in sight of Calicut. On Saturday, August 25, the fleet sailed a second time, this time anchoring almost out of sight of land. On Sunday a native boat came out and informed Gama that Diogo Dias was in the samorin's palace and that he would be brought on board if the hostages were released.

* Six of the hostages were Nairs, who refused to eat the "polluted" food of the Portuguese and would have starved. So these hostages were exchanged every day for six others.

Gama assumed that Dias had been killed, and believed that this was a ruse to detain his ships until the samorin and his Moslems were ready to attack. He ordered the Indians to leave the ship forthwith, threatening to fire on them with his bombards and menacingly advised them not to return without Dias or a letter from him. Unless these orders were obeyed at once, he said, he would behead his captives. And again he ordered anchors weighed and sailed along the shore a short distance.

When news of Gama's action and threats was taken to Calicut, the samorin forthwith summoned Diogo Dias and received him "with marked kindness, and assured him that his factor, and not he, had illegally demanded the 600 xerafins as customs duties. He then requested Dias to write a letter (with an iron pen upon a palm leaf) to be given to the King of Portugal. The tenor of this letter was as follows:

Vasco da Gama, a gentleman of your household, came to my country, whereat I was pleased. My country is rich in cinnamon, cloves, ginger, pepper, and precious stones. That which I ask of you in exchange is gold, silver, corals, and scarlet cloth.

On Monday, August 27, seven boats came out to the fleet with Dias and the other Portuguese. The Indians were afraid to face Gama's wrath, for the merchandise had not been returned, so they transferred the Portuguese to the commander's longboat which was moored to the stern of his ship. Dias brought a verbal message from the samorin, asking for a return of the hostages, promising to set up a padrão, and requesting that he, Dias, return to the city and remain with the merchandise. Gama gave the padrão * to the Indians in the boat and surrendered six of his prisoners, promising to surrender the others when the merchandise was restored.

Early Tuesday morning, August 28, oars were heard, a ladder lowered, and Monçaide, "the man of Tunis," clambered hastily over the rail. He was panic-stricken and told how all his property had been seized and his life threatened, for he was accused of being a Christian spy sent by King Manuel. He pleaded to be allowed to leave India with the fleet, so as to save his life, since his property was confiscated. This request Gama granted.†

* This padrão was dedicated to São Gabriel. There is no record in existence of its having been erected by the samorin.

† Monçaide arrived safely in Portugal and was later baptized.

Shortly after Monçaide had come aboard, several boats crowded with men rowed out to the fleet. Three of them carried striped cloth, which was part of the merchandise left ashore, and one of the men in the leading boat shouted up to Gama that if the hostages he held were returned, the remainder of the merchandise would be delivered. Always easily roused to anger, Gama ordered the boats away, telling them that the merchandise was of no importance to him, that he was taking his hostages to Portugal,* and that when he returned, as return he certainly would, he would teach the people of Calicut whether or not he and his men were thieves, as they had been accused by the Moslems.

On Wednesday, August 29, Gama held a council of his officers. The consensus was that the country which they had set out to discover had been visited, that samples of spices and precious stones had been found, and that it would be a waste of time to endeavor longer to establish friendly relations with Calicut in the face of the open hostility of the powerful and influential Moslems and their preponderant influence over the samorin. The council broke up, anchors were weighed, sails set, and the flags of the fleet broken out at masthead and yard-arm to the sound of trumpets and drums. The three ships that had made one of the most momentous and fateful voyages in history turned their prows slowly northward and westward toward Africa, the Cape of Good Hope, and Lisbon. Their mission had been successful. The sea route to the Indies had been found and Vasco da Gama, the commander of the expedition, had won an immortal place in the annals of mankind.

* This he had probably planned from the first. Five hostages arrived in Lisbon with Gama's fleet and were taken back to Calicut by Pedro Álvares Cabral in 1500.

NOTES

[1] Correa, who, as has been indicated, is not a reliable authority for this voyage, states that Nunes was "a man of subtle understanding" and that Vasco da Gama sent him ashore "in the guise of a buyer, with money to buy things to eat, and to look well all over the city . . . and not to speak or answer questions . . . and to return to sleep on board the ship."

[2] Monçaide is reported to have performed many valuable services to the Portuguese during their stay in Calicut. This brought on his head the enmity of his own people, and he returned with Gama to Portugal. There he became a convert to Christianity and remained in the country until his death.

Correa states that Monçaide was really one Alonso Perez, a native of Seville, Spain, who had been captured by the Arabs at the age of five and had been converted, "but that God in heaven . . . knew that his soul was Christian."

CHAPTER XIV

THE VOYAGE HOME

This is my loved, my happy land so sweet
Whereto if Heaven concede that I repair
In safety, with this enterprise complete,
Then may this life be ended with me there!
CAMÕES, *Os Lusíadas,* III, xxi.
Translated by J. J. Aubertin.

HE voyage back to the African coast began with an incident which might have had grave consequences. At noon on the day after setting sail, the wind dropped and the fleet was becalmed very near Calicut. Immediately about seventy boats crowded with armed men surrounded the ships. Gama cleared the decks for action and, waiting until the boats were within range, ordered the bombards fired. Meanwhile the wind sprang up. In spite of these volleys the boats continued to follow for about an hour and a half. Fortunately for both parties a thunderstorm rose and, filling the sails of Gama's ships, carried them out to sea; "and when they saw they could no longer do us harm they turned back, whilst we pursued our route." Feeble winds and alternating land and sea breezes kept the vessels near the coast for some days.

On Monday, September 10, 1498, Gama took advantage of his proximity to a small town to land one of his six hostages, a man who had lost an eye, with a conciliatory letter to the samorin, written in Arabic by Monçaide. In this letter the fleet's commander explained that he had carried off the Malabarese so that he could prove to his king the discoveries he had made, and averred that the only reason he had not left a factor at Calicut was his fear that the Moslems might murder him.*

On Saturday, September 15, the fleet sighted the Santa Maria islets and set up the third padrão, named Santa Maria, on one of

---

* One Portuguese chronicler states that the letter pleased the samorin and also the families of the kidnaped men!

them. Friendly fishermen came aboard and later helped in the erection of the padrão. On September 20 the ships arrived at the Angediva Islands (14° 15′ N. latitude, close to the Indian coast). There the fleet anchored and took on wood and water for the crossing to Africa. Samples of cinnamon (cassia?) were obtained, and fresh vegetables were taken on board. While the crews were engaged in this work, two fairly large vessels approached the anchorage. As the lookout at the masthead reported six more ships becalmed farther out at sea, Gama decided that the enemy was pursuing him and ordered the two ships sunk. One escaped, the other had a broken rudder; and when the Portuguese drew near, her crew fled in their ship's boat. Gama's men boarded the abandoned vessel but found only food, coconuts, palm sugar, and arms. The other seven vessels were fired on, but with what results is unknown. The next day some Indians coming on board informed the commander that these vessels had been sent from Calicut to destroy the Portuguese fleet, though of the truth of this there is no proof whatsoever.

On the following morning the *São Gabriel* and the *Berrio* were careened and cleaned. While the work was in progress two galleys (*fustas*) full of armed men approached, "rowed to the sound of drums and bagpipes. The hostages informed Gama that the galleys were pirate craft, intent on robbery and murder. Gama fired upon them as soon as they came within range, and they fled, pursued for some distance by Nicolau Coelho."

During the fleet's stay at the Angedivas, Gama was visited by a man who was destined to be of paramount value to the Portuguese in their Indian adventure. When he presented himself to the commander he appeared to be about forty years of age and was finely clad. Addressing Gama in the Venetian dialect, he told him that he was a Christian who had come to India from the West in his early youth, that he was at the moment in the service of the ruler of Goa (see p. 245). He added also that he had been converted to Islam, "although at heart still a Christian." On hearing that some Franks had arrived at Calicut, he had asked permission of his master to visit the ships. His request had been granted, with a message of welcome and friendship for the Portuguese. He was a garrulous man, "talking so much and about so many things that at times he contradicted himself."

While the stranger was speaking, Paulo da Gama inquired about him privately from the Hindus who had accompanied him, and he received the astonishing information that he was a pirate! Thereupon Gama ordered him seized, taken to the vessel on the beach and flogged, to make him confess. Though he told Gama that vessels were lying in wait to attack the foreigners when sufficient forces had been collected, he would not change his story about himself. Thereupon Gama without hesitation ordered him to be tortured. This was applied three or four times, so severely that the man could not speak, but with painful gestures admitted that he had come to learn all he could of the ships and their armament. He was then released but confined on Gama's ship. Some days afterward, when the ships were far out at sea, the captive confessed that his master had sent him to entice the fleet to his country, where he planned to employ the Portuguese in his wars with neighboring chiefs. He was taken by Vasco da Gama to Portugal, where he was baptized and received the name of Gaspar da Gama, though he is sometimes referred to as Gaspar da Índia. Later he accompanied Cabral to the East as an interpreter and served on several other Portuguese expeditions to India, being last heard of in 1510. It is recorded that he was a favorite of King Manuel, who made him a cavalier of his household. Lunardo da Cá Messer, Venetian ambassador to Lisbon in 1504, referred to him in a letter to the Signoria, in which he stated that Gaspar had married a Portuguese woman (though one authority gives him a wife at Cochin and another a wife and children in Calicut as well) and reported that he had received a state pension of seven hundred ducats annually in recognition of his services. Girolamo Sernigi, a Florentine, a resident of Lisbon at the time of Gama's return, met Gaspar, and spoke of him at length in a letter to a Florentine friend, first printed in 1507. Gaspar told Sernigi that he was a Jew whose parents had fled from Posen, in Poland, during the Jewish persecutions by King Casimir (ca. 1456) and who, after a short residence in Palestine, had moved to Alexandria, where Gaspar was born. Sernigi refers to him as "a pilot," whereas a letter of King Manuel (to Cardinal Jorge da Costa) speaks of him as a merchant and a lapidary.

The fleet remained at the Angedivas twelve days, and after burning the captured Indian vessel—though its captain offered a fair sum for its return—sailed on. The voyage across the Arabian Sea was a terrible one, lasting from October 2, 1498, to January 2, 1499, during which time the weather alternated between dead calms and adverse winds. All the vegetables were consumed, the water became foul, food ran low, and the terrible scourge of scurvy again attacked the crews. Thirty men died of this malady in addition to the thirty who had died previously; and the members of the crews well enough to work were so reduced in number that only seven or eight were left to navigate each ship, and even these few were too weak to do their work properly. Things "had come to such a pass that all bonds of discipline had gone," and even the iron-willed Gama enforced obedience with difficulty. Finally he called a council of his captains, who were so desperate that they decided "that if a favorable wind enabled us we would return to India whence we had come."

Finally fortune changed for the unhappy Portuguese; and "it pleased God in His mercy to send us a wind which in the course of six days carried us within sight of land, and at this we rejoiced as much as if the land we saw had been Portugal, for with the help of God we hoped to recover our health there."

Land was sighted at nightfall on January 2, 1499, and on the next day they found themselves, without pilots or other assistance, off a large town on an unknown shore.* Afraid to land, the Portuguese commander fired off many of his bombards—perhaps in rejoicing, perhaps in blind anger toward all strange peoples—and continued along the coast. On January 5 a thunderstorm struck the fleet, badly damaging the *São Rafael*; and to cap the climax, a pirate attacked with eight boats, but was driven off by Gama's bombards.

Finally, on Monday, January 7, Malindi was sighted and the weary mariners cast anchor in the familiar spot. They were welcomed, and sheep, oranges, eggs, and other foods were sent aboard by the friendly ruler. "But," adds the author of the *Roteiro* pathetically, "our sick did not profit by this, for the climate affected them in such a way that many of them died here."

When Gama realized how generous the ruler of Malindi was, he decided to ask further favors, "begging for a tusk of ivory to be given to the king [of Portugal] his Lord and asking that a pillar

* The town was Mukhdisho (Magadoxo on the Portuguese maps) (Lat. 5° N.).

[padrão] be placed on the land as a sign of friendship." The sultan sent the tusk and ordered the padrão erected.* He also sent aboard a young Arab boy who, he said, desired to go to Portugal—a boy who returned to his home in 1501 on one of Cabral's ships. The fleet remained at friendly Malindi for five days, sailing again on Friday, January 11, on its long voyage home. Passing Mombasa, the ships anchored off the São Rafael Shoals on Sunday, January 13. By this time the crews were so reduced in numbers and strength by death and severe illness that Gama decided that it would be impossible to navigate three vessels with the handful of men available. The *São Rafael's* contents and equipment were transferred to the other ships, and the remaining members of the crew were distributed between the two vessels. The figurehead † of the doomed ship was then carefully removed to Gama's vessel and the *São Rafael* was set on fire, the men sadly watching the end of the craft which had been home to them for over a year and a half, in storm and in calm, in peaceful waters and off enemy shores.

After fifteen days at the São Rafael Shoals, the ships sailed past Zanzibar and on February 1 anchored off the island of São Jorge, near Moçambique. On the next day a padrão was set up on the island where the crews had heard Mass on the outward journey. As the cross was being affixed to the pillar, a heavy rain swept down on the island, putting out the fire over which the lead for attaching the cross was being melted, so that the Portuguese were forced to leave the pillar without a cross and sail on in the storm.

On March 20 the Cape of Good Hope was doubled in a fair wind. The author of the *Roteiro* rejoiced at this point that the sur-

---

* The original padrão had disappeared when Cabral visited Malindi in 1501, having been removed at the demand of the people of Mombasa. Another, of sandstone and still standing, was erected in its place and is locally known as Vasco da Gama's Pillar.

† It is of interest to note that the 24-inch oaken figurehead of the *São Rafael* was treasured by Vasco da Gama during his lifetime, probably because of his deep love and devotion to his brother Paulo, the captain of the ill fated vessel; he took it with him on his two subsequent voyages to India. Thereafter the image was prized as an heirloom by the admiral's descendants. Count Dom Francisco, his great-grandson, carried it with him twice as viceroy; and a later scion, the Marquis of Niza, took it with him on his two embassies to France in 1642 and 1647. It was later placed in the church at Vidigueira (see p. 259). Removed to another church in 1840, it remained there until 1853, when it was removed to the Church of the Jeronimos at Belém, where the bones of the great Vasco repose, and is still to be seen there.

viving members of the crew "were in good health and quite robust, although at times nearly dead from the cold winds which we experienced."

For twenty-seven days after rounding the cape, the vessels ran before a fine wind until on April 16 they were in the vicinity of São Tiago, in the Cape Verde Islands, where they were becalmed for some days, finally nearing the Guinea Coast off the Bissagos Islands.*

Shortly after reaching the latitude of the Cape Verde Islands, the *São Gabriel* and the *Berrio* parted company for some unknown reason, perhaps separated by a storm. Coelho continued his voyage alone, perhaps, as has been suggested, in the hope of a reward, arriving at Cascaes and crossing the bar at Lisbon on Wednesday, July 10, 1499. Vasco da Gama, after waiting a day for the *Berrio*, proceeded to São Tiago. There João da Sá was given command of the flagship *São Gabriel*, with orders to proceed with all speed to Portugal.

Vasco da Gama had another task to perform, one so pressing that he laid aside all thought of the triumph that awaited his return to the capital. His brother Paulo, whom he loved better than all else in the world, was dying of tuberculosis, and Vasco planned to sail to Portugal faster than the *São Gabriel* could take him. A caravel was chartered, and the discoverer of the Indies and his brother set their course for Portugal. His efforts were in vain. Paulo became rapidly worse, so that Vasco was obliged to land at Angra, in Terceira of the Azores, for he feared that otherwise Paulo would die at sea and that his body would have to be consigned to the ocean—a thought abhorrent to him. Paulo was taken ashore, where he died the next day, "como muyto bô Christão que era." † Vasco was thus at least able to bury the gentle and kindly Paulo with all honors in Portuguese soil, in the Church of São Francisco, at Terceira. The church, founded in 1452, was demolished in 1666, and was reconstructed and rededicated in 1672. During the reconstruction knowledge of the site of Paulo's grave was lost. Careful search then and thereafter was unavailing. Three hundred and fifty years after Paulo's death

---

* At this point the *Roteiro* ends abruptly, and the remainder of the voyage must be pieced together from other sources.

† "Like the good Christian he was."

the governor of the Azores caused a marble slab to be placed in the main chapel of the church with the following inscription:

A memoria
do
Irmão de Vasco da Gama
o illustre capitão
Paulo da Gama
sepultado
neste convento
anno-1499
Erigio lhe esta lapida
il governador civil
A. J. V. Santa Rita
em
Janeiro-28-1849 *

As soon as the Gamas landed at Terceira, a caravel was dispatched with the news to Lisbon. Meanwhile, João da Sá continued on his way in the *São Gabriel,* arriving in Portugal shortly after Nicolau Coelho in the *Berrio,* on some unknown date prior to August 28, 1499.

* To the memory
of the
Brother of Vasco da Gama,
the illustrious captain,
Paulo da Gama,
buried
in this church
in the year 1499.
A. J. V. [José Viera] Santa Rita
the civil governor
erected this stone to him
on January 28, 1849

CHAPTER XV

THE RETURN OF VASCO DA GAMA

> "Climb up, climb up, O sailor,
> To the main topgallant mast!
> See if you can glimpse
> The lands of Spain, the shores of Portugal."
> "Good news, good news, my captain,
> I see the lands of Spain,
> The shores of Portugal!"
>
> —Anon.

HE sad task of burying his brother accomplished, Vasco da Gama sailed with a heavy heart from Terceira for Portugal. The Rock of Cintra was sighted, the ship rounded Cape Raso and passed the fishing village of Cascaes into the Tagus, finally dropping anchor at Restello, about four miles below Lisbon. As the cable ran through the hawsehole, Gama realized that the voyage to India and back was completed—a voyage that had lasted over two long, adventurous, strenuous years.

One might confidently assume that the Portuguese made a careful record of the date of the entrance of Vasco da Gama into Lisbon at the end of his great voyage. However, there is no notation to be found in official records referring to the event.* Neither is there any authentic contemporary writing which mentions the date or which gives any details.

Authorities through the succeeding centuries have disputed the day, the dates varying from August 29 to September 1, 1499.† As soon as King Manuel learned of the commander's presence at

---

* The historians of the 16th century attached little importance to dates, often referring to notable events without either the dates or the names of the persons concerned. E.g., in Dom Manuel's letter to the Spanish monarchs announcing the discovery of the sea route to India, he simply refers to "one of the captains who has returned" (probably Coelho), without naming him.

† Some historians believe that on his arrival Gama spent a novena in retirement because of the death of Paulo.

Belém, he sent Dom Diogo da Silva de Meneses, Count of Pôrto Alegre, together with many nobles, to receive him. They accompanied him to the palace, "where it was difficult to arrive because of the multitude of people gathered to see a sight so novel to them as Vasco da Gama appeared to them, not only because he had done such a great thing as discovering India but also because everyone thought that he was dead."

Accompanied by his escort of honor, the great Vasco entered the presence of King Manuel, who received him most solemnly and in great state in the presence of the whole court. No description of the reception or what transpired when Gama stood before his king and made his report has come down to us, nor are any of the speeches made on the occasion recorded.*

That Dom Manuel was highly pleased and elated at the outcome of the venture is undoubted. In fact, even before Gama had returned, the king sent out two letters reporting the discovery, one to his parents-in-law, the Spanish monarchs, the other to Cardinal Dom Jorge da Costa, at Rome.† In both of these letters the king rejoiced at the discovery and outlined its results very briefly. In the letter to Spain, Manuel put special emphasis on the opportunity offered the Church to extend its influence, the advantages offered by the discovery "for destroying the Moors of those parts," and for diverting "to the natives and ships of our kingdom the great trade which now enriches the Moors of those parts, through whose hands it passes without the intervention of other persons or peoples."

Two vessels of the four which had sailed for India in July, 1497, had arrived back in Lisbon, the *São Gabriel* and the *Berrio*. Of the crew which had departed so gaily to the flying of flags and the playing of martial music on that sunny day, fewer than half had returned. Though there was great rejoicing in the palace, there was much sorrow and weeping in the humble homes on the waterside where so many of the young men had lived, those lads who had braved unknown seas and faced the attacks of hostile savages and barbarians in faroff lands and who now lay in their graves on un-

---

* Many valuable records and documents of this period were destroyed in the terrible earthquake at Lisbon in 1755.

† A third letter was addressed to Pope Alexander VI, but it has not been found.

known coasts or at the bottom of the sea. No monument was raised to them, no eulogies were pronounced for them in palace or church, and their names were not inscribed on tablets for all to see; yet they formed the backbone of the expedition, and without them the project would have failed most dismally. Though nameless, they are equally the heroes with Vasco da Gama of the discovery of the sea road to India.

It seems passing strange to us, people of a different age, accustomed to the recording of the minutest events in the greatest detail in biography (including autobiography) and historical writings where even the unimportant and the ephemeral receive unwarranted attention, that so little has been preserved of the saga of Vasco da Gama's first voyage. The flimsy tradition that he himself wrote an account has never thus far been proven in any way. The chroniclers of the reigns of Dom Manuel and his successor, King John III have given scant space to the tale of the twenty-six months of storm and calm, of navigation with rude and inaccurate instruments through unexplored seas, of the devastating climate, the scourge of scurvy, of insufficient and often improper food, of the dangers encountered in the contacts with the peoples of the African coast and of India, and of the difficulties constantly arising in handling crews of ignorant men, saturated with superstition and ill equipped and trained to meet the frightful strains of such a voyage. More concerned with singing the glories acquired by their kings, the historians of an earlier age passed over the personal accomplishment of Vasco da Gama. His indefatigable energy and his iron will alone saved the expedition from failure and probably from disintegration or even absolute annihilation. He was everywhere at once, exhorting, driving, sacrificing his own comforts, giving his men the example of his own labors, picturing to them the wonders of India and the glory of the undertaking together with the rewards that awaited on the return home. When persuasive methods failed, he would unleash his terrible anger, shrieking, brandishing his fists, cursing and threatening dire punishments, so that to respect was added abject fear—fear even greater than the perils which always menaced the members of the expedition.

The people of Portugal were astonished beyond measure by the intrepidity, the courage, and the dogged perseverance by which so small a number of men had accomplished so much; and, ever since Gama's day, he and his men have held in the eyes of their fellow countrymen the place of Homeric heroes, and their historic mission to India stands forth in relief as the great national epic.

As to the material proofs brought back, they were few—the handful of spices and precious stones which his factors and crews had been able to obtain in exchange for their trade goods and personal belongings. There was enough, however, to confirm the tradition of great wealth to be found in the Indies; and the hostages, as well as Monçaide and Gaspar da Gama, were there to substantiate the tale as told to King Manuel.

The immediate results of Gama's successful undertaking were far greater than those of the discoveries of Christopher Columbus. Columbus had found naked savages and grass huts where he had expected to behold great palaces and civilized peoples and riches beyond the dreams of avarice; Vasco da Gama had found the sea road to the lands of spice, of ivory, of gold, and of precious stones, and had proved that the seas about India were not landlocked, as many of the old geographers had believed. Dias had doubled the cape; his expedition gave *boa esperança*; and Gama's voyage to Calicut made that "good hope" a *boa certeza*—a magnificent certainty.

The voyage to India was probably the greatest feat of seamanship on record down to that time, and more noteworthy as a feat of navigation in every way than that of Columbus. The latter sailed a much shorter distance in a matter of weeks, and for the greater part of the time had favoring winds to aid him, so that his course was more or less in a straight line after he had left the Canary Islands behind him. Gama's voyage had lasted twenty-six months, and the distance covered was thousands of miles more. Moreover, a comparison of the observations made by the two men proves that the Portuguese Gama was far more accurate than was the Genoese Columbus. The route found by Gama was that which was followed thereafter by ships proceeding to the East from Europe for nearly four centuries. It fell into disuse only with the opening of the Suez Canal—and it is still used when war closes the Strait of Gibraltar and the Suez route.

Even when stripped of the fictions of Camões's epic and of the myths that have grown up about Vasco da Gama, his first voyage was one of the epoch-making events in the recorded history of mankind, and marked the first meeting of an expedition of the men of the West with those of the East since the coming of Alexander the Great to India (327–324 B.C.). Though neither Europe nor Asia was able to realize it at the time, life in the world was never to be the same again. New and far horizons had been opened up by Gama and his ships. In the last two decades of the fifteenth century, the boundaries of the European's world had been pushed back thousands of miles in every direction by Bartholomeu Dias, Christopher Columbus, and Vasco da Gama. Oceans theretofore unvisited were traversed and charted, unknown shores were visited, new lands were explored. The men of the West were no longer to be limited or bound by the sea, and thenceforth they were to explore and settle far countries and to conquer and exploit strange peoples, a process which seems only to be reaching its limits in our own day.

Another momentous consequence of the finding of the sea route to India was the completion of the shift of the center of European history. In ancient times, from the first voyages of the galleys of Sidon and Tyre and Carthage, the Mediterranean had been the great arena of maritime enterprise. The development of the Hanseatic League with its stations along the western seaboard of Europe was marked by the growth of many Atlantic ports. The expansion of the Ottoman Empire and the piratical North African States, together with the fall of Constantinople, made the Mediterranean maritime trade routes ever more unsafe and precarious and greatly interfered with and damaged the caravan traffic. The discovery of America by Columbus and the finding of the route to India by Gama completed the process, until the Atlantic Coast became paramount in trade and power in European history, and the Mediterranean ceased thereafter to be the focus of Western commerce.

Still another great change was effected by Portugal's discovery. Prior to Gama's voyage the cities of Italy had, either directly or indirectly, drawn their wealth—and through it their ability to encourage and nurture culture and learning—from the trade of the East, which filled their coffers and gave them their power.

Hardly had the weary *São Gabriel* and *Berrio* dropped their anchors in the waters of the Tagus on their return from India when frantic letters were sent by the Italian ambassadors and spies in Portugal to their governments—for they quickly realized the serious threat to Italian prosperity. One Venetian diarist noted : "As soon as the news [of Gama's return] reached Venice, the populace was thunderstruck, and the wiser among them regarded the news as the worst they could have received." It inevitably meant that the flow of wealth would be transferred from the Italian cities to the coast of the Atlantic and that the centers of European civilization, following those of commerce, would move from the Mediterranean to the West.

Finally, the opening of the Cape route to India weakened the Ottoman hold by establishing a European power in the East, one which soon cut off a considerable part of the Turkish revenue. It thus gradually weakened the Moslem power which had threatened to overthrow Western Europe as it had disrupted and destroyed the Roman and other empires in the East.

In one important assignment of his mission, however, Gama had been unsuccessful. He had signally failed to employ that combination of shrewdness, tact, and patience so necessary in dealing with the peoples of the East. He left everywhere resentment and hatred, both on the coasts of Africa and in India. That resentment and hatred, coupled with the fear inspired by his arrogance and ruthlessness, his unbridled temper, and his ignoring of the truth when lies seemed better to serve his purpose, all combined to make the conquest and exploitation of the lands he had discovered difficult for those who came after him, and ultimately contributed in no small degree to the loss of Portuguese prestige and power in Africa and Asia.

CHAPTER XVI

PORTUGAL, 1499–1502

The Marchandy also of Portugal
By divers lands turne into sale.
—"The Libel of English policie":
HAKLUYT, *Voyages* (ed. 1598–1600), I, 189

MMEDIATELY upon receiving Coelho's (and perhaps João da Sá's) report of Gama's voyage, and even before the capitão-mór had arrived in Lisbon, Dom Manuel added to his title of "King of Portugal and of the Algarves on this side of and beyond the sea, in Africa," that of "Lord of Guinea and of the Conquests, Navigation and Commerce of Ethiopia, Arabia, Persia, and India." * A gold coin was also struck to commemorate the event. It weighed 712 grains and had a value of ten cruzados—approximately $25—and was called a "portuguez."

Gama's success had a strange effect on King Manuel, apart from the assumption of the grandiose new title—which, indeed, hardly accorded with the accomplishments of the first expedition to India. Frivolous and turbulent by nature, the king rushed into a program of public works with far more zeal than good judgment; moreover, the thirst for power engendered by the good news about India caused him to perform personal acts which bordered on madness.

John II, who had done so much to foster maritime exploration, and whom Manuel had succeeded, had been entombed in the Sé (cathedral) de Silves. One of Manuel's first acts after Vasco da Gama's return was to order the transfer of John's body to the Abbey of Batalha. This was done with what appeared to many of his people unseemly pomp and ceremony:

From place to place, accompanied by the grandees of the nation, archbishops, bishops, eighty chaplains and choristers, the king, preceded by a barbarous orchestra of trumpets, reed pipes, sackbuts, and drums

* First used in a letter to Cardinal D. Jorge da Costa, dated Aug. 28, 1499.

(and at night by torchbearers), crossed the plains of the kingdom for days on end, in the funeral cortege. At night, amid the silence of the grieving people, wherever they made a halt, the spirit of the [dead] king came into his [Manuel's] thoughts—and in the Church of Batalha, at night, when the ceremony [of transference] was over, the memory of the man who had prepared with so much constancy the great work whose consummation was now crowned with success brought him a morbid curiosity. Almost clandestinely he proceeded to the church and, ordered John's coffin opened, in order to see him. He beheld the body covered with lime dust, and ordered the monks to blow it off with tubes of cane, and he himself aided them, and then kissed the dead man's hands and feet again and again. It was a dramatic meeting, this of the dead and the living kings, and a sight for a man to look upon.

Shortly thereafter (December 10, 1500), Manuel ordered all of the olive trees in the city of Lisbon—a most picturesque feature— to be uprooted if they grew in any enclosure wherein stood a church, a monastery, or a feudal palace. He also decreed that a space should be cleared all around and contiguous to the city walls, and that certain other parts of the city be cleared and leveled as well.

Especially important was the beginning of the construction of new public buildings—the formidable group which embraced the majestic palaces of the Ribeira, the Casa da Índia, the Almaçens (royal warehouses), and of the Tercenas (storehouses) of Cataquefaras. In his impatience and desire to live in the excited atmosphere of building, noise, and confusion, he repaired the palace of Santos-o-Velho, and dwelt there while his new palaces were in course of construction.

The most ambitious project that King Manuel conceived at this time was the building of the Church of the Jeronimos at Belém, on the spot where stood the chapel in which Vasco da Gama and his men had worshiped before sailing on their adventurous voyage. This he planned as an eternal memorial to the discovery of India. It still stands as one of the greatest monuments of Portuguese Renaissance architecture and is of particular interest to students of the life and adventures of Vasco da Gama and Luis Camões.

The lands of Restello were obtained from the Brothers of Christ, who owned them, and were transferred in December, 1499, to the "principal and brothers of São Jeronymo, the saint to whom the

king paid his personal devotion—that they might there erect a
monastery, with the obligation, over and above the offices imposed
by its statutes, to offer their prayers for the soul of the Infante
[Henry], founder of the original chapel, of the monarch grantor
and his successors." Manuel then changed the name of the place
from Restello to Belém (Bethlehem). When the Brothers of Christ
surrendered their chapel, they unfortunately removed the stone
image of the Madonna and Child, seated on a wooden chair, which
stood there when Gama and his men kept their vigil the night of
July 7, 1497, before their ships left for India. The monks placed it
in the Conceição Velha, in the old Church of the Conception,
where it still stands, having survived a disastrous fire which
destroyed much of the church.

The foundations of the Jeronimos were begun late in 1499, and
on January 6, 1501, the cornerstone was solemnly laid with great
ceremony on the spot where the principal entrance was to be, in the
presence of the king, the royal family, the court, and a great con-
course of people. The construction of the great monastery continued
until 1551, when John III ordered that work cease. Additions and
alterations were made in the nineteenth century, but the building
stands substantially as it was in the middle of the sixteenth century.

Manuel's reputation for generosity was not great, but he appears
to have dealt very liberally with Vasco da Gama in his efforts to
compensate him for his great services to the crown. Unfortunately,
there are evidences that Gama was grasping and greedy, and that
he felt that no reward his sovereign might see fit to grant him was
sufficient.

He loved Sines, where he was born and where his father had
been alcaide mór. When asked to indicate what he desired, he did
not hesitate to petition for the seignory of the town. Sines, however,
belonged to the Order of São Tiago, of which the Duke of Coimbra,
bastard son of John II, was Master. Manuel granted Gama's request by Letters Patent issued December 24, 1499. These letters
provided that the town of Sines should be granted, together with
its privileges, revenues, and taxes, to Vasco da Gama, his heirs, and
successors, with the proviso, however, that the crown give the order
of São Tiago another town in exchange and that the Pope grant a

special dispensation to permit the transfer. The papal dispensation was given in 1501, but the Order of São Tiago refused to surrender possession of the town.* Manuel endeavored to placate Gama by the grant of an annual pension of 1,000 cruzados (about $2,000) "during the time that he shall not . . . be able to have enjoyment of the town of Sines." †

On January 10, 1502, exactly a month before he set forth on his second voyage to India, Gama was given an additional pension of 300,000 reis (about $1,500) for himself and his descendants. Together with this pension he also received the title of "Admiral of the Sea of India," and with it "the honors, preeminences, liberties, power, jurisdiction, revenues, privileges, and rights which he should have." In the same grant Gama was given the title of Dom not only for himself, but also for his brother Ayres, his sister Thereza (in the feminine form, Dona), and their descendants. To all this was added the right to bring or have brought in ships coming from India once a year 200 cruzados' worth of merchandise, paying only one tax—5 per cent to the Order of Christ. This decree states distinctly that it was issued and the grants made "sem nollo elle pedir nem outro por elle" (without his soliciting it, or anyone in his behalf), and terminates with the request and order that "the heirs of the said Vasco da Gama . . . should call themselves Gama in remembrance and in memory of the said Vasco da Gama."

In spite of all these gifts Dom Vasco was determined to have the lordship of Sines, and much trouble resulted from the contest on his return from his second voyage.

Evidently part of the first pension was not paid when due in 1501, and Dom Vasco was given a quantity of wheat in its place. The order of the king on his treasurer for this wheat (valued at 28,000 reis), bearing the admiral's receipt, is still in existence

---

* The reasons for the refusal to deliver Sines to Gama are not known. It may have been a question of the value of the lands offered in exchange, or perhaps the personal attitude of the Grand Master of the Order of São Tiago, Dom Jorge de Lencastre, Duke of Coimbra, a person of most unsavory reputation. Born in 1481, he married in 1500. After the death of his wife "he became the lecherous pursuer of the young girls of the palace" (he was fifty at the time) to such an extent that he tried to marry a lady-in-waiting of the queen who was sixteen years old. The sons of the king resisted his attempt, but "his amorous mania ceased only at his death in 1550."

† Decree dated Feb. 22, 1501.

and contains one of the three signatures of Gama that have survived.*

Except for the few details given above, and the fact that he married at this time in the city of Évora, where it is believed he lived from 1499 to 1502, very little is known of the life of the admiral between his first and second voyages to India. The exact time of his marriage cannot be fixed, and it can be approximated only by guessing at the ages of his sons at various times in their careers. The woman whom Gama took to wife was Dona Catharina de Athayde, daughter of Alvaro de Athayde and of Dona Maria da Silva.† Of Gama's marriage were born six sons: Francisco, Estevam, Pedro, Paulo, Christovão, and Alvaro de Athayde, and a daughter Izabel de Athayde.‡

* "I, Dom Vasco da Gama, declare that it is true that I have received the said 15 moios of wheat from said Go. de Sequeira. Dom Vasco da Gama."

† The chroniclers refer to Gama as a bachelor when he made his first voyage; on his second he was accompanied by his brother-in-law—Alvaro de Athayde.

‡ Younger sons of the period sometimes took the name of one parent, sometimes of the other.

CHAPTER XVII

THE VOYAGE OF PEDRO ALVARES CABRAL

In the yeere 1500. and in the moneth of March, one Pedro
Alvarez Cabral sayled out of Lisbon thirteene ships.
—Purchas, *His Pilgrimes,* Tenth Booke

ING MANUEL lost no time in following up the
opportunity offered him by the opening of the sea
road to the Indies. With the superiority of construction of the ships of the Portuguese, the experience
of their navigators, the greater accuracy of their instruments, and the accumulation of sailing data begun under the
direction of Prince Henry, the control of the Eastern seas and their
spice trade seemed Portugal's natural destiny. Manuel and his
people believed that God Himself had guided Dom Vasco to India
and home again in safety, and that it was a manifestation of His
will and desire that Portugal should rule the East and convert its
people to the faith. As had happened when Gama's first voyage
was planned, a group of Manuel's advisers opposed proceeding
further, pointing out the risks—Portugal's poverty and sparse population, and the overwhelming superiority of the Moslem power and
wealth. But Manuel persisted, as he had previously, impelled by
greed, by ambition for himself and his little nation, and by his
fanatical desire to win converts to the Church among the heathen
of Africa and the Eastern seas.

Vasco da Gama's voyage had accomplished great things, but
after all, his fleet had been a tiny one and his whole voyage an
exploratory one—or, as it has been called, "a reconnaissance in
force." Gama had, though clumsily and ineffectually, because of
his own intransigeant personality, acted the part of a wandering
foreigner seeking trade for his countrymen. Though the Moslems
of Calicut had opposed him and successfully blocked his freedom
of trade with the samorin's people, they did not seriously believe
that the arrival of the Portuguese ships off the Malabar coast

threatened any real—or at any rate immediate—danger to their strongly entrenched monopoly of the Indian trade and maritime enterprise. In order to obtain control of the Eastern spice trade it was imperative for the Portuguese to move swiftly, first to prevent other European nations from taking advantage of the discovery and, second, to arrive on the scenes of Gama's exploits before the Hindus and Moslems could prepare politically or militarily to oppose them successfully. Moreover, a larger force was necessary for the second expedition. There were neither narrow straits that could be easily controlled nor key points on the open seas and African coast between Guinea and Calicut. This meant that Portugal had to take swift and decisive steps to dominate the African coast at such points as the Portuguese would need as ports of call, and also to prevent other nations from obtaining a foothold along the route.

The man to whom the king naturally would turn to lead the expedition was Dom Vasco da Gama, now Admiral of the Indian Sea. In fact, by a grant dated October 2, 1501(?), King Manuel decreed "that of all the armadas which we shall order made and shall make during his lifetime for the said ports of India, whether they be only for traffic in merchandise or whether it is necessary to make war with them, he [Gama] may take and takes the chief captaincy [capytanya mór] of them—and when he thus wishes to take the said captaincy we may not place in them nor appoint another chief captain except him. . . ." This decree the king made irrevocable "without any impediment which might be placed on it." Thus the admiral could have led the second expedition had he so elected. But he was weary after his two years' voyage. It had been an extremely difficult and wearing experience, and he desired to relax and enjoy his newly won honors and pensions. Besides, he had just married, and wished leisure and at least temporary freedom from the hardships of a sailor's life.

On learning of Gama's unwillingness to exercise his option, Dom Manuel sought elsewhere for a leader. His choice fell on Pedro Álvares (or Pedralvares) Cabral. Cabral was born in 1467(?) near Covilhan, and so was thirty-two years old when Manuel chose him as the capitão-mór of the fleet. He had served as a page at the court of John II and later became a gentleman of the King's Council and a member of the Order of Christ. Little is known of his life. There is no proof whatever that he had even sailed in a ship before receiving his command in 1499 (to sail in 1500), nor is there a record of his having made a second voyage anywhere. From every point of view it appears to have been a political appointment, or the selection of a favorite without consideration of his fitness or ability. The choice is most surprising in view of the availability of commanders of the proved ability and caliber of Duarte Pacheco, Bartholomeu Dias, and Nicolau Coelho—all of whom sailed with Cabral but in subordinate positions. In Cabral's favor is the fact that he appears to have been acceptable to Vasco da Gama and to have been respected by his men in spite of his youth.

The expedition consisted of thirteen vessels fitted for voyages of eighteen months. In addition to Pacheco, Coelho, and Dias, the fleet carried Ayres Correia, who had in charge all matters relating to trade, and who was also empowered to negotiate commercial treaties. As the ships carried a large cargo for commercial purposes, rules and regulations for trade were provided. Detailed instructions were drawn up for the governing of the ships and for dealing with native rulers. Most of these written instructions have disappeared; but a very important portion, designed to guide Cabral after his arrival in India, is still in existence, as is a memorandum drawn up with the assistance of Vasco da Gama,* including advice as to sailing after leaving the Cape Verde Islands. In addition to these instructions, Cabral carried a letter to the samorin, offering friendship and trade, but containing a paragraph which threatened that if the samorin was unwilling or obstructive "our set purpose is to follow the will of God rather than of men, and not to fail through any opposition to prosecute this enterprise and continue our navigation, trade, and intercourse in these lands which the Lord God desires to be served newly by our hands, not wishing that our labors to serve Him be in vain."

Besides the captains and three factors, pilots, clerks (called *escrivães,* or writers), and interpreters, Monçaide, the five Hindus who had been carried off by Gama, and eight friars and priests accompanied the fleet. It also carried an astronomer—the only Portuguese Indian expedition which appears to have had one among its personnel.

The ships of the fleet were larger than those employed by Gama, and the tonnage of the thirteen ships was five times that of the

* The authenticity of this memorandum has been questioned.

admiral's. Contrary to the difficulty experienced in obtaining recruits for Gama's fleet, seamen and untried landsmen clamored for the opportunity of sailing with Cabral, and their pay was fixed in advance, without promise of special awards.

Manuel had learned from the mistakes of the first voyage to India. Accordingly, in addition to two boatloads of goods for the African negro traffic, a far better class of merchandise was carried for the Indian trade—copper, vermilion, mercury, amber, coral, woolen yardage, satin, velvets, and the like. As Portuguese money was not known to the Malabarese, coins of other countries, particularly of Venice, were carried on the flagship for making purchases for the home market.

On March 8, 1500, the fleet assembled at Belém, near the unfinished walls of the Monastery of the Jeronimos. One of the vessels (the *Anunciada*), it is interesting to note, was the property of Bartholomo Marchioni (the same Italian who had negotiated the letters of credit of Covilhan and Paiva [see p. 51] on their important mission overland to India), in partnership with other Florentines. Still another belonged to a Portuguese, the Count of Pôrto Alegre. The other vessels were owned by the crown.

After a pontifical Mass was said by Bishop Dom Drogo Ortiz in the presence of the king, Cabral was presented with a banner bearing the royal arms, and the crews boarded their ships to the strains of music from bagpipes, fifes, and drums. On the following day the ships set sail on a voyage even longer than that of Gama.

Misfortune followed the fleet from the first. On March 23 one ship was missing; and though some claim is made that it reached an unnamed port in safety, it is believed to have foundered in fair weather. On April 22 the coast of Brazil was sighted and the fleet dropped anchor offshore, remaining there until May 2, though but little if any exploration was made.[1] A ship was sent home to Portugal to announce the discovery; the remaining eleven turned their prows toward Africa. The crossing from Brazil to the Cape was long and arduous, and a comet seen on the night of May 12 was taken as a bad omen for the future. On May 24 the fleet ran into the bad weather for which the South Atlantic is notorious, and the ships were caught in a sudden violent storm. Four vessels were lost, including that of the venturesome discoverer of the Cape of Good Hope, Bartholomeu Dias, who went down with his ship. The remaining seven vessels were scattered, running before the high winds with damaged rigging and sails in ribbons. Cabral's flagship, with two others, sighted the cape and doubled it, first making a landing north of Sofala, in East Africa, thence proceeding to Moçambique, where they were joined by three more of the vessels. The ship commanded by Diogo Dias sailed too far to the east and discovered the island of Madagascar.[2]

After ten days spent in refitting in Moçambique, where the ruler, terrified by Gama's treatment of him a few years before, was friendly, the fleet sailed on, reaching Kilwa (Quiloa), an independent Arab kingdom whose ruler was unfriendly to the infidels, on July 26. When the king refused to sign a treaty, Cabral sailed on to Malindi, which he reached on August. 1. There the friendly ruler supplied pilots, and the six vessels continued on their way to the Angediva Islands on the Indian coast. Here the ships were careened and repaired. Finally, on September 13, Cabral's ships dropped anchor before Calicut, where, with flags flying, a salute was fired.

Cabral's fleet was greeted by the governor (*catual*) of the port, who welcomed the Portuguese in the name of the samorin. The next morning the five Hindu hostages who had been brought back from Portugal (all of whom had learned to speak Portuguese) were landed, dressed in fine clothes. All except one, Baltasar, were ignored, for they were of lower caste (fishermen) than Gama was led to believe. On the samorin's assurances of friendship and a safe conduct for carrying on business, Cabral arrogantly demanded hostages; and in token of good faith the samorin sent five Brahmins on board, to remain there during a visit from Cabral to the palace. A dwelling and a warehouse near the shore were assigned by the ruler as a residence and storehouse for the Portuguese trade goods.

Meanwhile, the Arabs had laid their plans to circumvent the Portuguese, and Ayres Correia, the factor, was warned that the warehouse would be attacked and looted. A few days later, on December 16, 1500, after nightfall, several thousand (according to Portuguese report) Arabs stealthily surrounded the warehouse and living quarters. One of Correia's servants heard an unusual noise and, looking out, saw the mob approaching. He at once set up a cry, "Ladrões, ladrões" (thieves, thieves). It was too late. The crowd of Arabs, Moplahs and Hindus climbed the walls into the compound. The stout doors of the warehouse and residence resisted them, but they swarmed up to the light roofs and threw arrows and darts down upon the Portuguese. These latter had but few bolts for their crossbows, and after they had discharged them they were helpless. Correia gave the order to run to the beach. Of the eighty men in the compound thirty were killed, and in the running attack on the fleeing Europeans fourteen more lost their lives, so that only thirty-six men, most of them very severely wounded, reached the boat. Ayres Correia was killed, and his little son who was with him barely escaped with the aid of a sailor. The mob was finally driven off by a rescue party. This inexcusable massacre ended all friendly relations with the samorin, who gave no excuse or apology for the outrage. Cabral held him responsible and in retaliation burned ten Arab vessels lying off the shore and then bombarded the town.

After this bloody affair Cabral sailed for Cochin, whose ruler (hostile and jealous of Calicut's prosperity) welcomed him and made overtures for trade. A cargo of pepper, cinnamon, benzoin, musk, porcelain, and fine weaves was purchased, and Cabral moved on to Cannanore. Cinnamon was loaded there, and on January 16 the fleet sailed for Portugal.

On the way home an Indian ship was hailed, but as its captain sent presents and was willing to acknowledge the supremacy of Portugal the vessel was released without molestation. Near Moçambique, Sancho de Toar's vessel ran aground because of the captain's refusing to follow the pilot's instructions. It began to take water; and though the crew and light objects and equipment were saved, the ship had to be abandoned. It was set on fire, for there was no space in which to stow the cargo on the other ships.

On reaching Moçambique, one of the ships was sent to Sofala to trade. The Portuguese obtained gold in exchange for worthless trinkets, for the people were simple Africans and were easily persuaded to give gold beads for glass ones. Before leaving, Sancho de Toar (who had Gaspar da Gama with him as adviser and interpreter) wheedled a letter out of the "king" to Cabral, "urgently requesting" him to send more ships to Sofala. Toar then sailed on to Portugal.

Meanwhile Cabral ordered the remainder of the ships to be careened and caulked at Moçambique, for they were beginning to show extensive damage. Shortly after sailing from Moçambique, a terrific gale was encountered and the ships were scattered. Some of Cabral's vessels rounded the cape on May 22, 1501, and finally sailed up the Tagus to Lisbon on July 31, 1501, and one of his ships (probably separated in the storm) had reached Portugal on June 23.

Thus, in the report of the voyage made by Giovanni Matteo Cretico, the Venetian nuncio to the Signoria:

seven ships have made the return voyage safely. One ship ran aground . . . only one ship . . . of 300 tons has returned to port . . . it is reported that others are near by . . . I happened to be with the Most Serene King, who summoned me and declared that I should congratulate him on his ships having returned from India with cargoes of spices, and I therefore did so in the manner that was proper for me. He had a feast held in the palace that night, and a ringing of the bells throughout the city, and on the following day he ordered a solemn procession throughout the country.

And the next time Cretico was with His Majesty, the king told him that thereafter the Venetians should send their ships to Lisbon for cargoes of spices, that "he would make them welcome and that they could feel themselves at home—. In short he feels that he has India under his control." *

Meanwhile, others of Cabral's ships straggled in. The cargoes of five of them were valuable enough not only to reimburse the crown for the investment, in spite of the great losses of ships and cargo, but even to bring in a handsome profit—100 per cent of all moneys invested.

* Many contemporary letters, notes, and diary entries telling of the success of Cabral's voyage and of its probable effect on Italian trade have survived. They may be found in Greenlee's excellent *Voyages of Pedro Alvares Cabral to Brazil and India.*

NOTES

[1] This book is not concerned with the discovery of Brazil by Cabral or with the many disputed points involved therein. A very full and annotated account may be found in William Brooks Greenlee, ed. and transl., *The Voyage of Pedro Alvares Cabral to Brazil and India,* printed for the Hakluyt Society (London, 1938).

[2] After the discovery of Madagascar, Dias's ship continued up the coast of Berbera (?), in Somaliland, with many sick on board. The coast Arabs pre-

tended friendship, and Dias landed fifty of the sick men together with ten others to care for them. This left on board the ship twenty men too sick to be moved and about twenty more able-bodied members of the crew. The Arabs seized and murdered the men on shore and sent out boats to attack Dias's ship. The chief gunner was sick but dragged himself from his pallet and fired the ship's guns, sinking three of the Arab boats and driving off the rest. Meanwhile, Dias and his crew hoisted sail and escaped. Three months later, after much suffering and many more deaths, the ship arrived at the Cape Verde Islands with thirteen surviving. There he rejoined Cabral on his homeward voyage. Dias and his men were the first Portuguese ever to sail around Africa from the Red Sea to the Strait of Gibraltar.

CHAPTER XVIII

LISBON IN 1502

And you, noble Lisbon, who in the world
Are easily the princess of the others.
—CAMÕES, *Os Lusíadas*, III, lvii

HE sea road to the Indies had been opened by Vasco da Gama. It was further explored by Pedro Álvares Cabral and by a small fleet of four vessels sent out under the command of João da Nova in 1501.* In pursuance of his plan to wrest the spice trade of the East from the hands of the Arabs and the Mameluke rulers of Egypt, and to secure for his own country the rich profits of the traffic, King Manuel decided to dispatch a large fleet to India. Its object was to lay a firm foundation for trade (and, if expedient, for conquest) and to divert to Lisbon as speedily as possible the traffic which had theretofore been almost exclusively carried on in Arab bottoms through Arabian and Egyptian ports.

Cabral, who was now a brilliant figure in the public eye and his discovery of Brazil and his Indian achievement the talk of the capital, was at first chosen by the king to lead the fourth Indian armada. Later, Gama received the royal commission, though the reasons for Cabral's refusal to accept the command or for his elimination from the eligible list are uncertain and obscure.†

With the disappearance of Cabral from the scene, the man to whom the king turned was the person best fitted for the post, the

---

* On the return voyage, Nova discovered the island of Saint Helena.

† One chronicler claims that Cabral refused the command when he learned of the small size of the fleet. Castanheda asserts cryptically that "for some good reasons Dom Manuel took the command from Cabral and gave it to Vasco da Gama." Other authorities state that Gama insisted on his rights under the royal decree authorizing him to take chief command in any fleet whose destination was India. Still another claim is that Manuel was displeased by Cabral's handling of the Calicut situation. And finally it is alleged that Gama asked for the command with the express purpose of avenging the treatment of the Portuguese in Calicut.

leader who had first traversed the uncharted seas and visited the unknown lands of East Africa and India—Vasco da Gama, now Dom Vasco, Admiral of India. The sovereign summoned Gama and laid before him his aims and plans, together with the reasons why he looked to Dom Vasco to develop and expand the trade which his first voyage had opened up for his countrymen. Gama accepted the commission, immediately took over the command, and pressed the preparations for the new venture to their completion.

Lisbon had changed immeasurably since the sailing of the first fleet from Restello on July 8, 1497. The reports brought from the East by the three fleets that had made the voyage had first astonished, then stimulated and stirred the Portuguese people as had no other event in their history. The public works ordered by the king had aroused the rich nobles and merchants to imitate his lavish building, and within and without the walls of the city a flame of feverish activity burned high. The squares and gates of Lisbon were crowded with townspeople and foreigners; for the thrilling news of the discoveries had spread like wildfire throughout Europe, and Venetians, Genoese, Florentines, Flemings, Germans, French, Spanish, and English all swarmed into Lisbon to take advantage of the golden opportunities offered there. Men, women, and children gathered around the swaggering sailors, listening in open-mouthed credulity to their highly colored and embroidered tales of India, Africa, and the islands of the sea. The taverns of the Ribeira at the waterside and the inns of the Alfama were thronged with idlers and workmen, and India, with its wonders and its fabulous wealth, was on all men's lips. Mingling with the crowds, insinuating themselves everywhere, were spies of the Signoria, of the Medicis, and of other foreign powers. The news of the Portuguese activities in the East were of vital concern to them, threatening as it did the very foundations of their prosperity, and reports and diaries still extant indicate that their agents were very active at King Manuel's court. Others crowding into the city were merchants from the Low Countries and England, intent on buying spices and other commodities from India; men seeking employment in the fast-growing capital, and unemployed condottieri in hopes of obtaining positions in castle and town.

The banks of the Tagus, from the city gates to Restello, were a hive of feverish activity. On hilltops and slopes palaces and villas were under construction, and the Cathedral do Mar and the Jeronimos' Church at Belém employed thousands of artisans. Where there had been wide stretches of yellow sand, warehouses were now rising for the storage of Indian cargoes. By the river's edge were the fish markets, displaying every color and variety of fish, the women screeching their wares shrilly at each stall, their bright-colored garments forming a vivid, variegated tapestry in the sunshine. Donkey drivers forced their way through the crowds, their baskets and panniers heaped high with strawberries and olives. There, too, were men and women cleaning, salting, and packing fish in tubs to be shipped all over Europe, and fishermen gossiping as they mended their brown nets. Idlers stood about, watching the laborers unloading bricks and cut stones for the buildings going up everywhere, or gazing at the boats with their rust-red sails coming in from the fishing banks along the coast.

Farther along the shore were the arsenals and royal warehouses. Great anchors, arms, and ammunition were being manufactured in foundries manned largely by negroes, who, to the eye of a contemporary German visitor, "seemed like the cyclops in the forges of Vulcan." Great stores of lead, copper, charcoal, saltpeter and sulphur were accumulated in the arsenals, together with "innumerable pikes, cannon balls, helmets, breastplates and every sort of equipment and gear that could be used on shipboard." On the stocks were vessels, large and small, in all stages of construction, for the Portuguese carrying trade was growing by leaps and bounds.

The narrow streets of the lower city within the walls seethed with activity and were filled from morning until night with the cries of food vendors. At street corners chestnut sellers sat crying their wares, the while fanning the flame in their braziers of clay. Men and women peddled oil, fish, water, and vegetables, carried, for the most part, on their heads. Bakers offered their loaves on great flat head baskets, and likewise fowl, squawking and screaming, were offered in cagelike baskets. From the street corners rose the reek of slaughterhouses and the odors of cooked food; and every few minutes the passers-by were startled into watchfulness by the cry—still heard in Lisbon—of "Agua vae!" (Look out for the water) as householders in the upper floors flung open their shutters and emptied buckets of water and domestic refuse into the streets, where all the drainage was carried off in open gutters in the middle of the roadway. Over the streets the washing was hung on poles to dry, as it still is today.

Through the many gates and up the narrow, steep thoroughfares climbed half-naked negro female slaves carrying jars of water from the fountains, and carts drawn by oxen and donkeys hauled great loads of cabbages, turnips, melons, olives, and fruits over the cobbled streets to the upper city. There the houses, often painted in bright colors, with graceful dark-red adobe chimneys, and decorated with many colored tiles, made a cheerful, gay picture in the strong southern sunlight, together with the pinnacles of the palaces and the domes and spires of the churches, monasteries, and convents all stamped as they were with the unmistakable traces of their Moorish origin. And high above all was the old Moorish palace of the king, gleaming with its arrowlike towers and high roofs like a crown.

In the lower city were the grain mills, horses turning the ponderous stones with a continuous dull rumble. Hucksters sold cooked food at the corners, the hammers of the armorers were constantly clanging, and the streets were filled with the stinging smoke from their forges. At the corners of the squares sat the *escrivães* (scriveners), who for a small sum would write a love letter, a petition, a contract, a set of verses—or an epitaph.

The slave market was always crowded with purchasers or idlers who spent their time watching the sales of human flesh, and who rejoiced in the stripping and exposing to their greedy gaze of the naked bronzed bodies of stalwart men and statuesque women whose physical excellences were vaunted aloud by the slave dealer and who were bargained for, and led off by, their new owners like cattle. . . .

When night came down over the city, the narrow winding streets were dangerous places, especially if one loitered in the shadows. The night watch was inefficient; all citizens carried knives; and scuffles, quarrels, stabbings, and worse were all too frequent. As the sun set, tentmakers could be seen sewing in their doorways; and the dying light gleamed on the armor of passing soldiers or shone on dark, gloomy, tonsured monks striding along in their long robes and sandals and on the potters in their white *aljubas* (vests) endlessly turning their wheels in the growing darkness. And later, when the shadows had lengthened and melted into black night, torches flared up and flickered in the city and on the riverbank; and the sound of lutes and timbrels, pipes and drums mingled in the taverns and low drinking places with the cries and laughter of men and women and the hoarse shouts and oaths of drunken men.

With the rising of the sun the city began to stir anew, and again the hum of human activity rose in the warm air. In the shipyards the hammers of the carpenters and caulkers rose in staccato accents, the forges in the quarter of San Francisco roared and sputtered merrily, the chanteys of the ships' crews on the river were wafted across the water; and with the passing of the morning hours all the multitudinous cries and noises of a busy, prosperous medieval city rose to the heavens in an ever increasing roar.

This was the Lisbon that Dom Vasco da Gama knew, this was the city through which he rode from Évora on taking command, and these the sights and sounds that were familiar to him as he made his daily rounds of ships and arsenals and warehouses and recruiting depots in the service of his king. Much of that Lisbon is gone, entirely obliterated by the terrible earthquake of 1755, but the sights and sounds and color of the daily life of the people in the city by the Tagus have changed but little, if any, since those far-off days of the year 1502.

The fleet under Gama was divided into three sections. The largest, under the immediate command of the admiral, consisted of ten vessels. The second section, of five ships, was commanded by Vicente Sodré, Gama's uncle. This section was under orders to cruise in the Indian Ocean and destroy or cripple the Arab sea trade. The third group consisted likewise of five ships, under the command of Estavão da Gama, the admiral's nephew.* In this fashion Gama contrived to have the subordinate commands in the hands of members of his own family, devoted to his (and their) personal interests. The arrangement was eminently satisfactory for all concerned.

* These ships (*redondos*) were to be left in Indian waters to guard the factories.

THE NARRATIVE OF THE SECOND VOYAGE

And in the yeere following, 1502, hee sent Vascus Gama againe
with ten ships giving him commission to make himselfe Lord of the
Sea, and to doe his utmost against the Mores.
—PURCHAS, *His Pilgrimes*, I, 11, 31

S with his first expedition, no record is in existence
compiled or written by Dom Vasco himself about his
second voyage to India. With the exception of one
surviving notation concerning the African coast city
of Kilwa,* we are dependent on outside sources for
information about the events of the voyage.

The sources are three in number. One is the narrative of the
voyage made by a Flemish sailor or officer who served on one of
the ships. The account, first printed in Antwerp in 1504, and entitled *Calcoen* (Calicut), is rough, clumsy in form and style, with
many omissions (and probably highly colored in spots), and appears
to be the work of an ignorant man.† Oddly enough, Vasco da
Gama's name appears nowhere in the entire narrative, but there is
no doubt about its being an original account of his second voyage
to the East. The dates, place names, and events correspond to those
known, and the account supplies interesting details not elsewhere
recorded. That a Fleming was serving on one of the Portuguese
ships is not surprising, as adventurers from the Low Countries were
faring forth early as mariners and merchants to the East. They were
some of those doughty men who were later to found and firmly
establish the Dutch power in the East Indies. In fact, Flemish
merchants had already reached Calicut by crossing through Egypt

* The document in question consists of a memorandum of instructions left
behind by Gama at Kilwa for the guidance of all Portuguese vessels arriving
in the port. Therein, with his usual directness and terseness, he describes the
attitude of the chief of the town.

† The only original known is in the British Museum. It consists of six pages
in Gothic characters. Though it bears no indication of the place or time of
printing, it is easy to date and place because of the style of type used.

or Persia, if we may believe an Italian translation of a letter of King Manuel written in 1505.*

The Flemish account opens with the words: "This is the voyage which a man wrote after he had sailed . . . from the river of Lisbon in Portugal to go to Calcicut in India in the year 1501." †

The second source for this voyage is the account of a Portuguese, one Thomé Lopes, who served as a writer (clerk) on a ship in Estavão da Gama's squadron, captained by Ruy Mendes de Brito (also known as Captain Giovanni Buonagrazia). Although the author did not join the main fleet until the rendezvous in the Angediva Islands, his full and well written account is a most valuable contribution to our knowledge of the voyage. The Portuguese original is not known, and the document was preserved only in an Italian translation in Volume II (page 133) of the famous three-volume collection of voyages edited by Giambattista Ramusio and first published in Venice in 1551–1559.‡

A third valuable but little used source was buried for many years in the voluminous *Diary* of the Venetian, Marino Sanuto.§ It consists of a lengthy letter from one Mateo di Begnino, factor of the Venetian, Francesco Affaitato, residing in Lisbon. Di Begnino served also on one of Estavão da Gama's ships. During the voyage home he spent his time from March 30, 1503, until the middle of April, 1503, partly at sea and partly in Moçambique, in writing an account of the events of the voyage and its results, dispatching the letter to Affaitato on April 19, 1503, with the first ship of the squadron that was leaving for Portugal. Di Begnino's long letter contains but few facts not already noted by Lopes and the unknown author of *Calcoen*; but it serves admirably as a check and criticism of these accounts and of the historians of the period, and, used together with them, it now makes it possible to piece out a fairly full presentation of the occurrences of the admiral's second voyage to India.

Dom Vasco's appointment to the command of the new Indian

---

* "Vi sono mercãdati d' tutte ql'le parti e d' mercantia como Bruges i Flandria, Venetia i Italia" (There are merchants from all those parts, and merchandise such as that of Bruges in Flanders and Venice in Italy).

† The date is an error. It should be 1502.

‡ This is the same volume which contains the first known Italian version of Marco Polo's *Description of the World*.

§ The most voluminous diary ever kept by any person in any language.

fleet was made probably before the end of the year 1501, as the ships were scheduled to sail in February. The royal orders conferred on him a new title—Almirante dos Mares das Índias Orientaes (Admiral of the East Indian Seas). The formal commission was delivered to Gama by His Majesty at a solemn Mass in the Cathedral of Lisbon on January 30, 1502. There, with all pomp and ceremony, the admiral received the royal standard from the hands of his monarch as the visible insignia of his command and was regaled with a speech from the throne extolling his merits. Alberto Cantino, the diplomatic agent of the Duke of Ferrara, was a witness of the ceremony, and there is in existence his letter to the duke describing it. As this account has appeared only in a pamphlet of which but ninety-nine copies were printed, it may be of interest here to see the scene through Cantino's eyes:

Today, the thirtieth [January, 1502], in the cathedral, the Most Serene King of Portugal installed as Admiral of the Indies one certain Dom Vasco . . . I should not forget [to describe] the ceremony which took place on the occasion of delivering the standard to the above-mentioned admiral.

First the sovereign went to Mass with great pomp, and after it had been celebrated the aforesaid Vasco, wearing a long surtout of crimson satin of the French type, lined with ermine, and a beret and tunic matching the surtout, and adorned with a neck chain of gold, placed himself at the side of the king, who was surrounded by his entire court.

A lord advanced to the center of the circle and delivered a speech praising the greatness and the virtues of His Lordship the King, to the degree that in all the parts of his discourse he exalted his glory above that of Alexander the Great.

Then, turning toward the admiral, he extolled his virtues and those of his ancestors in an abundance of words, recalling that by his genius and his courage he had discovered all this part of India.

When the oration was finished the herald-at-arms held out a book in his hand and caused the aforesaid Dom Vasco to swear eternal fidelity to the king and to his descendants. Then he [Vasco] knelt before the prince [king] who drew a ring from his own hand and slipped it on his finger.

Then a naked sword was given to the admiral, who was still kneeling. He took it in his right hand and received the standard in his left hand.

This done he rose and kissed the king's hand, as did all the lords and gentlemen. . . .

Finally, the ceremony was terminated by [the playing of] superb music.

After the conclusion of the ceremonies the participants marched in solemn procession to the river front.

The first two squadrons of the fleet sailed from the mouth of the Tagus on February 10, 1502, "em dia de Nossa Senhora da Março." Estavão da Gama followed with his ships on April 1 of the same year.

The first landfall of the voyage was the group of the Canary Islands, and thence the course was set southeast. At the end of February the Cape Verde Islands were sighted, and the ships put in at Porto Dala for wood and water. While this work was being carried on, a caravel arrived from São Jorge de Mina, on the west coast of Africa (now the Gold Coast), "under the command of Fernando de Montaroyo, and bringing 250 marks of gold, all in bracelets and jewels, which the negroes were accustomed to wear."

Three distinguished persons were traveling on the admiral's flagship. One was an ambassador returning from Lisbon to his sovereign, the Raja of Cannanore, and the two others were Hindu nobles of the aristocracy of the Indian State of Cochin. All three had been conveyed to Portugal by Cabral that they might see and appreciate the riches, power, and state of the Lusitanian kingdom. During their stay in Europe the agents of Venice, fearful of the rapidly growing Portuguese control of the Indian trade, had disparaged and made light of Portugal's political and economic position, and it was suspected that the Indians were carrying home with them an unfavorable report on the kingdom. The admiral immediately decided to use the arrival of the gold-laden ship to impress his passengers. Using Gaspar da Índia, who was with him as interpreter, he ordered the treasure brought out and spread before them, casually telling them "that ordinarily twelve to fifteen ships brought a like quantity of gold each year to Dom Manuel, King of Portugal and Lord of Mina. At this the Indians marveled greatly and admitted that the Venetians had represented Portuguese conditions far otherwise to them, but now they had seen for themselves and believed the words of Gama . . . and the case was his."

The author of *Calcoen* went ashore at Porto Dala and has left his visual impressions of the Cape Verde Islanders: "There the folk go entirely naked, both men and women. They are black, and have no shame since they wear no clothes and embrace their men openly like she-monkeys, and have no ideas of good or evil."

On June 14, 1502, the fleet anchored off the port of Sofala, on the east coast of Africa. Sofala (Arabic, *Saflá*—low ground) was an unhealthy city notable only as the export port for gold mined in the Monomotapa region of the interior. Here there was also a considerable trade in hippopotamus teeth—whiter, harder, and of better color than elephant ivory. The inhabitants were described as carrying assagais (Berber, *zaghay*—throwing spears) and using "arrows of middle size, the arrows not so long as those of the English." *

Jan Huyghen van Linschoten, the Dutchman who visited the East from 1583 to 1588, recounts that "there are some Moores [blacks] that carry other Moores on their backs like beasts, and are whollie accustomed there unto as if they were Horses, Moyles or Asses." †

Continuing the voyage after a short stop at Moçambique, the fleet arrived at the island of Kilwa, at the mouth of the Coavo River. It was a rich city, with fine houses of stone, whose people "all goe naked," or very slightly clad. Gama remembered that the Emir Ibrahim had treated Cabral badly and had refused to accept Christianity on his demand. This natural refusal was taken for impudence and hostility. Gama sent word that he would burn the town to the ground if Ibrahim would not submit to the Portuguese and pay tribute to Manuel. The helpless emir was forced to submit and swear fealty to the king. As guarantee for the payment of the tribute demanded, one Mohammed Ankoni, citizen of Kilwa (whom the Emir suspected of plotting to usurp his throne), was handed over to Gama. Mohammed knew that the sheik had no intention of paying the tribute from his own treasury and that the Portuguese would kill him, so he paid out the 2,000 mitcals (about

---

* The Portuguese had become well acquainted with English arrows through the English archers sent by John of Gaunt during the war with Spain.

† May this be the origin of Sinbad the Sailor's Old Man of the Sea in the *Arabian Nights*?

$5,000)* demanded and was released forthwith. The admiral received the money and never inquired who paid it. The important thing for him was that he had obtained both the submission of Kilwa's ruler and the coveted tribute.

The Flemish account has the following observations on Sofala and its people:

When, moreover, the king comes out of his court, they throw rice and water on his head, and they are very happy, clap their hands, sing, and leap about. The king and all the people, men and women, go naked, except that they wear an apron over their natural parts, and go every day to bathe in the sea. There are oxen without horns, but they bear on their backs a kind of saddle. There are also sheep with great tails, larger than were ever seen, and in these tails there is no bone, and the tail is worth more than half a sheep. . . . Moreover, figs grow there which are as large as two handbreadths.

From Sofala, Vicente Sodré's squadron (which joined Gama there) proceeded to Moçambique to await Gama, who wished to remain and explore the possibilities of Sofala for trade. The Fleming tells us of the natives of Caffraria and how the people live in walled cities. He tells of a conversation with a native of the country who had been taken as a slave by the ruler of Sofala, and how Caffraria "abounds in silver, gold, precious stones, and riches." Gama was able to obtain some of this gold in trade at Sofala.

Prefabrication of vessels is evidently not a modern invention, for at Moçambique a caravel was quickly constructed of sections brought from Portugal for the purpose and was put into service as a station ship for the African coast.

After remaining several weeks and erecting a factory for trade on the island, the fleet sailed. They were scarcely on their way when the ship of João da Fonseca was wrecked on the river bar.† By good fortune the crew was rescued and the cargo taken off, but the vessel itself was abandoned.

Before leaving Kilwa the admiral drew up the following instructions for all Portuguese ships arriving in Kilwa—instructions now in the National Library of Lisbon:

I, Admiral Dom Vasco, and so forth, give notice to all captains of whatever ships of my Lord the King, which arrive at this Port of

---

* Barros states that the sum was about 500 mitcals ($1,250).

† Castanheda states that the ship was that of Antônio Fernandez.

Quiloa, that I came here the 12 of the present month of July, 1502, and wished to treat with the king, in order to establish peace and amity with him, and that he did not wish to treat with me, but treated me very discourteously, wherefore I armed myself, together with all my people, prepared to destroy him, and drew up my vessels before his house and ran them up to the beach, and called upon him with far more rudeness than that with which he had met me. And he saw that it was to his interest to submit, and he came and I established peace and amity with him on the condition that he pay the King my Lord, 1,500 gold mitcals each year as tribute, and would pay at once the 1,500 mitcals for the present year in which we are, and that he avow himself a vassal of His Highness . . . and I notify all in general and command those arriving in these parts where I am that you should make no delay here but immediately continue on your way to Melinde, and if you do not meet me there to go on to Angediva, and if you do not reach me there to follow on the way to Cannanore, and to keep watch day and night in order that you do not pass me by.

While still at Kilwa, Vasco was joined on July 23 by Estavão da Gama and three of his ships, the others having been separated from them in a storm. Before sailing, Gama, suspecting the King of Kilwa, decided to teach him a lesson. Inviting him to visit his ship, he seized him and threatened "to hold him under the water until he died, and forced him to promise to be vassal of King Manuel and to pay tribute."

The next port the admiral steered for was Malindi, about one hundred miles distant from Kilwa, but was prevented by contrary winds and currents.

At Cape Santa Maria trading negotiations were carried on with the Moors, and the course was set for the Indian coast. From the accounts, Vasco did not sail direct across the Indian Ocean but nearer the land, past southern Arabia, and down the Indian coast.

The first place sighted was Cambay, which the *Calcoen* tells us is six hundred miles from "the city of Mecca where is buried Mahomet, the devil of the pagans.* A brief stop was next made at Goa, later to become the metropolis of Portuguese India.

"From there we proceeded and arrived at an island called Angediva, where we took on water and wood, and we also took ashore our sick, at least three hundred of them, and there we killed a lizard [crocodile] which measured not less than five feet

* Mohammed is buried in Medina, 250 miles northeast of Mecca.

long." During this part of the voyage scurvy broke out, and in spite of all efforts to curb it, over one-third of the crew were attacked, very many of whom died.

While at Angediva the ship of Ruy Mendes de Brito joined those of Dom Vasco, and from this point the narrative of the expedition is supplemented by the account of Thomé Lopes. Fourteen days later the last of the ships of Estavão da Gama joined the fleet at Monte Dely, and Vasco took over command of all the assembled ships.

The ships next arrived at Cannanore; and there Gama (again to quote the *Calcoen*) awaited the ships from Mecca, "and these are the ships which bring spices to our lands, and we wished to destroy them and thus the King of Portugal would alone have the spices there [in India] brought together."

After some days an Arab ship, the *Meri,* was sighted coming from the west. It was a vessel belonging to a brother of Khoja Kassim of Calicut on its return voyage from Mecca. In addition to a cargo of merchandise it carried 380 * passengers, men, women, and children, mostly people returning from a pilgrimage to the holy city to their homes in Calicut. The Portuguese commander gave. chase and quickly overhauled the Arab ship, which surrendered without resistance, as it would have been futile against such overwhelming numbers. Gama ordered the cargo to be handed over and all arms surrendered. The Arabs thereat denied possessing anything of value. Thereupon the admiral had two of them thrown into the sea, whereat the others confessed that they did carry some valuable cargo. The best of this was loaded on the ship of Diogo Fernandes Correa for the king, and the rest was distributed among Gama's crews. The transfer of cargo occupied two days. The admiral suspected that much was still concealed by the Mohammedans and that perhaps all the weapons had not been handed over. Thereupon, though he had met with no resistance and had pillaged a peaceful ship of a country with which he was not at war, Gama terminated this inexcusable act of piracy with the most dastardly and ferocious act of his whole career. Cold-bloodedly he ordered the passengers to be locked in the hold of the *Meri,* the ship to be set afire, and all on it burned to death. This, says Castanheda, he did in revenge for attacks made by the Moors on Cabral.

* The numbers vary in the account from 200 to 380.

The bombardiers to whom the horrible task was assigned set fire to the ship in several places, and the Portuguese vessels drew away far enough to be safe from the flames. The doomed Arabs, hearing and smelling the fire, managed to break out and rushed about the deck with buckets and axes, stamping out the fire which had entered the hull through the shot holes made by the Portuguese. Realizing the horrible fate awaiting them, they prepared to sell their lives dearly with the few weapons which they had managed to conceal. But first they made one more despairing plea for mercy. The women ran to the bulwarks, shrieking, wailing, and holding up their babies in their arms, pointing to them and to the few ornaments on their arms and fingers, lamenting pitifully in their native tongues and trying with wild gesticulations to melt the heart of the cruel unbeliever. It was all of no avail. Gama, who was on Estavão's ship, gave orders to grapple with the Arab craft and to set it afire again. He stood at a window of his cabin, looking stonily out onto the deck of the doomed vessel—a scene out of the Inferno, with black smoke and red and orange flames billowing out from the decks and hold of the *Meri*; the men, singed and fire-blackened, struggling pitifully to beat out the flames; the women and children screaming, running about to escape the flames and the missiles the Portuguese were now showering on them, while above all rose the derisive howls and shouts of the Portuguese pirate crews. In their frenzy the Arabs seized blazing sticks and timbers and flung them onto the decks of the Portuguese vessels, and Gama's men were kept busy extinguishing the flames. Dom Vasco could not be moved from his bloody decision. He brutally gave the order to board the ship and fire it again where the flames had been extinguished. The Portuguese vessels again closed in, the crews leaping from their high bulwarks onto the low-lying deck of the Arab. They met a fierce, insane resistance, the resistance of men fighting for their very lives and for those of their loved ones. The decks were slippery with blood, and again and again they repulsed the waves of Portuguese coming over the side.

Night fell, and the Portuguese ships drew off in fear that they in turn might be boarded or set afire by the despairing Arabs. The latter, exhausted and helpless, clung to the slender hope that wind and current might carry them far enough away during the hours of darkness to make good their escape even though the Portuguese vessels were all about them. Throughout the night the Arabs could be heard praying to Allah and calling upon Mohammed to save them. So the unequal struggle, unbelievable as it appears, continued for four days and four nights, the Portuguese repeatedly setting the ship on fire and the Arabs doggedly stamping out the flames. Though much of the ship was burned and many Arabs had been drowned when they threw themselves from the blazing deck into the sea, Gama's crews were beginning to weary of the fight, for they were losing men, ammunition, and time over a single looted vessel, no longer of any value to them. At this critical moment the Mohammedans were betrayed and destroyed by one of their own people. Lopes tells the tale:

The admiral went to the ship *Leonanda* and discussed the matter with six or seven other leaders of the fleet . . . that they had pursued [the fight] for four days and four nights with none of them being able to grapple with it, and only as they passed by it could they fire on it with bombards, and already our people were resolved not to continue further, when one of the Moors who had leaped into the sea came to tell our captain that if he would spare his life he would swim out and attach a rope to the hinge of the rudder of the ship, so as to set fire to it, and putting this into effect the admiral granted him his life and handed him over to João de Vera. He had with him coins [*xerafims*] of gold, and told of the great wealth which had been on the ship, and which had been thrown into the sea, moreover of the great quantities of provisions which it carried: he told us also that in the casks of honey and of oil they had hidden much gold, silver, and jewels, throwing everything overboard when they saw that we did not intend to spare their lives. And their fury was such that several times, in the midst of the melee we saw men wounded by arrows tear them out and fling them back at us by hand, and continuing to fight as though they felt no pain. And so, after so many struggles the admiral set that ship ablaze with much cruelty and without the least pity, and it burned with every one aboard.

Of all that shipload of helpless humanity, only some twenty boys were spared to be converted to Christianity and become monks at Belém! And none of all this atrocity was done in an outburst of passion, wrath, or revenge, but with cold, calculated, and unfeeling ferocity. It is an ineffaceable stain on the grim character of Dom Vasco da Gama, though the contemporary accounts do not seem to have found his action reprehensible.

After the destruction of the ship from Mecca, Gama sailed for Cannanore, with whose rajah he had sealed a pact of friendship on his first voyage—a man who was overjoyed at finding in the Portuguese an ally against his enemy the samorin of Calicut. It will be recalled that the same ruler had also aided Cabral during his visit in the country. There, says the author of *Calcoen*, "we bought all kinds of spices, and the king received us in great state and brought . . . two elephants and other strange animals which I cannot name." The rajah met Gama with great ceremony. Then, says Castanheda, the king and the admiral embraced, and they seated themselves on two high-backed chairs which Dom Vasco had ordered brought for this purpose, and the king sat on the chair to please Gama, though it was against his custom, and Gama gave him two hand basins filled with thick branches of coral, a thing very beautiful to see, and their friendship was sealed."

From Indian sources we have a more detailed account. "The King of Chirakkal came to the seashore with four thousand Nair swordsmen to greet the admiral, and their interview took place on a platform at the seashore. The rajah was given a sword of gold and enamel. A commercial treaty was discussed, and shortly thereafter the fleet sailed on, anchoring off Calicut on October 30, 1502."

The samorin was now aroused and frightened, for Gama was before his city with a large fleet; and the ruler at last realized that he had made a fatal error in scorning the admiral on his first voyage and in not preventing the treacherous attack on Cabral's men. He moved with alacrity and sent out officials with offers of friendship. Dom Vasco treated the envoys with contempt, telling them that his king could carve out a ruler equal to the samorin from the trunk of a palm. He demanded as the price of peace the immediate banishment of every Mohammedan in Calicut. To impress the samorin that he meant to follow up his ultimatum with action, the admiral perpetrated another inexcusable and inhuman outrage. On the arrival of the fleet a number of fishermen had put out in their boats to sell their catch to the crews. Gama had thirty-eight of the poor innocent fellows seized. Protesting and struggling, they were dragged on the ship and hanged from the yard-arms. At the same time Gama ordered his ships to bombard the city, which possessed but few, if any, cannon with which to reply.

At nightfall Gama ordered the bodies of the hanged men taken down. Their heads, hands, and feet were cut off and heaped up in a boat, and their dismembered bodies were flung overboard to be washed inshore by the tide. A message in Arabic was fastened to the heap of hands, feet, and heads, pointing out that this was but a warning and a forecast of the fate of the city if it resisted. Correa adds that the letter suggested that the samorin make a fine curry of the severed heads and limbs. The boat was then cast off to drift ashore.

The picture of the horrible night that followed is painted in lurid colors by Lopes. The inhabitants of Calicut gathered in crowds along the shore, staring at the ghastly sight; while many waited at the water's edge as the headless and limbless torsos were rolled up on the sand by the incoming tide, trying in the light of smoky torches to recognize their kin by their clothing or otherwise. When any were recognized they were carried off by their relatives, and the monotonous death chants of the Hindus could be heard rising and falling through the night.

On the following day the bombardment of the city was renewed, and a heavily laden ship which had been seized at the shoreline the day before was looted and then burned.

After committing this further act of piracy, Gama sailed off with his fleet to Cochin to load spices, leaving six ships and a caravel, under the command of Vicente Sodré, before Calicut to cut off any entry there by ships. Dom Vasco arrived at Cochin on November 7 and began loading his vessels with spices and other goods while he entered into a trade agreement and an exchange of gifts with the Rajah of Cochin.

Meanwhile, the Rajah of Cannanore sent a messenger with the information that he, too, had enough cargo to fill several of the Portuguese ships, and Gama dispatched two ships to take on the merchandise.

On January 3 a Brahmin and his son, together with two distinguished citizens of Calicut, arrived in Cochin, bringing letters from the samorin, who had tried in vain to attack and break Sodré's blockade, asking that the admiral return to Calicut to sign a treaty of peace and commerce. Gama departed in the *Flor de la*

Mar, commanded by his nephew, dispatching a caravel at the same time to his uncle at Cannanore, ordering him to join the *Flor de la Mar* at Calicut. The invitation of the samorin was a trap set to capture or kill Gama. During the night the latter found his ship surrounded by Arab vessels, and it was with difficulty that he escaped destruction from their fire. Had not Vicente Sodré come swiftly to his rescue with a ship and two caravels, the Portuguese would have fared very badly in the encounter.

Gama immediately took his revenge. He had released the Brahmin, but he strung up the boy and the other two prisoners at his yard-arm and sailed up and down several times before the city with his ship's gruesome ornaments swinging in the wind. Then he returned to Cochin and completed the loading of his vessels. As the work was drawing to an end, word was received that the Arabs were gathering a great fleet to attack the Portuguese. Gama immediately summoned all the ships of his armada to Cochin, and on February 10, 1503, sailed away to Calicut again. There, on the 12th of the month, he engaged the Rajah's fleet in combat. It was evidently not a very serious engagement. After a short encounter the Arab vessels fled, and with the dropping of the wind the heavier Portuguese ships could not pursue.

And now the admiral deemed that he had finished the task assigned him. The monsoon favorable for the return voyage was at hand, and on February 20 the fleet sailed from Cannanore straight for Moçambique. To quote the Flemish narrative further:

On March 5th we set our course to the southeast, 100 miles out at sea. On March 29th we had sailed at sea some 1,200 miles from Portugal; and we began to lose sight of the Great Bear, and the sun was over our heads, so that on April 2nd we could see no ghost or shadow of anything, nor any constellation. In this sea we saw fish with wings to fly so far that they could be shot at with the cross-bow, and they are as large as a mackerel, a herring, or a sardine. And for a space of about 300 miles we saw seagulls, black with white breasts, and they had tails like swans, and are larger than wild pigeons. They catch those flying fish even as they go flying by. On April 11th we had traveled so far ahead that at mid-day on the bridge we saw the sun toward the north. At the same time we saw no constellations of which we could avail ourselves, only our compasses and our charts.

Then we came to another latitude, where there was no living creature, neither fish nor flesh nor any other thing. On April 20th a contrary wind [began, which] blew us for five whole weeks [and] which drove us 1,000 miles out of our direct course, and for that reason we went 12 days without seeing land or sand. On May 22nd it was winter here, and the days did not have in this latitude more than eight hours' duration, and there was a great tempest of rain, hail, snow, thunder, and lightning. There was a clearing in the sky near the Cape of Good Hope, and it was stormy. When we arrived at the Cape we steered our course northeast. On June 10th we again saw the Great Bear and the North Star, and we again had knowledge of the sky, with which we were very content.

After a succession of storms, calms, and contrary winds, two ships sent with news of the voyage arrived in Lisbon on September 1, 1503. Dom Vasco and the main part of the fleet sailed up the Tagus and dropped anchor on October 11, 1503. "Ende alsoe," concludes the *Calcoen* narrative, "quamen wy wenderom behonden in Poertegael" (and so we returned safe and sound to Portugal). Deo Gratias.

Thus ended the second voyage of Dom Vasco da Gama to India. Again he had brought his sovereign added glory and gold. He had signed treaties and added far-off vassals and tributaries to the Portuguese crown, and he had laid the foundations of the conquest and exploitation of the East African Coast and the Indian seas for his people. But in so doing he had left behind him a hideous broad trail of fire, blood, and hatred—of the blood of innocents, needlessly shed, and of hatreds that could have been avoided by the exercise of tact, patience, and prudence. He had sown the wind. His successors were to reap the whirlwind, and in a few short generations his countrymen were to be stripped of the most valuable of their conquests and possessions. For himself, Dom Vasco had again given all too much evidence of the steely ruthlessness of his character, of his cold-blooded cruelty indulged in even when needless or futile. One seeks in vain in the record of the second voyage to India to find traits that might redeem him and soften the judgment of history and of ethics on this man who seemed to be, as Garcia da Orta remarked of Magellan, "the devil entered into a Portuguese."

CHAPTER XX

PORTUGAL, 1503–1524

Here is al the trat of the shippys that comyth from calicut and malaca with spices. . . . hit is called lusitania.
—ROGER BARLOW, *A Brief Summe of Geographie* (1540)

I

HERE has been much discussion among historians as to the treatment of Vasco da Gama by King Manuel after the former's return from his second Indian voyage. A number of documents are missing from the Portuguese archives, but those still extant indicate that on the one hand the admiral was not given what had been promised him, and on the other that he was grasping and arbitrary in his demands. His nature and that of his sovereign, whose niggardliness and overweening pride are well known, clashed. Without presenting the documents in full, we can glean from them the relationship between Dom Manuel and his admiral.

Nothing definite is known of Gama's movements between his return to Lisbon from Calicut in October, 1503, and March, 1507. The picture can be reconstructed in part from documents in the Torre do Tombo—repository of the Portuguese archives.

It will be recalled (p. 204) that by royal letters patent, issued December 4, 1499, Vasco da Gama was granted the seignory of his native town of Sines, the crown promising to give the owners, the Order of São Tiago, another town in exchange, and obtaining a papal dispensation for the transfer. The Order, however, refused to surrender the town.

The impatient and irascible Gama, at some time after his second return from India, decided to brook no more delays. So with his wife and family he entered Sines, took up his residence there, and began building operations as though he were really in possession as the lord of the town. Dom Jorge, Grand Master of the Order of São Tiago, thereupon appealed to the king, who issued a decree at Thomar, dated March 21, 1507. In most peremptory terms the admiral, his wife, and family were ordered to leave Sines within thirty days thereafter, and they were forbidden ever to enter the town precincts again without permission of the Grand Master, under penalty of a fine of 500 cruzados, and the usual punishment "meted out to those who do not obey the command of their king and lord." The same decree ordered suspension of any building operations that might have been commenced in Sines at Gama's orders, with like penalties for disobedience. Thus the great navigator was in a most humiliating fashion driven from the town of his birth, to which he felt justly entitled under the grant made him after his first voyage. As one modern Portuguese historian * strongly expresses it :

In the veins of the bastard [Dom Jorge] flowed royal blood, and this was sufficient to cause D. Manuel to force genius, glory and heroism to bow before it, and to oblige Vasco da Gama to recognize that his deeds and his services did not equal in value the few drops of regal blood which, in an hour of delirious pleasure, Don John II had transmitted to the veins of the son of D. Anna de Mendonça.

The admiral immediately obeyed the royal order and moved from Sines with his wife and family, but one may easily picture with what resentment, particularly as the decree was communicated to him through his own uncle, João da Gama. It is evident that King Manuel made efforts to placate the offended Gama, and existing documents reveal many grants and privileges made him. After the return from his first voyage he had been granted pensions amounting to \$3,500 a year. On February 4, 1504, this pension was increased to \$5,500. On June 13, 1513, a grant was made to him, relieving him of any charges for duty or freight on any goods brought in by him from any province of India. On August 22, 1515, a license was granted to Gama to hunt in the royal preserves of Niza, and on the same day letters patent were issued, granting him the right to send with the Indian fleet a representative to supervise and protect his interests. On the 29th of the same month Gama was granted an annual income of 200,000 reis from the excise taxes collected in Niza. On October 9, 1515, an annual salary of 6,000 reis was allotted to him as Admiral of India, and on October 19,

* Manuel Pinheiro Chagas, in Aragão's *Vasco da Gama e Vidigueira*, 3rd ed.

1515, a royal decree, later confirmed by John III, exempted the discoverer "and all the members of his house" from any real-estate or excise taxes wherever he should reside or own property. On December 17, 1519, a royal decree, issued in Évora, made him the grant of Vidigueira and of Villa de Frade. Letters patent were issued awarding him all fines collected from poachers in Niza. A law of March 30, 1521, granted Gama certain anchorages in India "by virtue of his office as Admiral," a law confirmed by a decree of John III. On the following day an additional anchorage for his use in the river of Goa was granted him.*

From what little can be learned from surviving tradition, it is probable that Gama went from Sines to Évora, the city of his boyhood education, and lived there for some time with his family. Tradition also points out some houses in which he is supposed to have lived and on the façades of which he is supposed to have ordered people, trees, and animals of India painted. In the middle of the nineteenth century these pictures were still to be seen above the doorways. The street on which the houses stand is known as the Street of Painted Houses (Rua das Casas Pintadas). Here Gama lived for twelve years, perhaps waiting to be recalled to the service of the king.

The admiral's wish—if he really desired to serve his country— was not realized during Manuel's lifetime. In 1518, deciding that he was condemned to live out the rest of his life in obscurity, he petitioned King Manuel for permission to leave Portugal and to offer his services to some foreign nation. He was not the first Portuguese to desire to offer his services to another country. Manuel had refused to consider Magellan's plans for a voyage, and the latter had, in October, 1517, left Portugal and offered his services to Charles of Spain.† The king's answer to Gama has been preserved:

FRIEND ADMIRAL: We are in receipt of this petition which you have presented, using the title of "Count" which you say we promised you, but which you have taken as though it were already conferred. We,

---

* Ca' Messer, the Venetian living in Lisbon at this time, remarked in a letter that Gama "is not very grateful [to the king], for he [Gama] is a man of bad temper, and unreasonable."

† Likewise, it may be noted, Columbus presented his projects to John II of Portugal. He was dismissed empty-handed and Portugal lost the opportunity of being the patron of the discoverer of the New World

because of the services you have rendered us, do not consent to give you the permission which you ask, to leave our kingdom, but by these presents we command you to remain in our kingdom until the end of December of this year, and we hope that by that time you will have seen the error which you are committing, and that you will desire to serve us as is befitting, and not to take the extreme step which you propose. But if at the end of that time you persist in the same plan of leaving our kingdom we shall, although this would cause us great regret, not hinder your departure, together with your wife, your children and your movable possessions. Done at Lisbon, August 17, 1518, by the Secretary.

THE KING.

This order may have been prompted by the departure of Magellan.

The time thus gained by King Manuel was employed in trying to find a proper reward for Gama. He had endeavored to cede to the admiral the town of Villa Franca da Xira, in the Valley of the Tagus, twenty miles from Lisbon, but the negotiations never were completed. Finally Dom Jayme, Duke of Bragança, a nephew of the king, signified his willingness to surrender the town of Vidigueira and the title of Count that went with the seignory, and on October 24 the king gave his consent to the exchange. The agreement was signed on November 4, 1519. The duke surrendered the towns of Vidigueira and Villa de Frade, and Gama surrendered to him the hereditary king's pension of 1,000 cruzados (400,000 reis) and a cash payment of 4,000 cruzados in gold. This transaction was signed at Évora on November 7, 1519,* whereupon the king, on December 17, confirmed the transfer and made it irrevocable for all time, "in virtue of the many and important services which we have received from the said admiral, especially in the discovery of the Indies—which have redounded and redound—to the crown of our kingdom—and in general to its inhabitants and to those of all Christianity." Thus, in a little over a year after Manuel's letter to Gama forbidding him to leave the kingdom, the admiral obtained his coveted seignory, even though it was not that of his beloved Sines.

On December 29, 1519, a representative of the navigator took possession of Vidigueira, and on the same day the king, in Évora, conferred upon Vasco da Gama "the title of Count of the City of

---

* Gama's wife's name appears in full for the first time in this document.

Vidigueira, and we create him Count [of that city] with all the prerogatives and franchises enjoyed by the Counts of the kingdom by virtue of the very great and signal service which Vasco da Gama performed in the discovery of the Indies." Twenty years had passed since Gama's return from his great voyage. Such is the gratitude of kings.[1]

There is little evidence of the residence of Vasco da Gama in Vidigueira. One authority states that "probably in 1520 he removed there from Évora . . . and that in the four years from 1520–1523 the development by the admiral of his new dominions doubtless occupied his time." Beyond this gratuitous and baseless speculation, we have no information as to what Dom Vasco's activities were before his appointment as Viceroy of India in 1524, except one brief remark. Frei Luiz de Sousa (1555–1632), in his *Annals of King John III*, mentions among those present when King John took the oath as king (December, 1521), "Dom Vasco da Gama, Count of Vidigueira, Admiral of the Seas of India." Other than in this notation, history is silent.[2] The real reasons for Gama's inactivity between the years 1502 and 1524 will probably never be known. The misunderstanding and bitterness over his failure to receive Sines may well be one. His stubborn and uncompromising nature, his hot temper, irritability, and his greed may have been others. It is easy to see that there could be no love lost between a man of his nature and his king.

2

Manuel was a man to whom, seemingly, real gratitude and appreciation for faithful and meritorious services rendered him were unknown.* Other traits of the king also probably entered into his relations with Gama—the jealousy of a very mediocre man, his vanity, his capriciousness, and his fear of giving too much power to any one of his officials.† Manuel's career was a remarkable one of prosperity and fame, which were both entirely unearned and un-

---

* Duarte Pacheco Pereira, one of the greatest public servants of the reign, and author of the *Esmeraldo de Situ Orbis* (1505), was allowed, after a religious procession in his honor, to die in neglect, disgrace, and misery in the Hospital of the Misericórdia.

† It is interesting to note that one English author believed that there was no hostility between Gama and his sovereign, but that the admiral's marriage, his raising of a family, and the management of his estates offered many more inducements than the hard life of the commander of a fleet. '

deserved. He was not a great man, nor was he a wise king. The Persians have a proverb: "An ounce of luck is equal to a pound of talent"—and Manuel had the luck. That luck has earned him the name through the centuries of Manuel the Fortunate. The span of his lifetime saw the greatest, most famous, and most prosperous period of Portugal's history. He had neither distinction nor an attractive personality, but he had loyalty to his country and good fortune at home and abroad. The discovery of India was the most decisive event in Portugal's history and fixed the direction and course of that history for a hundred years. Manuel saw his country at the zenith of its national life, but, though he could not know it, the seeds of decay at home and abroad had been sown before his death.*

Damião de Goes (1501–1574), in his *Chronicle of Dom Manuel*, has left the following description of the king:

He was of good stature, rather delicate than stout, with a round head, which he held erect, covered with chestnut hair. His face was round also. His eyes, which were greenish, had a pleasant expression, and altogether he appeared handsome and cheerful. His arms, which were fleshy, were so long that the fingers of the hands reached below his knees. His legs, long and well made, were in accordance with the proportions of his body. . . . His voice was clear and well modulated.

He discussed matters while dining, and always had learned men and foreigners by him. He was very musical, summoning musicians from all over Europe. . . . He was the first European monarch to possess elephants, brought from India, and once he had paraded through the city [Lisbon] a rhinoceros and a panther, gifts from the King of Ormuz [in Persia]. He was chaste, clean in person and well dressed, wearing something new nearly every day. He gave away so many clothes that at his death there were few at court who did not possess some of them. He was a good businessman, and worked quickly. He was temperate in eating and drank only water. Nor would he use oil or eat food cooked in it. He paid little attention to what he ate. He was a good and strict Catholic.

This description, written by a court chronicler, sheds no light on the character of the man. His acts and his decrees are far more revealing.

* His shameful treatment and final expulsion of the Jews from his realm, in order to win the favor of Spain, was one of the causes of Portugal's economic deterioration, even during his lifetime.

At the end of 1521 an epidemic swept over Portugal. It did not spare the person of the king, who, in the words of the chronicler, "rendered up his soul to his creator, on the ninth day of his illness, in his palace in Lisbon on December 13." He was buried in the Monastery of the Jeronimos at Belém and was succeeded by his nineteen-year-old eldest son, who assumed the title of John III. All unknowing that his country had passed the zenith of its power and prosperity, John celebrated his accession with great joy and ceremony.

He rode to his coronation mounted on a handsome gray horse. He was clad in a long brocade robe, with a long train lined with the fur of martens. He was preceded by a prince of the blood royal, bearing in his hands the baton of a marshal, while John's bridle was held by another royal prince. The third of the princes, who was also a cardinal, awaited him at the church, accompanied on foot by the Duke of Bragança, the Duke of Coimbra—and by the counts, many of whom walked . . . the illustrious Count of Vidigueira, Dom Vasco da Gama, and so forth.

The chronicler, Garcia de Resende (1470–1536), who lived through three reigns, commented on the occasion that "never had he seen such pomp," and that "the King of the world appeared in power and in perfection." This John III was the young king who was to recall Vasco da Gama to his country's service and to send him as viceroy to India.

The Lisbon of 1521, when John III ascended the throne, was probably the greatest commercial city of Europe. It had spread far beyond the limits of the city of John II. The anchorages of the Tagus were crowded with ships from India, Africa, the Mediterranean ports, and the harbors of northern Europe. The markets of the city were overflowing with the products of Asia and Africa, brought in Portuguese bottoms. From Afghanistan came musk. Sind and Cashmere sent their finely woven shawls and scarfs. From Gujarat came drugs, indigo, silks, gold, and precious stones. The bazaars overflowed with pepper, ginger, and every other manner of spices. Teak from the Farther Indies was heaped high. Men and women bargained for calicoes and brocades and the fine muslins of Bengal. Everywhere jewelry and precious stones were offered. From Cairo and Baghdad came fine weaves; from Persia, rugs and carpets; and from Arabia, frankincense and myrrh. Sejuia supplied fine metalwork; the Moluccas, cloves and nutmegs and mace.

Timor was stripped of its sandalwood for the Portuguese market, and ivorywork and silks and porcelains from far-off China were to be found by the connoisseur. Out of Africa came slaves, Moroccan leather, ebony, and elephants' tusks, as well as gold in nuggets and dust. Brazil was represented by sugar and whale oil and feather mantles. All this wealth poured unceasingly into Lisbon, the new center of world trade. Through her streets rode nobles and cavaliers with short-stirruped saddles, and bridles mounted in silver and gold. In the monastery at Belém stood the great monstrance wrought from the first gold brought from the East.* All Lisbon seemed to be rich and happy, with a future great beyond men's dreams. \

There was another side to this bright picture, a far darker side, which was to overshadow and finally eclipse the fortunes of Lisbon and Portugal. The little country had, in a generation, become first a fighting, then an exploring, and finally a trading country. Agriculture was gradually being neglected and disdained. The Holy Office had penetrated the land, the Jews and Moors had been expelled, and slaves were taking the place of free men. The country was being drained of its men, whom the colonies greedily absorbed and destroyed, and there were none in the tiny country to replace them. An early historian claimed that between 1497 and 1527, 80,000 Portuguese, mostly men, left the country for the Indies; and another declared that only one-tenth·of these ever returned to their homes in Portugal.

* It is believed by many that the goldsmith who made the work was the famous poet Gil Vicente.

NOTES

[1] Vidigueira and Villa de Frade are two villages which lie very near each other in the southern foothills of the Alemtejo, about 200 feet above sea level. The name Vidigueira is probably derived from "videiras" (vines), as wine is produced in the country thereabouts.

[2] In the clock tower of the Hermitage of the Holy Spirit in Vidigueira there is preserved a precious relic. It is the bell which strikes the hours and which the count-admiral ordered cast. It measures in inside height 64 cm. and in diameter, 59. It shows in relief on one side the cross of the Order of Christ, and on the other the arms of the Gamas, with the coat of arms bearing the additions which King Manuel granted him. Beginning outside, and around the lip, there is the following inscription in Gothic letters: "This bell the Count Dom Vasco Admiral of India caused to be cast in the year 1520" (Este sino mandou fazer o Sr. Conde Dom Vasco Almirante da India era da millcv vinte). This was probably one of the first gifts of Vasco da Gama, after the purchase of Vidigueira was consummated in 1519, to some church of the town. He was already a count, as the inscription states.

CHAPTER XXI

INDIA, 1502–1524

The Portuguese entered India with the sword in one hand and the Crucifix in the other; finding much gold they laid aside the Crucifix to fill their pockets.
                    —João de Castro, Viceroy of India, 1548

The first conquistadores of India appear to have been stimulated solely by the greed for gold, which almost invariably carries with it the thirst for blood.
                    —Alphonse Rabbe, *História de Portugal*

The Portuguese was not the corrupted in India. He was the corrupter, not the victim.
                    —Gilberto Freyre, *The Masters and the Slaves*

1

THE Portuguese people had an unparalleled opportunity to expand and develop through Gama's discovery of India. Unfortunately, they possessed certain characteristics which, from the first, militated against their success. They seem to have had no fixed ideals, a too-easy willingness to compromise with ethical principles, an unbelievably cold-blooded cruelty, combined with a stupidity and ineptitude in dealing with foreign, particularly with native, peoples, together with fanaticism and absolute hatred of peoples not of their faith. These foredoomed their empire in the Indies, in spite of dazzling successes at the outset, to a short life and a speedy decline.

2

The fleets which the king of Portugal sent out to India between 1500 and 1504 were merchantmen—armed, it is true—for no conquest seemed to be contemplated. All that was desired was the obtaining of monopolistic control of the export trade of India. During the first years of the century an effort was made to establish factories (warehouses and shipping facilities) in the friendly cities of Cochin, Cannanore, and Coalão. The king relied on the friendly rajahs and petty princes to protect the factories and the Portuguese who remained to carry on the trade. The constant quarrels and fighting with the samorin of Calicut, the most powerful state on the Malabar coast, not only made trade with that port almost impossible, but had a very deleterious effect on the relations between the Europeans and their Indian allies.

Events in India following Cabral's voyage changed the whole policy of the Portuguese government toward India. Valuable knowledge had been gained of the various ports, of the manners and customs, as well as of the fighting strength of the coastal Indian peoples. A very important factor in the policy was the discovery that the Indians were not a Christian people and were not, therefore, in the ethics of the time, entitled to any of the fundamental rights assumed by the Christian peoples to be their prerogatives. After several attacks by the Rajah of Calicut on the Portuguese in Cochin, King Manuel realized that dependence on scattered factories and the looting of native vessels could not continue. If Portugal was to maintain her place in the Indian trade, some sort of a system was necessary to maintain law and order and to assure a steady stream of merchandise flowing into Lisbon. It was decided to create a new office, that of Viceroy of India, the term of the viceroy to be three years. The first man selected was the navigator, Tristão da Cunha. When, however, he was stricken with temporary blindness, Dom Francesco d'Almeida was chosen. A wise and tried soldier, he sailed from Lisbon in March, 1505, clothed with full power to make treaties, regulate commerce, and, if necessary, to wage war. A system of government was prepared for any lands that might be acquired. The beginning of the lack of manpower available in Portugal manifested itself even on this expedition. The fleet was large, and 1,500 soldiers sailed in it. But many of the sailors in one of the caravels were recruits from the farms. The tale is told that they knew so little of the sea that they did not know the difference between "starboard" and "port." The captain of the ship thereupon hung a bundle of garlic over one side and a bunch of onions over the other, and issued orders to the helmsman to "Garlic your helm" and "Onion your helm."

Almeida's aim was to secure the monopoly of the export trade of India for his king. He therefore planned to drive the Mohammedan traders from the sea, to replace them with Portuguese, and to divert all Indian trade, some of which passed through the Persian Gulf and the Red Sea, to the Cape route. On land his idea was to make alliances with the various princes, guaranteeing them the protection of the Portuguese ships in exchange for their promises to supply cargoes and guard the factories against attack.

Almeida's first act was to build and man a fort at Kilwa, on the East African coast, the second was to loot and destroy several towns near by! On his arrival in India a fort was built at Cannanore, which Gama had visited on his first voyage, and Portuguese were landed to settle in Cochin. Meanwhile, his ships had treated the Mohammedan traders with a high hand, killing and looting indiscriminately.

The Portuguese control of the sea was challenged by the Mameluke Sultan of Egypt, whose fleet, in 1508, attacked a Portuguese squadron and killed Almeida's son. The viceroy swore vengeance, and, meeting the Egyptian fleet at Diu, off the west coast of India, soundly defeated it on February 3, 1509, the artillery of the Europeans being far more than a match for the primitive weapons of the Egyptians and their allies from Calicut. Shortly after this victory Almeida's term as viceroy came to an end, and he was succeeded by Affonso d'Albuquerque,* though he held his office until 1509.†

D'Albuquerque had come out to the Indies in 1507, with orders to subdue the Persian city of Hormuz. Though there was no quarrel between Manuel and the boy king of Hormuz, D'Albuquerque saw no reason not to attack. Three towns were ruthlessly sacked and burned, and the slaughter of the helpless natives was horrible. The prisoners taken were all mutilated, the women having their noses and ears cut off, the men their noses and right hands. All this was done in cold blood, for the Portuguese were the aggressors, and very few of them had been killed. Hormuz surrendered after the Portuguese artillery had attacked the Persian fleet, an annual tribute was

* On the voyage home Almeida was killed while leading a punitive expedition against a tribe of Hottentots at Table Bay (Capetown).

† Only a short sketch of D'Albuquerque's term in India is possible here. His exploits in Arabia, Persia, and Malaya have no place in this narrative. The subject has been fully covered in Elaine Sanceau's *Indian Adventure* and elsewhere.

exacted, and a fort was built. To terrify the Persians still more completely, D'Albuquerque threatened the emissaries of the king that if he was interfered with he would "build the walls [of his fort] of Mohammedans' bones, nail their ears to the door, and set up his flagstaff on their skulls." Finally the Hormuz expedition failed because of the disloyalty of some of the Portuguese captains, and D'Albuquerque sailed for India. After a defeat by the Nairs of Calicut, the viceroy began to put into execution a plan for the control of the East. We are interested here only in the Indian portion of his policy, which involved the occupation of Goa as a colony and as the center of Portuguese power on the Indian coast. This, in the words of the historian Jayne, "meant for Portugal the final step from mere command of the sea to territorial empire in the Orient."

Goa (from the Hindu *Gomant*, "the district of cowherds") is an old city on the central west coast of India, just north of 15° N. latitude, and was, next to Calicut, the principal seaport on the coast. It is situated on an island formed by tidal creeks. Its soil is fertile and it was easily defended by a fleet. It was a most strategic place in which to found a colony. D'Albuquerque sailed for the city in January, 1510, with a fleet of twenty-three ships. The town, to his surprise, surrendered after one of its small forts was captured, and on March 1 the governor entered the city and took possession of it, with all its warehouses, horses, elephants, and dockyards.

After only two months of peace a Mohammedan force of 60,000 attacked the forts. When D'Albuquerque saw that he was in danger of being defeated, he retreated from the island, but first ordered a massacre of the inhabitants. He spared a few of the richest men for ransom, "the more beautiful of the women to marry, and some of the children to turn into Christians." He and his men then fought their way to their ships. Fortunately for the viceroy, fourteen ships arrived from Portugal, and he pressed them into his service. Attacking the city on November 20, D'Albuquerque forced his way in and succeeded in retaking the island. After a solemn religious service of thanksgiving had been held, he issued orders to sack the city and to destroy every Mohammedan man, woman, and child remaining in it. Three hideous days of slaughter, rape, and torture followed. D'Albuquerque sent a dispatch to his sovereign that 6,000 men, women, and children had been massacred. In February, 1512, while

D'Albuquerque was away at Malacca, Goa was again besieged by the Shah of Bijapur, ruler of Goa, who had been driven out of the city. Caught between the governor's fleet and the fire from the walls, the Mohammedans were driven off. They surrendered nineteen Portuguese deserters. D'Albuquerque promised to spare their lives. He kept his word, but in a letter to his king he wrote, "I gave them their lives . . . but I ordered their noses, ears, right hands, and left thumbs to be cut off, for a warning and in memory of the treason and evil that they did." Half of the poor wretches died under the tortures, and the others dragged out a miserable existence. D'Albuquerque devoted much of his time to putting the administration of the Indian factories in a satisfactory condition. The fear inspired by his cruelty and efficiency was such that even the ruler of Calicut permitted the building of a Portuguese fort in his city.

In 1515, while compaigning in the Persian Gulf, D'Albuquerque received word that his term had expired (he had served as viceroy six years) and that his successor was to be Lopo Soares de Albergaria. A harsh and cruel man, D'Albuquerque none the less must be recognized as the real founder of the Portuguese dominion in India. His last letter to his king told the truth in a few lines:

Sire, I do not write to your Highness in my own hand because it trembles greatly when I do so, and this forecasts death. . . . As for the affairs of India . . . everything is settled. . . . And so I have done that with which your Highness charged me. . . . I advise you . . . that if you would keep India secure, continue to make it self-supporting.

The letter was signed by D'Albuquerque himself. After dispatching the letter, he set sail, mortally ill, from Hormuz to Goa. As the ship crossed the Goa bar, he had himself dressed as a commander of the order of São Tiago, with spurs on his feet and a sword in his belt. There he leaned against his cabin door and looked for the last time on the city which he had twice won for his sovereign. A few hours later, at sunrise, as the ship was dropping its anchor, he died. In the quaint language of the *Commentaries*:

So great was the weeping and lamentation that it seemed as though the very river of Goa itself was pouring itself out. . . . When they [the Hindus] beheld his body . . . his long beard reaching down to

his waist,* his eyes half open, they declared . . . that he was not
dead, but that the Gods had need of him for some other war, and
had sent for him.†

With a small fleet and badly trained and armed men, D'Albuquerque had established and maintained the control of the trade
routes of the Indian Ocean. He had founded a colonial empire and
had an understanding of the political and economic aspects, problems and duties of government. He was a real leader, and men followed him. His was a brutal, savage, fanatical, and ruthless age,
and it did not judge him harshly. All in all, he must be considered
one of the greatest among all those Europeans who have ruled in
India.

One of D'Albuquerque's colonial schemes for colonizing the
Indies should be mentioned here, for it had a devastating effect
on later efforts of the Portuguese to hold their dominions. It was the
plan to colonize by bringing men to India and having them marry
native women. To D'Albuquerque and his fellow countrymen this
was nothing abnormal. African slaves had been brought into the
country from the time of Prince Henry the Navigator and had
been absorbed into the population. The native women in India became nominally Christians but maintained their relations with their
people. The Portuguese quickly lost their vigor in the enervating
climate. Symptoms of decay set in very early. "This mixed breed,
the result of these unions, never invigorated by contact with the
sterner race, some of whose blood was in its veins, approximated
more and more the type of the country where it originated." ‡

Lopo Soares de Albergaria, the successor of D'Albuquerque, was
his very opposite, and his weakness, after D'Albuquerque's strength,
quickly had its effect on Portuguese relations with their allies and
subjects. Where D'Albuquerque would not allow Portuguese to
trade, Soares opened the door to every kind of abuse by permitting
rascals of all types to prey on legitimate Indian commerce, and even

---

* When Goa was retaken by the Mohammedans, D'Albuquerque vowed
never to cut his beard until he had retaken the city. Apparently he had never
cut his beard thereafter. The *Commentaries*, written by D'Albuquerque's
illegitimate half-caste son, make most interesting reading.

† Thus the first two Portuguese rulers in India died far from the land of
their birth, neither living to reap the honors that their services had deserved
at the hands of King Manuel.

‡ Whiteway, *The Rise of Portuguese Power in India*, p. 178.

piracy was soon rampant. Soares interfered in the administration at every point; and finally many of D'Albuquerque's finest officers, disgusted with such proceedings as the auctioning off of D'Albuquerque's private property to fill Soares's own treasure chest, left India.* After a thoroughly discreditable administration, Lopo Soares departed in 1518, hated and unregretted.

Lopo Soares was succeeded as governor by Diogo Lopes de Sequeira. His term, from 1518 to 1522, was not distinguished by any great events (in India), and he himself extorted wealth on every hand.

The fifth governor of India was Dom Duarte de Menezes, a thoroughgoing rascal, licentious and greedy even for his times. He arrived in India just three months before the death of King Manuel. After carrying on what seems to have been a perpetual war with Hormuz, Menezes turned his attention to Indian affairs.

The Portuguese historians are strangely silent about most of the events of Menezes' governorship. The most famous event seems to have been the "discovery" of the tomb of the Apostle St. Thomas near Madras.

The Portuguese government by this time had finally become aware of the terrible straits into which the Portuguese administration had fallen, and realized that a thorough housecleaning had to be made. It would be almost impossible, were it not for many records of the time, to believe that such deterioration could have set in in two decades. Several narratives have supplied most vivid descriptions. The Portuguese captains would often receive money from the king to buy provisions and would steal half the money, forcing the men to live on half-rations throughout the voyage. One Italian who visited India wrote: "There come from Portugal every year 2,500 or 3,000 men and youths of the lowest class imaginable. Most of them come to a bad end." An old Portuguese soldier describes the horrors of the voyage, often lasting seven months, and how the crews and soldiers, landing half-dead, were received with a salvo of greeting and cries and foul names, not only from the boys and natives, but from the people of their own nation and fatherland. "He who has no money or letter for friend or relatives sleeps under the eaves of the church, or within the boats drawn up on the shore . . . the second and third day are spent pawning or selling

---

* Soares's deeds in Persia, Aden, and elsewhere cannot be discussed here.

their cloak or sword. . . . And they go, four by four or six by six, entering houses, stupefied and starving, so that many . . . die." Incredible stories are told of thefts and false entries by tax collectors and other officers, who would bribe messengers to show them secret dispatches from which they could derive profit, shamelessly pocketing public funds and extorting all they could from the hapless natives. These people lived, as one chronicler has it, "in the luxury of a sultan and the greed of a rag-picker. . . . At the end of the three-years' term of one of the early viceroys [the Count of Vidigueira, grandson of Gama] . . . the ships [taking him back to Portugal] hardly sufficed to take all the baggage and chests of the viceroy and those near him, and were overflowing with precious things and infamy."

The practice of rewarding men like Gama and later officials with grants made for personal commerce, or of money, and so forth, finally made the official positions less public offices than royal liberality, a drain that neither the homeland nor the colonies could long sustain. Almeida, the first viceroy, advised against permitting private trading by officials, but no steps were ever taken to enforce decrees designed to put an end to the abuse. The salaries of officials were small, but in their stead were given captaincies, commands of fortresses, auditorships, rights of trade, and so forth.

The soldiers who were sent to garrison the Indian settlements were in general a poor lot, and their fate in India was a pathetic one. They were recruited from the farms and the slums. They brought nothing with them to India, where they were jeeringly called *descamisados* (literally, "men without shirts"). Many of them became robbers and thieves, for there were in India none of the controls which had kept them in their place in Portugal. With them worked the desperate adventurers and jailbirds who had enlisted in the crews. Cheating, gambling, debauchery were the common pleasures of the Portuguese in the India of King Manuel. One traveler who wrote shortly after this period bitterly remarked that "the prevailing characteristic of the first fifty years [of the Portuguese in the East] was ferocity." Added to all the evils enumerated above was the growth of slavery in the colony. The slaves were bought, sold, and treated like animals. Both men and women were stripped naked on the auction block on the rua Direita, in Goa, to exhibit their good points. In order to prevent trickery, girls offered as virgins were examined by women before they were purchased as concubines by the Portuguese. African women were preferred to Asiatics. Some Portuguese kept as many as five or six of these women.* Slaves were brought to Goa from every part of the Indies, as well as from Africa. In addition to the female slaves, Goa swarmed with native women, who consorted with the soldiers, crowding the taverns and cheap lodgings. These women are quaintly described by Garcia da Orta, a famous botanist of the time, who lived many years in India, as "ardent Malabar she-dogs, many pretty, of tropical temperament, perfumed with sandal, aloes, camphor, musk . . . and rose water. They could converse in bad Portuguese, dance, play, and sing with much grace."

One of the great causes of the severity and difficulty of life for the Portuguese in India was the almost complete absence of women from the homeland. Most of the men took native or half-caste women as their wives. These sat around in idleness, waited on by slaves, and having no conception of the real position of a wife.

Added to all of these evils, the Portuguese were an easy prey to tropical diseases. Weakened as they often were by the long voyage, bad food, and outbreaks of scurvy, they fell easy victims to cholera, dysentery, and malaria, as well as to syphilis and other diseases which they had themselves brought to the Indies. One Dutch writer avers that "although a man were of iron or steel, their un-chaste life with women [together with drink and disease] was able to grind him to powder and sweep him away like dust, which costeth many a man's life." He tells further, that of five hundred who entered the public hospital every year, only a few came out alive.

The Portuguese empire in India was, because of all these forces, rapidly becoming decadent, though not even a generation had passed since the opening of the sea route. The colony was in sad straits. The feudal evils of the Portuguese system in Lisbon had found their counterpart in India. No one was concerned with the common weal. From the governor down to the lowest official it

---

* These women were often also bought by the half-caste and native wives of the adventurers, and sent out on the streets to solicit men, their mistresses shamelessly and greedily taking the money so earned. These same wives used datura extensively, to drug their husbands when they wished to carry on amours with others. This practice was so extensive that several travelers mention it.

was each for himself, and greed and lust ruled instead of moderation and an efficient administration.*

What India needed, and needed badly, was a wise governor and an efficient, honest administration, if, indeed, it were not too late. The new king, John III, was certainly not a man of great parts, and made many errors of judgment in government, but the blame for the debacle in India cannot be placed altogether on his shoulders. The enterprises of Manuel had grown too large for a tiny nation like Portugal to carry. The effort was too great; the crash was bound to come. And more profound than all else was the disintegrating effect of India on Portugal. The enterprise was not an ordinary colonization of a virgin land, or one inhabited by an inferior people. India had a civilization as high as that of Portugal of the sixteenth century, but a civilization that was far different. The contact of the two was fatal to the Portuguese efforts. India had a civilization which combined fabulous riches with widespread and abject poverty, the opulence of the few accompanied by the starvation of the many, clamoring for a handful of rice. It was a country of absolute rulers, where a head was lopped off at the nod of a prince. In the picturesque words of a Portuguese narrator: "It was a mixture of perfume and the odor of blood, and of duplicity and cruelty with abject cowardice, all of which accorded with the base passions of the conquerors."

It was to this Portuguese India that Vasco came as viceroy in 1524.

* In all fairness it must be added that in spite of all the evils enumerated above, the Portuguese did much to improve the quality of spices and fruits of the Malabar coast. They also developed the cultivation of the coconut, and introduced its fiber, coir, into world markets.

CHAPTER XXII

THE THIRD VOYAGE OF VASCO DA GAMA, HIS VICEROYALTY AND DEATH

And it was to Dom Vasco da Gama . . . to whom he [John III] gave the government of India, with the title of viceroy.
—CASTANHEDA, *História da Índia,* Livro VI, Chap. lxxi

HE circumstances which brought about the appointment of Vasco da Gama as Viceroy of India are not known, and no documents of appointment have been found. There is, however, in the National Archives, the oath of fealty which the admiral swore before witnesses in Évora, dated February 28, 1524, though a document of February 5 of the same year refers to him as viceroy. In this document John III guaranteed that in case of the death of the admiral his eldest son would succeed to his title and estate without formalities or delays. The cautious Gama, realizing that much might happen during his term of office, evidently desired to provide for all contingencies. His two sons, Dom Estevão, who went as Captain-Commander of the Sea of India, and Dom Paulo, accompanied their father on the voyage. The admiral was the same harsh, hardfisted mariner who had led the first expedition in 1497, and his life in Portugal seems to have made him more arrogant and fond of pomp and ceremony than ever. The fleet was composed of fourteen ships * and carried 3,000 men, many of them fidalgos, cavaliers, and men who had served in the household of the king, among them many of breeding and education. In addition to the crew, there was a reserve group to man the ships already stationed in the Indian Ocean.

Because of the frequent deaths of high officials while on duty far from home, the king instituted, on this voyage, a procedure which became standard thereafter. The admiral carried with him three sealed documents. The first contained the name of the man who

* Seven ships, three galleons, and four caravels.

was to succeed the viceroy if he died in office; the second appointed the successor to the viceroy's successor if he died in office, and the third provided for the successor to the successor, if such a need arose. These documents were to be retained in the hands of the Comptroller of India, in Goa, the second highest official in the colonial empire, and opened only on the death of the viceroy. This practice eliminated the great confusion that had heretofore occurred on the death of a governor.

The ships sailed from Lisbon and crossed the Tagus bar on April 9, 1524, Vasco da Gama leading the way on his flagship, the *St. Catherine of Mount Sinai.* Just before the ships weighed anchor off Belém, the admiral, knowing from experience the difficulties encountered when women were surreptitiously taken on board for the voyage,

both for their souls' sake and an account of quarrels and plots, ordered proclamations to be made on shore, and posted as well at the foot of the masts, to the effect that any woman who would be found in the ships after leaving Belém would be flogged publicly, even though she were married, [and in that case] her husband would be sent back to Portugal in chains, and if she were a captive or a slave she would be sold for the ransom of a captive. Also, any captain who found a woman on his ship and did not surrender her would lose his commission in consequence.

Nevertheless, when the fleet reached Moçambique and dropped anchor for repairs, three women who had stowed away or been hidden by the crews were handed over to Gama and locked up until the arrival of the fleet at Goa.

After leaving Moçambique, the fleet ran into difficulties. Great storms were encountered, and three ships were lost with all on board. The crew of the caravel commanded by Gaspar Malhorquim mutinied, murdered their captain, left the fleet, and sailed away to engage in a piratical career in the vicinity of the Strait of Bab el Mandeb, at the entrance to the Red Sea.* Scurvy and other diseases broke out among the other crews, and many died before reaching their destination.

The Indian coast was finally reached in the neighborhood of

---

* In 1525 the caravel was captured by Antônio da Miranda d'Azevedo, near Cape Guardafui. The ship was taken to India, where many of the crew (Correa says all) were hanged, the others degraded.

Dabul, where they lay becalmed. Suddenly, early in the morning watch of September 8,* "the ships began to pitch and roll so that all thought they were on shoals . . . and lowered the boats into the sea with great shouts and cries and firing of cannon. Soundings with the lead revealed no bottom, and they cried to God to have mercy, because the ships tossed so violently that the men could not stand upright, and chests were thrown from one end of the ship to the other." The submarine earthquake was a most violent one, with alternate tremors and subsidences for an hour, with the waters of the sea boiling in an alarming manner about the fleet. A doctor on board the flagship recognized the phenomenon and explained it to Gama. The story is told by one narrator that Gama was in no way terrified by the earthquake, but fearlessly called his crew around him and said, "Friends, rejoice and be happy, for even the sea trembles before us." † Soon afterward the ships anchored at Chaul, where the viceroy appointed a new captain for the fortress, ordering him to obey no orders that might be given by the retiring governor, Menezes. Thence he proceeded to Goa, where he arrived a few days later.‡

Gama was welcomed with real joy by the better class of both Portuguese and natives, for they felt that his coming would bring a change for the better. He was received under a' rich canopy, with festivities and speeches, and was led in a great procession, first to the cathedral and then to the fortress. The council of the city dispatched a letter to King John, announcing the admiral's arrival and rejoicing that at last an honest and efficient administrator had arrived.

Correa, the most important chronicler of Gama's third voyage, lived in India for many years and was an eyewitness to many of the events that followed the count's landing in India. He describes most vividly the manner in which the admiral lived in India:

The said Dom Vasco brought great state, being served by men bearing silver maces, by a major-domo, and two pages with neck

* Other contemporaries give the date as Sept. 6 or 7.
† Of this incident Camões wrote:

> How trembles and boils the sea, even in calm,
> Oh, powerful race, and of what high thoughts
> That even the elements do fear them.
> —*Os Lusíadas*, II, xlvii

‡ It is impossible to reconcile the dates as given by the chroniclers.

chains of gold, many equerries and body servants, very well dressed and cared for. He had rich table service of silver, and fine Flanders tapestry, and the cover of the table at which he dined was of brocade. They brought to him at table dishes as large as those of a king, with his towel-bearer bringing him a pitcher, and all things pertaining to a king. The ornaments of his wardrobe, bed, and chapel were complete. . . . He had a guard of two hundred men, with gilded pikes and dressed in his livery. He kept a fine table, and there dined with him all the gentlemen and honored people.

Though some authors call this "ostentation," Gama knew that the way to win the people whom he was sent to govern was to impress them with his power and magnificence, as they were accustomed to judge their own native rulers in the same way.

The viceroy had been granted plenary powers, executive, judicial, and legislative. His reputation had preceded him, and he was much feared and respected. He immediately set about using these powers in an earnest effort to correct the abuses that he found rampant and to restore respect and obedience for the government. One of the first things he discovered was that the king's officers had sold many pieces of artillery to the merchants of the colony. He immediately issued an order commanding the return of all such property within thirty days, under the penalty of losing both property and life. Most of the artillery was quickly returned! In the words of the letter referred to above, from the Council of Goa to the king, he refused, when "many persons went to him with gifts such as is customary to make to newly arrived governors, to take anything from Christian or Moor, and still less from this city, which we all look upon as strange, as it is the custom for all to be accepted." He found the hospital crowded with men who were using it as a lodging, and drove them out. He forbade the hospital to receive anyone wounded in a brawl, "saying that they brawled on account of women." Crews of ships were to remain aboard while in harbor and receive their rations there.

The next step was to make an example of the three women who had shipped in the fleet at Lisbon and who had been locked up ever since they had been turned over to him at Moçambique. He issued an order that the three women be flogged in public, while the government crier proclaimed: "The justice of the King, our Lord, It commands that these women be flogged because they did not fear

his justice, coming to India contrary to his prohibition." Upon the
announcement of the approaching punishment, people of all classes,
"gentlemen," bishops and friars and the Brothers of Mercy, interceded on behalf of the women and offered a large sum of money to
buy them off. He even refused, on the day of the carrying out of
the sentence, to listen to priests carrying a crucifix from the Fran-
ciscan church. The order for flogging was carried out; and though
he was adjudged a cruel man, it had a very salutary effect among
would-be evildoers.

Just before his death, Gama did his best to mitigate the fate of
the three women. He sent each of them 300,000 reis, "which were
to be given them with much secrecy, and if they should not choose
to accept them, this sum was to be doubled and given to the Santa
Casa de Misericórdia. These women, with this money, found good
husbands and were married and became honest women." Thus the
chronicler Correa.

The viceroy was already ailing but persisted in his task of reor-
ganizing the government of the Portuguese Indies. After spending
some time in restoring law and order in Goa, Gama sailed south to
confer with the Portuguese governor of Cochin. He labored unceasingly and, in spite of the heat and his increasing illness, did not
take the customary siesta, but worked through the entire day.

During this time the retiring governor, Dom Duarte de Menezes,
who had been cruising in Persian and Indian waters, gathering
more ill gotten gains to take back to Portugal with him, came to
Cochin to greet the viceroy. Gama forbade Menezes to land and
placed him under arrest for malfeasance in office. He allowed him
to remain on parole in his (Menezes') vessel, however, until he
reported to the king in Lisbon. But Dom Duarte transferred to
another of his vessels, for he had learned that the viceroy was ill,
and hoped that he might die, and that he (Duarte) could regain
the governorship. When Gama heard of this, he sent for Dom
Duarte, who discreetly sailed for Portugal. To prove that Gama's
severity toward Menezes was justified, one has but to read Correa's
account of how he escaped with the money that he had stolen
or extorted during his term. When he came to Cochin to meet
Gama, he had a chest "full of rich gold stuffs, pearls, and jewelry,
which were worth a large price." Two of his men landed with a
boat,

and they two took the chest, with an iron shovel . . . they made a hole in the sand, into which they put the chest and on the top of the sand they placed the skull of an ox, and they took the bearings . . . but not very exactly, as it was night. . . . It appears probable that some one who passed by kicked the skull . . . for when the priest [one of the two men who had buried the chest] came at night and thrust in a stake where the skull was, he did not find the chest . . . they underwent much labor in seeking for it every night. . . . After many days had passed, they fell in with it, when they were already despairing of finding it; for God did not choose that so great a treasure should be lost.

And now the great viceroy's illness was becoming more severe, being aggravated by the heat, his overwork, and the strain of his struggles with Menezes and other dishonest or inefficient officials. Again we turn to Correa:

For some days the viceroy had been suffering from severe pains in his neck, which had become awry, and some boils came to the surface at the base of the neck.* They were very hard, and would not come to a head in spite of all the remedies that were applied. They were of no avail, and they gave him such torment that he could not turn his head in any direction. . . . He took to his bed, and issued all necessary orders there, with great travail of spirit, which caused him to be over-taken by mortal illness, with such pain as deprived him of speech.

The viceroy, realizing the gravity of his illness, had himself carried from the fortress of Cochin, where he had been lodging, to the house of Diogo Pereira. There he summoned his secretary and other responsible officials and made the last disposition of official matters, including memoranda for the governor who might succeed him. The official business finished and put aside, "he confessed and par-took of the Holy Sacrament, with much perfection as a Catholic Christian." He then summoned his sons and made his testament, and

set his affairs in order, like a good Christian, with all the Sacraments of the Church, and ordered that his bones should be conveyed to the Kingdom [of Portugal], as they were conveyed later. Speaking always with his full understanding, he ended the number of his days when he surrendered up his soul on the eve of Christmas of the holy birth

* The disease which carried the admiral off has been diagnosed as a cervical anthrax.

of Christ, at three o'clock after midnight, on the twenty-fourth day of December of this present year of 1524. God be praised.

He was, according to the best authorities, about sixty-four years old.
    The viceroy's death was kept secret,

without weeping or lamentation, and the doors were closed all the day till the hour of "Ave Maria," when all was ready. Then his sons and servants gave out the announcement of his death with very great lamentations, and many gentlemen, relations, and friends came in to assist them. Soon thereafter all the people of the city came into the courtyard of the church, each showing his sorrow.
    The body, dressed in silk clothes, and over them a mantle of the Order of Christ, with a sword and gilded hilt, and gilt spurs fixed on dark buskins, and on its head a dark round biretta, was placed in the hall, uncovered on the bier of the Brotherhood of Mercy. It was borne on the shoulders of the Brothers, clothed in the mantles of their order, many tapers being lighted, and it was followed by all the people.

The body was buried with great ceremony in the monastery chapel of St. Anthony * pending its transfer to Portugal, in conformity with the admiral's wishes on his deathbed.

    There the next day a solemn religious service was performed, and all the Brothers were present, and the sons [of the Admiral] were placed among them, and at night they betook themselves to the monastery, and made their lamentations, as was fitting on losing so honored a father, and a man of such deserving fame in the Kingdom of Portugal.

    * The monastery no longer exists. Another church stands on its site.

CHAPTER XXIII

THE BURIAL PLACE OF VASCO DA GAMA

For the whole earth is the sepulchre of famous men.
—THUCYDIDES, Book II, Chap. 43

HE body of Vasco da Gama, first Count of Vidigueira, was brought, in 1539, to Portugal from Cochin, where it had lain since the interment of 1524. Though it is not known definitely who made the transfer, it was probably one of his sons who made repeated voyages to the East. It was buried in the ancient Church of Our Lady of the Relics of Vidigueira, in accordance with the contract made with the friars of the church, a contract confirmed by a decree of King John III on May 24, 1524. No record of this burial has been found. In 1533, before the return of the coffin from India, Vasco da Gama's son, Francisco, who had succeeded him as the second Count of Vidigueira, established a fund in perpetuity for the saying of daily Mass for the souls of both the discoverer and his wife.

The present Church of Our Lady of the Relics was completed in 1593. Again the remains of the great discoverer, once exhumed in Cochin in 1539, were removed from their resting place in the old church and transferred to the new one. Though there is no record of the transfer, it is supposed that Dom Miguel da Gama, a grandson of the admiral, and a very generous contributor to the building of the church, removed the remains and those of others of the family. The bones of Vasco da Gama were supposed to have been placed in an ossuary on the epistle (right, as one faces the altar) side of the chancel. The lid was formed of four stone slabs, only slightly polished on the upper surface, on which was carved the following epitaph:

AQUI JAZ O GRANDE ARGONA
VTA DOM VASCO DA GAMA PR.*
CONDE DA VIDIGVERA AL

MIRANTE DAS INDIAS ORI
ENTAES E SEV FAMOSO DES
COBRIDOR.*

In this tomb the bones of the admiral rested in peace for some 250 years.

On May 28, 1834, the monastery, church, and enclosure of Our Lady of the Relics of Vidigueira were included in a severe government decree designed to suppress a number of Portuguese religious institutions. The last Mass was celebrated at seven in the morning of June 28, by the prior of the monastery. Thereafter all the orna-ments and silver service were packed, and the edifice was vacated the same evening. The church was abandoned, thieves broke in, forced open the lids of the graves, and carried off whatever they thought of value, many of the bones being scattered about and the tombstones smashed. This wanton destruction continued unchecked until September 21, 1841, when the church was offered by the government at public sale as the property of a suppressed monastic order, the government not giving a thought to the fact that the building contained the bones of one of Portugal's most famous sons, the man who by his voyage had given his country an empire and raised Portugal to the position of a great world power. Fortunately, the successful bidder, Dom José Gil, restored the church and re-established religious services. Thus the last resting places of genera-tions of the Gama family are now protected from further damage or profanation.

The abbot Antônio Damaso de Castro appears to have been the first to conceive the idea that the great discoverer should have a fitting burial place in the Monastery of the Jeronimos at Belém. There his bones would repose on the site of the little chapel at Restello, where he had kept vigil that faraway evening of July 7, 1497, just before setting sail for India. De Castro appeared before the Portuguese Chamber of Deputies in 1844. An investigation was made and a report was filed by the governor of Beja, telling of the sad state of the chapel and its desecration. The tombs were thereupon sealed by the government, with orders that they were not to be opened except on orders from the king. There the matter

* Here lies the great argonaut Dom Vasco da Gama, First Count of Vidi-gueira, Admiral of the East Indies and their famous discoverer.

rested, and no action was taken. A second petition from De Castro in 1846 met with greater success.*

In 1871 the historian A. C. Teixeira de Aragão interested the president of the Council of State in the matter, and a commission was appointed by the king on February 24 of the same year, with power to arrange for the removal of the remains to the Jeronimos. Rafael de Castro was commissioned to design the tomb. Nine years passed. On April 13, 1880, a paper was read before the Royal Academy of Sciences, requesting the government to take part officially in the ceremonies of transferring the remains of both Vasco da Gama and Luis de Camões (the tercentenary of whose death was to be commemorated on June 10, 1880). The government consented and named a committee to arrange for the transfer of the remains of Gama. Teixeira de Aragão, one of the commission, has written a minute account of what occurred.

After obtaining permission from Dom Thomas, Count of Vidigueira, and descendant of Vasco da Gama, the committee, followed by a crowd of townspeople, proceeded to the chapel, and, the seals having been broken, the stone lid was raised. Unfortunately, when the remains were placed in the sandalwood casket especially made in the marine arsenal, no medical examination was made of the bones. They were a confused mass, having been disturbed by the desecrators of the graves. "We had hardly time to place the bones in the casket," wrote Aragão, "but observed that there were skulls, thighbones and leg bones which appeared to belong to four skeletons." The casket was placed on a catafalque, with a guard of a veteran of the Royal Marines on either side. With solemn ceremony a military and civil cortege was formed, a religious service was held in the church, and the casket was officially turned over to the government. Four marine veterans then raised the casket, which was draped with the Portuguese flag. As the casket was carried to the funeral car, bells rang and fireworks were detonated, the town band played and the military bands joined in. With the casket was carried the wooden figurehead of the *São Rafael,* the flagship of Vasco da Gama on his first voyage. There followed the laying of a cornerstone of a new school in Vidigueira, to be called the Vasco da Gama School. Thence the convoy proceeded with the

* The Gama tombs were repaired in 1843 through the efforts of José Sylvestre Ribeiro.

playing of the national hymn and cheers from the crowd. Ovations greeted the remains at each station. At Barreira the casket and the figurehead were placed on a royal barge and conveyed to the corvette *Mindello,* whose sailors manned the yard-arms and whose officers were drawn up at the gangplank. The vessel proceeded down the Tagus to the Arsenal of Lisbon, where spectators lined the banks of the river in great crowds. At the arsenal the casket and figure were placed on the royal brigantine, where were gathered the family of the Count of Vidigueira and a marine guard of honor. From the arsenal the vessel proceeded to Belém, where the waterfront was decorated for the occasion, the Portuguese and foreign vessels in the harbor firing salvos of artillery. The casket was taken ashore and placed on a naval artillery caisson, followed by officers of the army and navy and by the admiral's descendants. At this point the procession joined that bearing the remains of Luis de Camões, who was to be interred in the church at the same time.

The procession passed between long lines of soldiers, presenting arms and restraining the crowds, while cannon were fired, bells rung, and bands blared forth military marches and hymns. King Dom Luis, with the queen, met the cortege at the entrance to the Church of the Jeronimos. The court costumes, plumed generals, gold, scarlet, white and red uniforms, the robes of the clergy—all these were a colorful background for what was a great national event. The royal party entered the church with the casket, a religious service was held, and the casket was conveyed to the epistle side of the chancel. There the casket was opened, its contents verified, and a certificate of its receipt was signed by their Majesties and other notables present. The king and queen then placed on the casket a beautiful silver wreath, and the ceremonies were closed.*

Thus, on June 8, 1880, 382 years and 11 months after his sailing from the shore by the chapel of Restello, it was believed that the great admiral had at last found his final resting place. But the story is not yet complete. There is one more chapter to add to the wanderings of the bones of Dom Vasco da Gama, Count of Vidigueira, Admiral of the Indies.

* It is to be noted that the caskets containing the remains of both Vasco da Gama and Luis de Camões were received in the same ceremony at and inside the church.

It will be recalled that the committee charged with removing the remains opened the grave on the *epistle* side of the chancel, and that the stone lid of the grave bore the name of the admiral. It also was stated that the ossuary contained four incomplete skeletons, of which one was supposed to be that of Vasco da Gama.

Some time after the conveying of the bones to the Jeronimos on June 8, 1880, Teixeira de Aragão found a manuscript which had belonged to the Monastery of Our Lady of the Relics of Vidigueira, and which was dedicated to the first Marquis of Niza. The manuscript bears on its title page the following: "The Establishment of the Monastery of Our Lady of the Relics of the Order of the Carmelites, and how this Lady appeared, and of the graves of the lords of the House of Vidigueira which are in the Church." The statement is added that the writing of the manuscript was ordered in 1646 by the prior of the monastery, Frei João das Chagas, and that Frei Alvaro da Fonseca was charged with the task. Then follows the very significant statement:

The first lord of the House of Vidigueira whom we have to place among those who are buried in this monastery of Our Lady of the Relics, is the great D. Vasco da Gama, founder of the house of the Counts of Vidigueira, and its first Count, who was married to the Countess D. Catharina de Athayde. This monastery has cared for these bones in the chancel, on the *evangelist* [left, facing the altar] side, near the great altar; it was the great D. Vasco da Gama, first discoverer of the East Indies, royal Admiral of the same, and first Count of Vidigueira. *He has no inscription on his grave.*

The MS continues with the information that in front of the grave of Vasco da Gama, on the *epistle* side, were buried "in a grave lined with black velvet and covered with a pall of black velvet" other members of the Gama family, and on that grave was a temporary epitaph on wood.

Frei José Pereira de Sant' Anna, in his book the *Chronicles of the Carmelites of Portugal,* written in the middle of the eighteenth century, makes the same statement, that the admiral's grave was on the *evangel* side. If one of these two authors, writing one hundred years apart, had made the statement one might admit an error, but with two, both priests, such an error may be ruled out. In addition Sant' Anna states that the grave of Vasco da

Gama bore an epitaph on stone, as did the grave of the other Gamas.* Moreover, as the evangel side is the principal side of the chancel, it would be only natural to suppose that it was there that the admiral, founder of his house, should have been interred. The added fact that parts of several skeletons were found by the committee when they opened the tomb on the epistle side makes the identification of 1880 still more suspicious.

After studying the manuscript of Frei Fonseca and the book of Frei Sant' Anna, Teixeira de Aragão decided to make further investigation of the matter. So, in his own words:

On the 11th day of July, 1884, at 11 A.M., in the chancel of the Church of Our Lady of the Relics, we raised the tombstone which covered the ossuary on the evangel side, and we verified among the fragments of a chest lined with black trimmed velvet, and with gilded nails, the existence of the bones belonging to a single skeleton. This therefore corresponds to a real proof in corroboration of what is stated both in the MSS. of Frei Alvaro da Fonseca and the *Carmelite Chronicle,* and, therefore, in view of this examination and of the reasons which we have presented, we feel that we can be sure that the ashes of D. Vasco da Gama are still lying in the ossuary on the evangel side, where they were placed when the church was finished in 1593.

Aragão states that the lettering on both tombs is in the character of the end of the seventeenth or the beginning of the eighteenth century. He suggests that perhaps the inscriptions were originally carved on the wrong stones, but that it was more likely that the grave robbers changed the stones. Since there were probably no objects of value in the admiral's tomb after the transfer, first from India to the chapel, in 1539, and again, in 1593, to the church, the robbers would have quickly discovered that and not disturbed the bones. That they should have moved heavy tombstones and then put them back on the wrong ossuaries is very unlikely. The answer will probably never be known. What is reasonably certain is that the bones transferred in the great celebration of 1880 to the Jeronimos were not those of Vasco da Gama, and that in 1884, when Aragão visited the church, the bones were still there, and those in the tomb at Belém were those of Dom Francisco da Gama, fourth viceroy of India, together with those of others of his family.

* Both gravestones are of the same size.

The publication of Teixeira de Aragão's findings in the *Journal of the Geographical Society of Lisbon* in 1889 did not arouse the government to make any move to correct the flagrant error of 1880. A speech (published in the same *Journal* in 1896) by the famous historian Luciano Cordeiro likewise had no effect. Aragão then published his findings in a book containing the *Journal* articles expanded and in this he pleaded with the government to remedy the mistake.

The mistake was finally rectified, though the only information obtainable by the author is a page in a strange book written by Maria Telles da Gama, in 1902, facts verified in a personal letter from Colonel João A. L. Galvão, Secretary of the Geographical Society of Lisbon.

In 1898, on the occasion of the celebration of the fourth centenary of the discovery of the sea road to the Indies, the bones of Vasco da Gama were exhumed and transferred in almost the identical fashion—this time by night on the steamer *Dona Amelia,* and were received by the Minister of Marine and other officials.* The remains were placed in the tomb on the morning of May 9, 1898, with a simple ceremony. The sepulcher, given to the nation by Simão José da Luz Soriano, is of marble, supported by six couchant lions. It is ornamented in relief with the Gama arms, ships, and so forth, and Gama is represented as he was prepared for burial in Cochin, according to the description of Correa, his hands joined in prayer. The inscription just under the lid is from Canto IV, Verse lxxxvii, of Camões's *Lusíadas*:

> Partimos nos assi do sancto templo
> Que nas praias do mar está assentado.†

Thus after many wanderings, Vasco da Gama rests from his long voyage on the very spot where he knelt and offered up his prayers in the little chapel of Restello.‡

---

* Both Teixeira de Aragão and Luciano Cordeiro were among the invited guests, and it must have been a source of patriotic satisfaction to the formei to see his labors justified.

† Thus we departed from the holy fane
   Which on the margins of the sea is built.

‡ It is curious to note that the remains of many of the great discoverers and explorers, e.g., Marco Polo, Christopher Columbus, and Hernán Cortes, have had strange wanderings and vicissitudes.

CHAPTER XXIV

VASCO DA GAMA THE MAN

Through all the world
Shall I proclaim in song
Those who by their valorous deeds
Hold such a place
That from death's law
They are released.
—CAMÕES, *Os Lusíadas*, I, ii

UDGING from the scanty remarks of his contemporaries, Vasco da Gama was a man of medium height and inclined, at least in later life, to corpulence. One chronicler speaks of his bearing as "noble deportment." Faria y Sousa, who wrote two generations after Gama's death, describes him as "of a florid complexion, with somewhat Israelitish features, large eyes, heavy eyebrows, hooked nose, and a beard, which in his later years was white."

There are several portraits in existence of the admiral, but there is no proof that any of them was made in his lifetime. In the Government House of Goa is a large portrait, painted by Gaspar Correa. This portrait has been repainted and restored so much that it is impossible to recognize the original. There are two oil portraits of Gama in the hermitage of Nossa Senhora das Salas. The best known portrait is the one in the Gallery of Fine Arts in Lisbon, traditionally painted from life. In the cloister of the old Monastery of the Jeronimos, at Belém, there is a stone medallion, said to represent Vasco da Gama.

A statue of the discoverer stands in Old Goa, in a niche of the Porta da Ribeira, also called Arch of the Viceroy. It was erected in 1597 by the Viceroy Francisco da Gama, to commemorate his grandfather's exploits. Hatred of his despotic rule caused his enemies to pull the marble statue down at night and break it into four pieces and expose it in different quarters of the city. The statue standing in the niche at present is one authorized by the Municipal

Chamber of Goa in 1609. Other statues of Gama stand in Lisbon and elsewhere.

The biographers dismiss the character of Gama with adjectives of which the following are the commonest: "daring, harsh in command, fearfully violent in anger, severe in justice, brave, morally courageous, never fearful of responsibility, of indomitable constancy, intrepid, persevering, passionate, of absolute probity, merciless, ferocious, tenacious, hot-tempered, valiant, proud, despotic, irascible, brusk, daring, haughty, pitiless, domineering, masterful."

Perhaps it would be well to pause at this point and consider the men of the era of John II and Manuel—not to extenuate or palliate the actions of Vasco da Gama in Indian waters, but to throw light on them. The period was one which has well been called "abnormal and disequilibrated," and all of Europe was in a similar condition. The continent was in the birth throes of the early Renaissance, and the minds and souls of men were so profoundly stirred that both their virtues and their vices were exacerbated by the mighty ferment of the age. Human thoughts and actions swung to great excesses— excesses both of good and evil. When we read with horror of the dastardly deeds of the Portuguese in the East, we must remember what was going on at the same time in Europe. When we shudder and are saddened by the unrelieved savagery of Gama in burning the Arab ship and putting his hapless and innocent prisoners to death, we must ever keep in mind that we are reading of the early sixteenth century. In Italy, where marvelous works of art were being created, where letters and sciences were being revived and developed along lines undreamed of before, unspeakable scenes of violence were daily occurrences. We find the Duke of Valentino hanging old people by their arms and then burning the soles of their feet until they died under the torture, in order to extort money from them. The same duke amused a brilliant company of lords and ladies by firing arrows with his own hand into the trussed-up body of a condemned criminal. We see a Benvenuto Cellini, one of the great artists of his or of any other age, assassinating his enemies on the streets in broad daylight, and getting off scot-free because he has the right sort of a "protector" in a high place. We read of Hercules d'Este's ordering an eye gouged out and a hand cut off of each of 280 prisoners, before selling them as slaves.

These horrible acts occurred in the civilized lands of Europe, which were bearing aloft the torch of culture and progress. It was caused (as in some countries in our own day) by the disorientation of men's minds, without reason or restraint to guide them. It was an age of heroes and saints, of wickedness and debauchery, during which the modern world had its birth pangs. In the words of a brilliant student of the era: "The man of the period vibrated like a taut string set in motion by a bent bow—splendid vigor, genial invention and dazzling fantasy, but very prompt to mount to the heights of purest heroism, or to descend to the excesses of wantonness or to the cruelty of wild beasts." *

If these things could happen so easily and so casually in Europe, it makes the actions of the Portuguese in India far more comprehensible to us. They had for years fought the Moors on the battlefields of Arzila and Azamor, and had conquered, looted, and raped along the coast of Africa for years. They were trying to seize the earth and its riches with both hands. The heart of the nation was beating frantically, and the pulses throbbed at the extremities—in the far-off seas and on the coasts which had been discovered by Dias and Gama and Cabral. The Portuguese, carrying in their brains and blood the hot ferment and turmoil that were seething in Europe, found themselves isolated in the Orient, thousands of miles from the homeland, and surrounded by hostile peoples on whom, if they were to impose their rule, they deemed it necessary—not knowing differently—to force themselves by terror and savagery. At least they could, or felt they could, plead the inexorable pressure of circumstances, the choice of crushing by every resource at their command or of being destroyed by the sheer weight of enemy numbers. Hence were written the short but bloody chapters, of which Gama's voyages are a part, of the conquest and rule of the East by the Portuguese.

While great deeds were spreading the name of Portugal throughout Europe, a profound change for the worse was taking place under the surface; a subtle poison was seeping into the veins of the nation's life. We perceive all this easily now, but at the time it was not recognized or evaluated by many. Lisbon was rapidly becoming the most important port in Europe. Its warehouses were bulging with Indian goods of every kind, and the strongboxes of the king-

* Conde Ficalho, *Garcia da Orta e Seu Tempo.*

dom were gorged with the gold of Africa and the precious stones
of the East. The very air was filled with the heavy odors of sandalwood and cloves, nutmeg and cinnamon. Great as these riches
were, the reports grew and were exaggerated as they spread from
mouth to mouth throughout the cities and towns of Europe. People
flocked into the capital from the small towns and the farms of
Portugal. The local life of the provinces slackened and then stopped.
"At the smell of cinnamon the kingdom became depopulated," for
more and more men—and women—sought quick fortunes in the
newly found lands. Grain became scarcer and dearer. Famine seized
upon the land, and the poor died in great numbers in their hovels
alongside warehouses bursting with the wealth of the Indies. As
ever, pestilence trod hard on the heels of famine, and Manuel's
court fled from the contagion, from city to city—from Montemór
to Évora, from Évora to Chamusca. This sordid story is largely
avoided by chroniclers, absorbed as they were in the life of the
court. Little heed was given to the sufferings or needs of the populace. All the records were of the pageantry and vain pomp of kings
and courts, of cavaliers and ladies. Of the people, nothing—or next
to nothing.

Taine, in his "Essay on Titus Livius," has endeavored to define
the biographer's attitude in words that should be used in judging
Vasco da Gama:

The historian gives no thought either praising or blaming. He seeks
neither to exhort his readers to virtue, nor to instruct them in politics.
It is not his aim to excite hatred or love, to elevate hearts or spirits.
He has for his sole duty and desire to eliminate the distance of time,
and to bring his readers face to face with his subject.

The few and scanty notes on the personality of Gama to be found
in contemporary chronicles or records probably indicate that he
was neither an attractive man nor a sympathetic character. We find
no warmth in him, no traits that might have endeared him to those
about him, no love of nature, nothing of the dreamer, the man with
a vision. To him the great voyage was not the result of an irresistible
inner urge that drove him, as it did Columbus. His discovery was
the result of a task set before him by his king. To it he brought to
bear such talents as were his: seamanship, the leadership of men,

the ruthless destruction of all who stood in his way, and the cold, cruel, pitiless religious fanaticism of his country and age.

That Gama had little, if any, of the gentler traits is the unfortunate conclusion that a study of his life brings. We know absolutely nothing of his family life. That he did love his brother Paulo dearly is revealed in the chronicles, but with that brother's death at the Azores passes the last glimpse of brightness and affection from our picture of Gama. He inspired fear more than love, and the fearsome portion has kept all the other characteristics—if there were any—from the record.

Gama's greed and grasping for money and place occurs again and again. It is part of that great greed for gold and rank that seemed, in his age, to drive out the finer, nobler sentiments, and crass, selfish interest is reflected in all the documents and narratives of his relations with King Manuel. We may go further and point out that our own twentieth century has revealed that these evil traits of Gama and his century are with us still, but little beneath the surface, and that man has to travel far, very far, before he can call himself really civilized.

CHAPTER XXV

THE CONTRIBUTION OF VASCO DA GAMA
AND HIS DISCOVERY OF THE
SEA ROAD TO THE INDIES

No great man lives in vain. The History of the World is but the Biography of Great men.—CARLYLE, *Heroes and Hero Worship*

ASCO DA GAMA, unlike Columbus, had forerunners, and because of their labors had a clean-cut problem given to him to solve, a problem based on the voyages of Bartholomeu Dias and his predecessors. None the less, his nautical performance was not inferior to that of Columbus, though Magellan's was greater than that of either. To solve Gama's problem required great seamanship, personal courage and fortitude and a driving personality, one that could face all odds and not recede a foot's breadth.

As a seaman, Gama's greatest claim to fame probably lay in his courageous decision to abandon the timid creeping southward along the African coast that had characterized the voyages of his predecessors, and to steer instead boldly west-southwest out into the middle of the unknown Atlantic. His daring lay in his doing this at a period when that portion of the Atlantic had not been explored and when there were great uncertainties of navigation—for there was no means available of accurately ascertaining longitude. Moreover, the charts of the African coast were, when in existence, extremely inaccurate. He sailed thousands of miles out of sight of land, going into regions whose winds and currents were all either unknown or a matter of conjecture. This took him almost within sight of South America, which was later accidentally(?) discovered by Cabral on his Indian voyage.

The route thus followed by Vasco da Gama through trial and error is still the true sailing route from Europe to the Cape of Good Hope, and it was followed as long as sailing ships plowed the South Atlantic. He was three months out of sight of land, and even the unfamiliar stars and constellations could not be of the assistance that those visible in the Northern Hemisphere were to Columbus. Considering the type and size of his vessels, the long, alternating spells of storm and calm, and his absolute ignorance of his environment, his choice of route has, in the words of the former Director of Operative Staff of the British Admiralty, "a strong claim to rank as the finest feat of pure navigation ever accomplished." *

The casual reader of the story of Vasco da Gama will probably be impressed mostly with the lurid tales of murder and rapine that fill its pages. But that would not alone have secured for him the place he occupies in history. Besides his seamanship he contributed much. His command of men, harsh and unrelenting though it was, accomplished results. He always kept on the course he had laid out for himself, and none of his men dared swerve, "because the captain-major did not choose." With all his cruelty and other faults, he was the embodiment of the conquering spirit of Portugal, the spirit which enabled a tiny nation to make miraculous conquests—and, it must be added, sadly enough, the cruel and fanatic spirit that aroused the hatred of the Westerner in the hearts of the natives of Africa and Asia which has not ceased until this very day.

Gama, like Columbus and Magellan, is one of the heroes of that period which came once in the world's history but which can never be repeated, that era which marked the sudden expansion of the knowledge of the world by the Western nations through daring and unprecedentedly long sea voyages. These discoveries shifted the center of gravity of European civilization from the shores of the Mediterranean, where the great scenes of the ancient and medieval world had been enacted, to the coast of the Atlantic, and the centers of commerce and political activity moved thenceforth westward. One historian has well called this era of exploration "one of the most important and fateful epochs in man's history on earth." †

Vasco da Gama was one of the greatest figures of this era, and, unlike most of the others, he had not only the good fortune to live to see and to profit greatly by his discovery, but to become the central figure of the great Portuguese epic of Luis de Camões, the *Lusiads*. The immediate results of his voyage far exceeded those of Columbus. The latter discovered a land which required many gen-

* Admiral G. A. Ballard.
† Arthur P. Newton, in *The Great Age of Discovery*.

erations for its development and a profitable return. Gama's discovery brought Europe in contact with a rich civilization, and the returns on the investment were speedy and fabulous.

Gama's voyages not only revolutionized the history of Europe, but also ushered in a new era in Asia, and for the first time the sea became important in Indian political history.

We have examined what references his contemporaries and later historians have made to Vasco da Gama. When all his great exploits have been weighed against his defects of character and personal attitudes, Gama appears as one of history's great figures, "fit for all that was intrusted to his conduct as Captain, as Discoverer and as Viceroy." * He belongs not only to the history of Portugal, his tiny homeland, and to the history of India, but to world history. In the words of Correa, his contemporary:

It pleased the Lord to give this man so strong a spirit, that without any human fear he passed through so many perils of death during the discovery of India, as is related in his history; all for the love of the Lord, for the great increase of his Catholic faith, and for the great honor and glory and ennobling of Portugal.

* Thomas Astley, *Collection of Voyages.*

NOTE:

THE DESCENDANTS OF VASCO DA GAMA

The offspring of the marriage of Vasco da Gama and Dona Catharina de Athayde were seven. The oldest was Dom Francisco da Gama, second Count of Vidigueira, Admiral of the Indian Sea, and equerry to King John III. The second was Dom Estevão da Gama, who accompanied his father on his third voyage to India and served as governor of India from 1540 to 1542. The names of these two elder sons appear in the list of pages of King Manuel. The third son, Dom Pedro da Silva, made many voyages to India. The fourth son, Dom Paulo da Gama, was governor of Malacca in 1538, and died in India. The fifth son, Dom Christovão da Gama, went to India, and thence to Ethiopia, where he was killed. The sixth son, Dom Alvaro de Athayde, succeeded his brother Dom Christovão as governor of Malacca. Gama had one daughter, Dona Izabel de Athayde. She married Inácio de Noronho, but was so ill treated that she left him and entered the Convent of Santa Clara of Lisbon. There she died, making her brother Dom Estevão her heir. Her grave is in the chapel of Our Lady of the Conception in the convent, and the tombstone bears the inscription:

> Here lies D. Isabel de Athayde, daughter of the Count Admiral who discovered India, who, because of her devotion, withdrew to this convent. She died March 17, 1568.

No knowledge of Gama's family life has survived.

The line of the Gamas has not been broken, and many of his descendants are living today, the head of the family still proudly bearing the title of Count of Vidigueira.

BIBLIOGRAPHY

Abd-er-Razzak, *Narrative*. See Major, R. H.

Academia das Ciências de Lisboa. "Nomes Proprios de Navios Portugueses," February, 1931.

Aiya, V. Nagam, *Travancore State Manual*, 3 vols. Trivandrum, Travancore, 1906.

Alaux, Jean-Paul, *Vasco da Gama, ou l'Epopée des Portugais aux Indes.* Paris, 1931.

Albert-Montémont, *Biblioteca Universale dei Viaggi*, 8 vols. Venice, 1834.

Albuquerque, Braz de, *Commentarios do Grande A. Dalboquerque*, 4 vols. Lisbon, 1557.

Alguns Documentos do Archivo National da Torre do Tombo acerca das Navegações e Conquistas Portuguezas, ed. J. Ramos Coelho. Lisbon, 1892.

Ali, A. Yusuf, *Mediaeval India: Social and Economic Conditions*. Oxford, 1932.

Almada, André Alvares d', *Tratado Breve dos Rios de Guiné do Cabo Verde*, ed. Diogo Köpke. Oporto, 1841.

Almeida, Fortunato de, "Causas da Decadência do Império Português," in *O Instituto*, Vol. 72. Lisbon, 1925.

———, *História de Portugal*, 5 vols. Coimbra, 1922-1927.

———, "Últimas Dias de Vasco da Gama," in *O Instituto*, Vol. 72. Lisbon, 1925.

Alvares, Father Francisco, *Narrative of the Portuguese Embassy to Abyssinia During the Years 1520-1527*, transl. by Lord Stanley of Alderley. London, Hakluyt Soc., 1881.

Alvarez, Sir Francis, a Portugall Priest, The Voyage of, in Purchas: *His Pilgrimes*, Vols. VI, VII, Maclehose reprint. Glasgow, 1905.

Ameal, João, *História de Portugal*. 2nd ed., Oporto, 1942.

Ammianus, Marcellinus, *History*, transl. by John C. Rolfe, 3 vols. London and Cambridge, 1935-1939.

Anonymous, *Calcoen: A Dutch Narrative of the Second Voyage of Vasco da Gama to Calicut*, printed at Antwerp *ca.* 1505, with Introduction and Translation by Jean Philibert Berjeau. London, 1874.

———, *First Voyage of Vasco da Gama*. See Velho, Alvaro.

———, ("G. R."), *História de la Colonización*, 2 vols. Barcelona, 1933.

————, *Índice Cronológico das Navegações, Viagens Descobrimentos e Conquistas dos Portuguezes nos Paizes Ultramarinos desde o Principio do Seculo XV.* Lisbon, 1841.

————, "Navegação as Índias Orientaes por Thomé Lopes" (2nd voyage of Gama), in *Collecção de Notícias para a História e Geografia das Nações Ultramarinas,* Vol. II. Lisbon, 1812.

————, "Navegações de Luiz de Cadamosto," in *Collecção de Notícias para a História e Geografia das Nações Ultramarinas,* Vol II. Lisbon, 1812.

————, "Navegação do Capitão Pedro Álvares Cabral," in *Collecção de Notícias para a História e Geografia das Nações Ultramarinas,* Vol. II. Lisbon, 1812.

————, *Paesi Novamente Retrovati.* Milan, 1508 (attributed to Amerigo Vespucci).

————, *Sete Unicos Documentos de 1500.* Referentes à Viagem de Pedro Álvares Cabral. Lisbon, 1940.

Astley, Thomas, *New General Collection of Voyages, etc.,* 4 vols., ed. Thos. Green. London, 1745–1747.

Avezac, M. d', *Note . . . sur le Degré d'Habilité des Portugais, etc.* Paris, 1846.

Axelson, Eric, *South-East Africa, 1488–1530.* London and New York, 1940.

Ayalla, Frederico Diniz d', *Goa Antiga e Moderna.* Lisbon, 1888.

Azevedo, J. Lucio de, *Epocas de Portugal Economico.* Lisbon, 1929.

Azevedo, Pedro A. d', "Os Escravos," in *Arquivo Histórico Portugues,* I, 289–307. Lisbon, 1903.

Azurara, Gomes Eannes de, *Chronicle of the Discovery and Conquest of Guines,* transl. by Beazley and Prestage, 2 vols. London, 1896–1899. See also De Zurara.

————, *Conquests & Discoveries of Henry the Navigator, Being the Chronicles of Azurara,* ed. by Virginia de Castro e Almeida, and transl. into English by Bernard Miall. London, 1936.

Baio, Antonio, *et al., História da Expansão Portuguesa no Mundo,* 3 vols. Lisbon, 1937–1940.

Baker, B. Granville, *A Winter Holiday in Portugal.* London, n.d.

Baker, J. N. L., *A History of Geographical Discovery and Exploration.* Boston, 1931.

Ballard, G. A., *Rulers of the Indian Ocean.* Boston, 1928.

Barata, Antônio Francisco, *Vasco da Gama em Évora.* Lisbon, 1898.

Barbosa, Antônio, "Instrumentos Nauticos da Epoca dos Descubrimentos," in *Revista Militar.* Lisbon, 1925.

Barbosa, Duarte, *The Book of Duarte Barbosa,* transl. by Mansel Longworth Dames, 2 vols. London, 1918–1921.

————, *Description of the Coasts of East Africa and Malabar in the Beginning of the Sixteenth Century,* transl. from the Spanish by Henry E. J. Stanley. London, Hakluyt Soc., 1866.

————, *Livro,* in *Collecção de Notícias para a História e Geografia das Nações Ultramarinas,* Vol. II. Lisbon, 1812.

Barlow, Roger, *A Brief Summe of Geographie,* ed. by E. G. R. Taylor. London, 1932.

Barros, João de, e Diogo de Couto, *Décadas da Asia,* 24 vols. Lisbon, 1778–1788.

Barros, João de, *Tweede Scheeps-Togt van Don Vasco da Gamma.* Leyden, 1706.

Barthold, H. V., *La Découverte de l'Asie.* Paris, 1947.

Beazley, C. Raymond, *Prince Henry the Navigator.* New York and London, 1914.

———, "Prince Henry of Portugal and His Political, Commercial and Colonizing Work," in *American Historical Review,* XVII. New York, 1912.

———, "Prince Henry of Portugal and the African Crusade of the Fifteenth Century," in *American Historical Review,* XVI. New York, 1910.

Bell, Aubrey F. G., *Diogo do Couto.* Oxford, 1924.

———, *Gaspar Correa.* Oxford, 1924.

———, *Gil Vicente.* Oxford, 1921.

———, *In Portugal.* London, 1912.

———, *Portugal of the Portuguese.* New York, 1915.

———, *Portuguese Portraits.* Oxford, 1917.

Bensaude, Joaquim, *Histoire de la Science Nautique Portugaise résumé.* Genève, 1917.

———, Introduction à l'Edition Fac-simile du *Regimento do Astrolábio e do Quadrante.* Munich, 1915.

———, Lacunes et Surprises de l'Histoire des Découvertes maritimes. Coimbra, 1930.

Benson, E. F., *Ferdinand Magellan.* London, 1929.

Bettencourt, E. A. de, *Descobrimentos, Guerras e Conquistas dos Portuguezes em Terras do Ultramar nos Seculos XV e XVI.* Lisbon, 1881–1882.

Biblioteca Nacional de Lisboa. *Guia de Portugal,* 3 vols. Lisbon, 1927.

Blackham, Robert J., *Incomparable India.* London, n.d.

Blake, John William, *Europeans in West Africa, 1450–1560,* 2 vols. London, 1942.

Botelho, Simão, "Tombo do Estado da Índia," in *Subsidios.* Royal Academy. Lisbon, 1868.

Boulting, William, *Four Pilgrims.* London, n.d.

Bovill, E. W., *Caravans of the Old Sahara.* London, 1933.

Boxer, C. R., "Portuguese Roteiros, 1500–1700," in *The Mariner's Mirror,* Vol. XX, No. 2, April, 1934. London, 1934.

Bowra, C. M., *From Virgil to Milton* ("Camões"). London, 1945.

Braamcamp Freire, A., "Emmenta da Casa da Índia," in *Boletim da Sociedade de Geographia de Lisboa.** Lisbon, 1907–1908.

Braga, Theophilo, *Camões.* Oporto, 1907.

———, *Centenário da Descoberta da América.* Lisbon, 1892.

Bragança Pereira, A. B. de, *Arquivo Português Oriental* (nova ed.), Vol. I, 1498–1599. Bastorá, India Portuguesa, 1936.

* Hereafter *B.S.G.L.*

Branco, Manuel Bernades, *El-Rei D. Manuel*. Lisbon, 1888.

British Foreign Office, *Peace Handbooks*, Vols. XIII, XIX, covering Portuguese Colonies in Africa and Asia. London, 1920.

Brown, A. Gordon, ed., *South and East African Year Book and Guide*. 47th ed., London, 1947.

Brown, Lloyd A., *The Story of Maps*. Boston, 1949.

Buel, James William, *Heroes of Unknown Seas and Savage Lands*. Philadelphia, 1891.

Bulhão Pato, R. A. de, *Cartas de Albuquerque*. Lisbon, 1884.

Burton, Harry E., *The Discovery of the Ancient World*. Cambridge, 1932.

Burton, Richard F., *Camoëns: His Life and His Lusiads, A Commentary*, 2 vols. London, 1881.

———, *First Steps in East Africa*. London, 1856.

———, *Goa and the Blue Mountains*. London, 1851.

Ca' Messer, Leonardo da, "Relazione di Leonardo da Ca' Messer alla Serenissima Repubblica di Venezia sopra il Commercio dei Portoghesi nell' India dopo la Scoperta del Capo di Buona Speranza (1497–1506)," in *Archivio Storico Italiano*, Ser. I, Append., Vol. II. Firenze, 1845.

Cabral, Pedro Alvares. See Anonymous, "Navegações do Capitão Pedro Alvares Cabral"; also, Greenlee, W. B.

Ca da Mosto, Luiz de, *Voyages*. See Caddeo, Rinaldo; also Crone, G. R., and Anonymous, "Navegações de Cadamosto."

Caddeo, Rinaldo, *Navigazioni Atlantiche di Alvise Ca da Mosto, etc.* Milan, 1929.

Cambridge History of the British Empire, *South Africa, Rhodesia and the Protectorates*, Vol. VIII, Chap. III. London, 1936.

Cambridge Shorter History of India, The (Allan, Haig and Dodwell). Cambridge, 1934.

Camões. See Camoëns, Luis de.

Camoëns, Luis de, *Os Lusíadas*, ed. Basto. Oporto, 1945.

———, *The Lusiads*, transl. by J. J. Aubertin, 2nd ed., 2 vols. London, 1884.

———, *Os Lusíadas*, Englished by Richard F. Burton, 2 vols. London, 1880.

———, *The Lusiad*, transl. by William Julius Mickle. 5th ed., London, 1900.

———, *Os Lusíadas*, ed. by J. D. M. Ford. Cambridge, Mass., 1946.

———, *The Lusiad*, transl. by Richard Fanshawe, ed. by Jeremiah D. F. Ford. Cambridge, Mass., 1940.

Cândido, Zeferino, *Brasil*. Rio de Janeiro, 1892.

Canestrini, Giuseppe, "Memoria Interno Al Relazioni, etc." in *Archivio Storico Italiano*, Ser. I, Append. Vol. III. Florence, 1846.

Cantera, Francisco, *Abraham Zacut*. Madrid, 1835.

Capistrano de Abreu, João, *Descobrimento do Brasil pelos Portugueses*. Rio de Janeiro, 1929.

Cary, M., and E. H. Warmington, *The Ancient Explorers*. London, 1929.

Castanheda, Fernão Lopes de, *História do Descobrimento e Conquista da Índia pelos Portugueses*, 4 vols. (reprint of Edição Princeps). Coimbra, 1924.

——, *História do Descobrimento, etc.* (thirty-one chapters of the "lost" Livro IX, ed. by C. Wessels). The Hague, 1929.

Castanhoso, Miguel de, *Dos Feitos de D. Christovam da Gama*, ed. by Francisco M. E. Pereira. Lisbon, 1898.

Castro, João de, *Roteiro de Lisboa a Goa*. Lisbon, 1882.

Cavalheiro, Rodrigues, and Eduardo Dias, *Memórias de Forasteiros*. Lisbon, 1945.

Chagas, Manuel Pinheiro, *Os Descobrimentos Portugueses e os de Colombo*. Lisbon, 1892.

——, *Migalhas de História Portugueza*, 2nd ed. Lisbon, 1925.

Charton, Edouard, *Voyageurs, Anciens et Modernes* (containing the French translation of Velho), 4 vols. Paris, 1854–1855.

Chatterton, E. Keble, *Ships and Ways of Other Days*. Philadelphia and London, 1913.

Clifford, Hugh, *Further India*. London, 1904.

Coelho, J. M. Latino, *Vasco da Gama*, 2 vols. Lisbon, 1882.

Coelho, J. Ramos, ed., *Alguns Documentos do Arquivo Nacional Acerca das Navegações e Conquistas Portuguezes*. Lisbon, 1892.

Collecção de Notícias para a História e Geografia das Nações Ultramarinas, Vol. II. Lisbon, 1812; 2nd ed., Lisbon, 1867.

Comité Départmental du Calvados, *Quatrième Centenaire de la Découverte de la Route Maritime de l'Inde*. Cen, 17 mai, 1898.

Commissão Portugueza, *Centenário do Descobrimento da America: Memórias* (article by João Braz d'Oliveira, "Os Navios de Vasco da Gama"; article by Prospero Peragallo, "Carta de el rei D. Manuel ao Rei Catholico, narrando-lhe as Viagens Portuguezas á India desde 1500 até 1505). Lisbon, 1892.

Conti, Nicolò de, "Travels in the East," in R. H. Major's *India, etc.*

——, "Travels in the East," in *Marco Polo, Travels, etc.*, transl. by John Frampton, ed. by N. M. Penzer. London, 1929.

——, *Viaggi in Persia, India e Giava*, ed. Longhena. Milan, 1929.

Cordeiro, Luciano, *De Como e Quando Foi Feito Conde Vasco da Gama*. Lisbon, 1892.

——, "Diogo Cão," in *B.S.G.L.*, Ser. 11, No. 4. Lisbon, 1892.

——, *Questões Histórico-Colonais*, V. 7, 8. Lisbon, 1936.

——, "Os Restos de Vasco da Gama," in *B.S.G.L.* Lisbon, 1896.

Cordier, Henri, "L'Arrivée des Portugais en Chine," in *T'oung Pao*, Vol. XII. Paris, 1912.

——, *Histoire Générale de la Chine*. 2 vols., Paris, 1920.

Correa, Francisco Antônia, *Conseqüencias Econômicas dos Descobrimentos*. Lisbon, 1937.

Correa, Gaspar. See Stanley, Henry E. J.

——, *Lendas da Índia*, Vols. 1–4. Lisbon, 1858–1864.

——, transl., *Three Voyages of Vasco da Gama, and His Viceroyalty*. London, Hakluyt Soc., 1869.

Corsali, Andrea, "Lettere," in Ramusio (*q.v.*), I, 176 ff.

Cortesão, A. Z., *Subsidios para a História do Descobrimento da Guiné e Cabo Verde.* Lisbon, 1931.
Cortesão, Annando de, *Cartografia e Cartógrafos dos Seculos XV e XVI,* 2 vols. Lisbon, 1935.
Cortesão, Jaime, *Do Sigillo Nacional Sobre os Descobrimentos* in *Lusitania,* Vol. I. Lisbon, 1924.
———, *L'Expansion des Portugais dans l'Histoire de la Civilisation.* Antwerp, 1930.
———, *A Expedicão de Pedro Álvares Cabral e o Descobrimento do Brasil.* Lisbon, 1922.
Costa, Fernandes, *A Viagem da India.* Lisbon, 1896.
Cottineau de Kloguen, Denis L., *An Historical Sketch of Goa,* 2nd ed. Bombay, 1922.
Coupland, R., *East Africa and Its Invaders.* Oxford, 1938.
Couto, Diogo de. See Barros, *Décadas.*
———, *O Soldado Prático.* Lisbon, 1937.
Cox, Edward Godfrey, *Reference Guide to the Literature of Travel,* 2 vols. Seattle, 1935–1938.
Crawfurd, Oswald, *Portugal, Old and New.* London, 1880.
Crone, G. R., *Voyages of Cadamosto, etc.* London, 1937.
Crooke, William, *Things Indian.* London, 1906.
Cruz, Gaspar da, *Tractado das Cousas da China e de Ormuz.* Barcelos, 1937.
Cunha, V. de Bragança, *Eight Centuries of Portuguese Monarchy.* New York, 1911.
Dames, M. Longworth, "The Portuguese and Turks in the Indian Ocean in the Sixteenth Century," in *Journal of the Royal Asiatic Society,* 1921.
Danvers, Frederick Charles, *The Portuguese in India,* 2 vols. London, 1894.
———, *Report to the Secretary of State for India in Council on the Portuguese Records Relating to the East Indies, Contained in the Archivo da Torre do Tombo, etc.* London, India Office, 1892.
Dark, Richard, *The Quest of the Indies.* Oxford, 1912.
Daux, A. A., *O Portugal de Camões.* Paris, 1889.
Day, Francis, *The Land of the Permauls, or Cochin, Its Past and Present.* Madras, 1863.
Diarii e Diaristi Veneziani, studii del Prof. Rinaldo Fulin, Terzo Congresso Geografico. Venice, 1881 (Estratto dall' Archivio Veneto, Vol. XXII, Part 1).
Dias, Carlos Malheiro, *et al.,* *História da Colonização do Brasil,* 5 vols. Oporto, 1921.
Dias, Eduardo, *Islão na India.* Lisbon, 1942.
Dieulafoy, Marcel, *Art in Spain and Portugal.* New York, 1929.
D'Orsey, Rev. Alex J. D., *Portuguese Discoveries, Dependencies and Missions in Asia and Africa.* London, 1893.
Dos Remedios, Mendes, *História da Literatura Portuguesa desde as Origens até a Actualidade,* 6th ed. Coimbra, 1930.
Dubois, Abbé J. A., *Hindu Manners, Customs and Ceremonies,* transl. by Henry K. Beauchamp, 3rd ed. Oxford, 1924.

Ducasse, André, *Negriers, ou le Trafic des Esclaves*. Paris, 1948.
Dujarday, Mme. H., *Résumé des Voyages, Découvertes et Conquêtes des Portugais, etc.*, 2 vols. Paris, 1839.
East, Gordon, *The Geography Behind History*. London, 1938.
Eça, Almeida d', *Luiz de Camões, Marinheiro*. Lisbon, 1880.
Eça, Vicente M. M. C. Almeida d', *Normas Económicas na Colonização Portuguesa até 1808*. Coimbra, 1921.
Empoli, Giovanni da, "Lettera a Leonardo su Padre, etc.," in *Archivio Storico Italiano*, Ser. I, Append. XXX, Vol. III. Florence, 1846.
Encyclopedia Pela Imagem (various articles, issued in fascicules). Oporto, n.d.
Erdmann, C., "Kreutzzuggedanke in Portugal," in *Historische Zeitschrift*, Vol. 141. Berlin, 1929.
Falconbridge, Alexander, *An Account of the Slave Trade on the Coast of Africa*. London, 1788.
Faria e Sousa, Manuel de, *Ásia Portuguesa* (Port. transl.), 6 vols. Oporto, 1945.
———, *Asia Portugueza*, 3 vols. Lisbon, 1666–1675.
Fasoli, Gina, *La Serenissima*. Florence, 1937.
Ferrand, Gabriel, *Introduction à l'Astronomie Nautique Arabe*. Paris, 1928.
———, "Le K'ouen-Louen," in *Journal Asiatique*, Paris, 1919.
———, "Le Pilote Arabe de Vasco da Gama," in *Annales de Géographie*, Paris, 1922.
———, *Rélations de Voyages et Textes Géographiques Arabes, Persans et Turks Relatifs à l'Extrême Orient, du VIII au XVIIIe Siècles*, 2 vols. Paris, 1914.
Ferreira Paes, Simão, *Famosas Armadas Portuguesas*. Rio de Janeiro, 1937.
Ficalho, Conde (Francisco Manuel Carlos de Mello), *Garcia da Orta e Seu Tempo*. Lisbon, 1886.
———, *Viagens de Pedro da Covilhan*. Lisbon, 1898.
Figueiredo, Antero de, *D. Pedro e D. Inês*, 10th ed. Lisbon, n.d.
Figueredo, Fidelino de, "The Geographical Discoveries and Conquests of the Portuguese," in the *Hispanic American Historical Review*, Vol. 6. Durham, N. C., 1926.
Firestone, Clark B., *The Coasts of Illusion*. New York, 1924.
Fiske, John, *The Discovery of America*, 2 vols. Boston and New York, 1892.
Fitzmaurice-Kelly, James, *A History of Spanish Literature*. New York, 1898.
Fonseca, Faustino da, *A Descoberta do Brasil*. Lisbon, 1900.
Fonseca, Ignacio Joâchim de, *Descobrimento do Brasil*. Rio de Janeiro, 1895.
Fonseca, José Nicolau de, *An Historical and Archaeological Sketch of Goa*. Bombay, 1878.
Fonseca, Quirino da, "Nomes et Proprios de Navios Portugueses," in *Boletim da Academia das Ciências de Lisboa*, February, 1931.
———, *A Representação Artística das Armadas da India*. Lisbon, 1933.
Fonti Italiani per la Scopèrta del Nuovo Mondo: Raccolta Colombiana. Rome, 1892.
Fontoura da Costa, A., *As Portas da India en 1484*. Lisbon, 1935.

Fontoura da Costa, A., *A Marinharia dos Descobrimentos*. Lisbon, 1939.
———, ed., *Roteiros Portugueses Inéditos da Carreira da Índia do Seculo XVI*. Lisbon, 1940.
Pereira da Silva, Luciano, "O 'Roteiro' da Primeira Viagem do Gama e a Suposta Conjuração," in *O Instituto,* Vol. 72. Lisbon, 1925.
Fordyce, W. Dingwall, *In Search of Gold*. London, 1924.
Fosse, Eustache de la, "Voyage à la Côte Occidentale d'Afrique en Portugal et en Espagne, 1479–1480," in *Revue Hispanique,* 4ème Année, Paris, 1897.
Foster, William, ed., *Early Travels in India*. London, 1921.
Freyre, Gilberto, *The Masters and the Slaves,* 4th ed., transl. from *Casa-Grande e Senzala* by Samuel Putnam. New York, 1946.
Galvano, Antonio, "The Discoveries of the World," in *Purchas: His Pilgrimes,* Vol. X, Maclehose reprint. Glasgow, 1905.
———, *The Discoveries of the World,* Portuguese text and translation, ed. by Vice-Admiral Bethune, C.B. London, Hakluyt Soc., 1862.
Galvão, Antônio, *Tratado dos Descobrimentos,* 3rd ed. Lisbon, 1944.
Gama, D. Maria Telles da, *Comte-Amiral D. Vasco da Gama*. Paris, 1902.
Geddes, M., *The History of the Church of Malabar*. N.p., 1694.
Gibson, Charles E., *The Story of the Ship*. New York, 1948.
Gil Vicente, *Obras Completas,* 6 vols. Lisbon, 1942.
Giles, H. A., *The Travels of Fa-Hsien*. Cambridge, 1923.
Gillespie, James Edward, *History of Geographical Discovery, 1400–1800*. New York, 1933.
Godinho, Vitorino Magalhaẽs, *Documentos Sôbre a Expansão Portuguesa,* Vols. I, II. Lisbon, n.d.
Godinho de Eredia, *Malaca, l'Inde Méridionale,* transl. by M. Léon Janssen. Bruxelles, 1882.
Goes, Damião de, *Chronica d'el Rei D. Manuel,* 5 vols., in Biblioteca de Clássicos Portuguezes, Vols. LIX–LXIV.
———, *Chronica do Principe dom Joam segundo do nome*. Lisbon, 1567.
———, *Opúsculos Historicos,* transl. from the Latin by Dias de Carvalho. Oporto, 1945.
Gonçalves, Luiz, "A Cathedral de Goa," in *B.S.G.L.,* Ser. 17, No. 5. Lisbon, 1901.
Gordon, Helen Cameron, *My Tour in Portugal*. London, 1932.
Gowen, Herbert H., *A History of Indian Literature*. New York, 1931.
Grandidier, Alfred, *Histoire de la Découverte de Madagascar par les Portugais*. Paris, 1902.
Grands Navigateurs et Colons Portugais du XVe et du XVIe Siècles, ed. Virginia de Castro e Almeida, 6 vols. (only 5 printed). Bruxelles and Paris, n.d.
Green, Thomas. See Astley's *Voyages*.
Greenlee, William Brooks, *The Voyage of Pedro Alvares Cabral to Brazil and India*. London, 1938.
Greiff, B., "Tagebuch des Lucas Rem, etc.," in "Sechsundzwanzigster Jahres-Bericht des historischen Kreis-Vereins im Regierungsbezirke von

Schwaben und Neuburg für das Jahr 1860." Augsburg, 1861 (Peutinger Letters).

Griaule, Marcel, *Les Grands Explorateurs*. Paris, 1946.

Gubernatis, Angelo de, *Memoria interno ai Viaggiatori Italiani nella India Orientale dal Secolo XIII a Tutto il XVI*. Florence, 1867.

———, *Storia dei Viaggiatori Italiani nelle Indie Orientali*. Leghorn, 1875.

Günther, Siegmund, *La Epoca de los Descubrimientos*. N.p., n.d.

Hamy, E. T., *Études Historiques et Géographiques*. Paris, 1896.

Handbook for Travellers in India, etc., 15th ed. John Murray, London, 1938.

Harlow, Vincent T., ed., *Voyages of Great Pioneers*. Oxford, 1929.

Harrisse, Henry, *Americus Vespuccius*. London, 1895.

———, *Document Inédit Concernant Vasco da Gama*. Paris, 1889 (privately printed).

Hart, Henry H., *Venetian Adventurer: the Life, Times and Book of Messer Marco Polo*, 3rd ed. Stanford University Press and Oxford University Press, 1947.

Hawkridge, Emma, *Indian Gods and Kings*. Boston and New York, 1935.

Hennig, Richard, *Terrae Incognitae*, 4 vols. Leyden, 1936–1939.

Herodotus, *The Persian Wars*, in *The Greek Historians*, 2 vols. New York, 1942.

Heyd, W., *Histoire de Commerce du Levant au Moyen-Âge* (Edition Française), 2 vols. Leipzig, 1936.

Hieronimo di Santo Stefano, "Journey," in R. H. Major's *India, etc.*

Hildebrand, J. R., "The Pathfinder of the East," in *National Geographic Magazine*, Vol. LII, No. 5. Washington, 1927.

História da Colonização Portuguesa do Brasil, ed. by Carlos Malheiro Dias, 3 vols. Oporto, 1921–1924.

História da Expansão Portuguesa no Mundo, ed. by Baião, António, *et al.*, in parts. Lisbon, 1939.

Homer, *Odyssey*, transl. by A. T. Murray, 2 vols. London and New York, 1930.

Hoskins, Halford L., *European Imperialism in Africa*. New York, 1930.

Hudson, G. F., *Europe and China*. London, 1931.

Hümmerich, Franz, *Quellen und Untersuchungen zur ersten Indienfahrt des Vasco da Gama*. Munich, 1897.

———, *Quellen und Untersuchungen zur Fahrt der Ersten Deutschen nach dem Portugiesischen Indien*. Munich, 1918.

———, *Vasco da Gama und die Entdeckung des Seewegs nach Ostindien*. Munich, 1898.

Hume, Martin, *Through Portugal*. New York and London, 1907.

Hyde, Walter Woodburn, *Ancient Greek Mariners*. New York, 1947.

Ibn Batuta, *Travels in Asia and Africa*, transl. and selected by H. A. R. Gibb. London, 1929.

———, *Voyages, texte Arabe, traduction par Defrémery et Sanguinetti*, 4 vols., 3 ed. Paris, 1893.

Idrisi, *Géographie*, transl. by P. A. Jaubert. Paris, 1836.

Inchbold, A. C., *Lisbon and Cintra*. London, 1907.

Ingrams, W. H., *Zanzibar*. London, 1931.

Instituto, O, Vol. 72. Coimbra, 1925.

Jayne, K. G., *Vasco da Gama and His Successors, 1460–1580*. London, 1910.

Jervis, W. W., *The World in Maps*. New York, 1937.

Johnson, A. H., *Europe in the Sixteenth Century*, 7th ed. London, 1925.

Johnston, Harry H., *A History of the Colonization of Africa by Alien Races*, 2nd ed. Cambridge, 1899.

——, *The Opening up of Africa*. New York and London, n.d.

Jorge, Ricardo, *O Obito de D. João II*. Lisbon, 1922.

Journal of the First Voyage of Vasco da Gama, A, 1497–99, transl. by E. G. Ravenstein. London, Hakluyt Soc., 1808.

Julien, Ch-André, *Histoire de l'Afrique*. Paris, 1946.

Kaeppel, Carl M. C., *Off the Beaten Track in the Classics*. Melbourne, 1936.

Kammerer, Albert, "Découverte de la Chine par les Portugais au XVIème siècle et la Cartographie des Portulans," in *T'oung Pao*, Supplement to Vol. XXXIX. Leyden, 1944.

——, *Mer Rouge, l'Abyssinie et l'Arabie Depuis l'Antiquité*, 2 vols. in 5 parts. Cairo, 1929–1935.

Kayserling, M., *Christoph Columbus und der Antheil der Jüden an die Spanischen und Portugieseschen Entdeckungen*. Berlin, 1894.

——, *Christopher Columbus*. New York, 1894.

Keith, A. Berriedale, *Classical Sanskrit Literature*. Calcutta and London, 1923.

Keltie, J. Scott, and O. J. R. Howard, *History of Geography*. New York and London, 1913.

Kimble, George H. T., *Geography in the Middle Ages*. London, 1938.

Koebel, W. H., *Portugal, Its Land and People*. London, 1909.

Lafitau, Joseph François, *História dos Descobrimentos e Conquistas dos Portuguezes no Novo Mondo*, 4 vols. Lisbon, 1786.

Lagõa, Visconde de, *Grandes e Humildes na Epopeia Portuguesa do Oriente*, 2 vols. Lisbon, 1942.

Landini, Gaspar Dias de, *O Infante D. Pedro*, 3 vols., in Biblioteca de Clássicos Portuguezes. Lisbon, 1893–1894.

Lane, Edward W., *The Manners and Customs of the Modern Egyptians*. London, 1914.

Lane, Ferdinand, *The Mysterious Sea*. London and New York, 1947.

Lane-Poole, Stanley, *The Story of Cairo*. London, 1906.

Langer, William L., *An Encyclopedia of World History* (for genealogical tables of the Portuguese kings). Boston, 1940.

Lannoy, C. de, and H. Vanderlinden, *Expansion Coloniale des Peuples Européens, le Portugal et l'Espagne*. Brussels, 1907.

Lelewel, Joachim, *Géographie du Moyen Age*, 5 vols. Bruxelles, 1857.

Leo Africanus, *Geographical Historie of Africa*, ed. by R. Brown, 3 vols. London, 1896.

Lewis, Rev. Thomas, "The Old Kingdom of Congo," in *Geographical Journal*, XXXI.

Ley, Charles David, ed., *Portuguese Voyages, 1498–1663*. London, 1947.

Light, Richard Upjohn, *Focus on Africa.* American Geographical Society, New York, 1941.

Lisboa, João de, *Livro de Marinharia,* ed. by Brito Rebello. Lisbon, 1903.

Liske, Javier, *Viajes de Extranjeros por España y Portugal en los Siglos XV, XVI, e XVII,* transl. by F. Rozanski, Madrid, 1879.

Livermore, H. V., *A History of Portugal.* Cambridge, 1947.

Lloyd, Christopher, *Pacific Horizons.* London, 1946.

Lobo, A. de S. S. Costa, ed., *Memórias de um Soldado da Índia Complidas de um Manuscripta Portuguez do Museo Brittanico.* Lisbon, 1877.

Logan, William, *Malabar.* Madras, 1906.

Logan, William A., *Malabar,* 2 vols. Madras, 1887.

Lopes, David, *Expansão da Lingua Portuguesa no Oriente nos Séculos, XVI, XVII, e XVIII.* Barcelos, 1936.

Lopes, Fernão, *Crónica de D. João I,* ed. by António Sergio, 2 vols. Lisbon, n.d.

———, *Chronica de el-Rei D. Pedro I,* in Biblioteca de Clássicos Portuguezes. Lisbon, 1895.

Lopes, Thomé. See Anonymous, "Navegação as Índias Orientaes por Thomé Lopes."

Macdonell, Arthur A., *A History of Sanskrit Literature.* New York, 1900.

McClymont, James Roxburg, *Pedralvarez Cabral.* London, 1914.

Maçoudi, *Les Prairies d'Or,* transl. by De Maymard and De Courtelle. Paris, 1861.

Major, R. H., *India in the Fifteenth Century.* London, 1857.

Marden, Philip S., *A Wayfarer in Portugal.* London, 1927.

Mariz, Pedro de, *Diálogos de Varia História dos Reis de Portugal, etc.* Lisbon, 1672.

Marlowe, Christopher, *The Plays and Poems.* London, n.d.

Martens, Otto, and O. Karstedt, *The African Handbook,* 2nd ed. London, 1938.

Martins, J. P. Oliveira, *The Golden Age of Prince Henry the Navigator,* transl. by J. J. Abraham and William E. Reynolds. London, 1914.

———, *História de Portugal,* 3rd ed., Vol. I. Lisbon, 1880.

———, *Portugal Nos Mares,* 2 vols., 3rd ed. Lisbon, 1924.

Maugham, G. C. F., *Portuguese East Africa.* London, 1906.

Mendonça, Henrique Lopos de, *Vasco da Gama na História Universal.* Lisbon, 1925.

Metropolitan Museum of Art, The, *The Age of Exploration.* New York, 1942.

Mocquet, Jean, *Voyages en Afrique, Asie, Indes Orientales et Occidentales.* Paris, août, 1830.

Moor, E., *The Hindu Pantheon,* new ed., Simpson. Madras, 1864.

Moraes Sarmento, José Estavão, *D. Pedro e a Sua Época.* Oporto, 1924.

Morais e Sousa, L. de, *Ciência Nautica dos Portugues nos Seculos XV e XVI,* 2 vols. Lisbon, 1924.

Morelet, Arthur, *Journal du Voyage de Vasco da Gama en MCCCCXCVII.* Lyons, 1844.

Morison, Samuel Eliot, *Admiral of the Ocean Sea,* 2 vols. Boston, 1942.

Morison, Samuel Eliot, *Portuguese Voyages to America in the Fifteenth Century*. Cambridge, Mass., 1940.

Mosto, Andrea da, *Alvise da Mosto e la Sua Famiglia*, in Archivio Veneto, Ve Serie, Nos. 3–4. Venice, 1927.

Muirhead, Finley, *Southern Spain and Portugal* (Blue Guides Series). London, 1929.

Münzer, Jerónimo, *Viaje por España y Portugal en los Años 1494 y 1495*, Spanish transl. by Julio Puyol. Madrid, 1924.

Murias, Manuel, *História Breve da Colonização Portuguesa*. Lisbon, 1940.

Navarrete, Martin Fernandez de, *Colección de los Viajes y Descubrimientos que Hicieron por Mar los Españoles*, 2nd ed., 5 vols. Madrid, 1837.

Nehru, Jawaharlal, *The Discovery of India*. New York, 1946.

Newton, Arthur Percival, ed., *The Great Age of Discovery*. London, 1932.

——, *Travel and Travellers of the Middle Ages*. London, 1926.

Nordenskiöld, A. E., *Facsimile Atlas to the Early History of Cartography*. Stockholm, 1889. .

——, *Periplus*. Stockholm, 1897.

Norris, Herbert, *Costume and Fashion*, 3 vols. London, 1938.

Nunez do Liam, Duarte, *Chronicas del Rey João I e as dos Reyes Dom Duarte e Dom Affonso V*, 2 vols. Lisbon, 1780.

Oaten, Edward Farley, *European Travellers in India*. London, 1909.

Odoricus Raynaldus, *Annales Ecclesiastici*, Vol. IX. Cologne, 1694.

Oliveira Martins, J. P. *O Brazil e as Colónias Portuguezas*, 5th ed. Lisbon, 1920.

Oliveira, J. B. d', "Navios Portuguezes do Tempo dos Descobrimentos e Conquistas," in *Revista Portuguesa Colonia e Maritima*. Lisbon, 1897–1898.

Olschki, Leonardo, *Storia Letteraria delle Scoperte Geographiche*. Florence, 1937.

Olsen, Orlan, *La Conquête de la Terre*, 6 vols. Paris, 1933.

Oman, Sir Charles, *The Sixteenth Century*. New York, 1937.

Orta, Garcia da, *Colloquies on the Simples and Drugs of India*, transl. by Sir Clements Markham. London, 1913.

Osorio, Jerome, *The History of the Portuguese During the Reign of Emmanuel*, transl. from the Latin by James Gibbs, 2 vols. London, 1742.

Osório, Jerônimo, *Da Vida e Feitos de el-Rei D. Manuel*, Port. transl. from Latin, by Manuel do Nascimento, 2 vols. Lisbon, 1944.

Outhwaite, Leonard, *Unrolling the Map*. New York, 1935.

Pais, Pero, *História da Etiopia*, 3 vols. Oporto, 1945.

Pannikar, K. M., *Malabar and the Portuguese*. Bombay, 1929.

Parks, George Bruner, *Richard Hakluyt and the English Voyages*. New York, 1930.

Peattie, Donald Culross, *Cargoes and Harvests*. New York, 1932.

Pedros o Sebastião José, *Resumé Histórico ácerca da Antiga Índia Portugueza*. Lisbon, 1884.

Pedroso, Z. Consiglieri, *Catálogo Bibliográfico das Publicações Relativas aos Descobrimentos Portugueses*. Lisbon, 1912.

Peregallo, Prospero, "Viaggio di Matteo da Bergamo in India sulla Flotta di

Vasco da Gama (1502–03)," in *Bollettino della Società Geografica Italiana,* Ser. IV, Bol. III, Anno XXXVI, Vol. XXXIX. Rome, 1902.

Pereira, A. B. De Bragança, *Arquivo Português Oriental* (nova edição), Tomo I: *História Política, etc.,* Vol. I, 1498–1599. Bastorá, India Portuguesa, 1936.

Pereira, Duarte Pacheco, *Esmeraldo de Situ Orbis,* transl. by George H. T. Kimble. London, 1937.

Pereira, Gabriel, "De Lisboa a Cochim em 1505," in *B.S.G.L.,* Ser. 17, No. 5. Lisbon, 1900.

———, "Diogo Gomes: As Relações do Descobrimento da Guiné, versão do Latim," in *B.S.G.L.,* Ser. 17, No. 5. Lisbon, 1900.

Pereira da Silva, Luciano, *A Astronomia das Lusíadas.* Coimbra, 1915.

Peres, Damião, *História de Portugal,* 7 vols. Barcelos, 1928–1936.

———, *História dos Descobrimentos Portugueses.* Oporto, 1943.

Péringuey, L., "Inscriptions Left by Early European Navigators on Their Way to the East," in *Annals of the South African Museum,* Vol. XIII. Cape Town, 1913.

Peschel, Oscar, *Abhandlungen zur Erd- und Völkerkunde,* Leipzig, 1877.

———, *Zeitalter der Entdeckungen.* Leipzig, n.d.

Phillips, George, "The Seaports of India and Ceylon," *Journal of the Royal Asiatic Society,* North China Branch, Vols. XX, XXI. Shanghai, 1885.

Pigafetta, Antonio, *Magellan's Voyage Around the World,* ed. by J. A. Robertson, 3 vols. Cleveland, 1906.

———, *Relazione del Primo Viaggio Intorno al Mondo,* ed. Manfroni. Milan, 1929.

———, *Storia del Primo Viaggio Intorno al Mondo,* ed. Ginocchietti. Rome, 1944.

Pina, Ruy de, *Chronica del Rey Dom João II,* ed. by Correa da Serra. Lisbon, 1790.

Pinho Leal, Augusto, *Portugal Antigo e Moderno,* 12 vols. Lisbon, 1880.

Pinkerton, John, *A General Collection of Voyages and Travels, etc.,* 17 vols. London, 1814.

Pires, Tomé, *Suma Oriental,* 2 vols. London, 1944.

Plattner, Felix Alfred, *Jesuiten zur See.* Zurich, 1946.

Pliny, *Natural History.* London, 1855.

Plutarch, *Lives,* Vol. I. New York, n.d.

Pohl, Frederick J., *Amerigo Vespucci, Pilot Major.* New York, 1944.

Pons, R. Giorgi de, *I Grandi Navigatori Italiani.* Florence, 1929.

Poujade, Jean, *La Route des Indes et ses Navires.* Paris, 1946.

Pratt, Sir John, *The Expansion of Europe into the Far East.* London, 1947.

Prestage, Edgar, *The Chronicles of Fernão Lopes and Gomes Eannes de Zurara.* Watford, 1928.

———, *Portugal: A Pioneer of Christianity,* 2nd ed. rev. Lisbon, n.d.

———, *The Portuguese Pioneers.* London, 1933.

Purchas, Samuel, *Hakluytus Posthumus, or Purchas His Pilgrimes,* Maclehose reprint, 20 vols. Glasgow, 1907.

Pyrard, Francisco de Laval, *Viagem,* 2 vols. Oporto, n.d.

Pyrard, Francisco de Laval, *Voyage,* English ed. by Albert Gray *et al.,* 2 vols. London, 1887–1889.

Rabbe, Alphonse, *História de Portugal.* N. p., n.d.

Raccolta di Documenti e Studi, pubblicati dalla R. Commissione Colombiana, Pt. I, Vol. III, Tav. LXX, autograph of Columbus.

Ramusio, Giovanni Battista, *Delle Navigationi e Viaggi, etc.,* 3 vols. (1613 ed.). Venice, 1554.

Randall, H. J., *The Creative Centuries.* London and New York, 1947.

Ravenstein, E. G., *The First Voyage of Vasco da Gama.* See Velho, Alvaro.

———, *Martin Behaim, His Life and His Globe.* London, 1908.

———, "The Voyages of Diogo Cão and Bartholomeu Dias, 1482–88," in *Geographical Journal,* XVI, 625–655. London, 1900.

Rawlinson, H. G., *Intercourse Between India and the Western World from the Earliest Times to the Fall of Rome,* 2nd ed. Cambridge, 1926.

———, *India, A Short Cultural History.* London, 1937.

Raynal, Abbé, *Histoire Philosophique et Politique des Establissmens et du Commerce des Européens dans les Deux Indes.* Paris, 1778.

Reade, H., "Vasco da Gama," in *Journal of the Royal Asiatic Society,* p. 589. London, 1898.

Reparaz, Gonçalo de, in *Biblos.* Coimbra, 1920.

Reparaz, Gonzalo de (Hijo), *La Época de los grandes Descubrimentos Españoles y Portugueses.* Barcelona and Buenos Aires, 1931.

Resende, Garcia de, *Chronica de el-Rei D. João II,* 3 vols., in Biblioteca de Clássicos Portuguezes, Vols. XXXII–XXXIV. Lisbon, 1902.

Rey, Charles F., *The Romance of the Portuguese in Abyssinia.* London, 1929.

Ribeiro, João, *História de Portugal.* Rio de Janeiro, 1928.

Ricardo, Jorge, *O Obito de D. João II.* Lisbon, 1922.

Ridley, Henry N., *Spices.* London, 1912.

Robins, F. W., *The Story of Water Supply.* Oxford, 1946.

Rodrigues, Francisco, The Book of (in Pires [*q.v.*], Vol. II).

Rogers, J. A., *Sex and Race,* 3 vols. New York, 1940–1941.

Rogers, Stanley, *The Indian Ocean.* London, 1932.

Rohr, Christine, "Neue Quellen zu den Endeckungsfahrten der Portuguesen im Indischen Ozean," in *Beiträge zur Historischen Geographie, Ethnographie und Kartographie, vornehmlich des Orients.* Leipzig and Vienna, 1929.

———, "Neue Quellen zur Zweiten Indienfahrt Vasco da Gamas," in *Quellen und Forschungen zur Geschichte der Geographie und Völkerkunde.* Leipzig, 1939.

Rose, J. Holland, *Man and the Sea.* Cambridge, 1935.

Ross, E. Denison, "The Portuguese in India and Arabia Between 1507 and 1517," in *Journal of the Royal Asiatic Society.* London, 1921.

Rostovtzeff, M., *Caravan Cities.* Oxford, 1932.

Roth, Cecil, *A History of the Marranos.* Philadelphia, 1932.

Saint-Martin, Vivien de, *L'Histoire de la Géographie, etc.* Paris, 1875.

Salisbury, W. A., *Portugal and Its People.* London, 1893.

Sanceau, Elaine, *D. João de Castro.* Oporto, n.d.

————, *Henry The Navigator.* London, n.d.
————, *Indies Adventure.* London and Glasgow, 1936.
————, *The Land of Prester John.* New York, 1944.
————, *O Sonho da India* (Alfonso de Albuquerque). Lisbon, n.d.
Sanuto, Marino, *Diario* (1466–1535). Venice, 1879–1902.
Sassetti, Filippo, Lettera à Francesco I de' Medici in Angelo de Gubernatis: *Storia* (*q.v.*).
Schefer, M. Charles, *Navigation de Vasque de Gamme.* Paris, 1898.
Schoff, Wilfred H., *The Periplus of Hanno.* Philadelphia, 1913.
————, *The Periplus of the Erythraean Sea.* New York and London, 1912.
Scott, Hugh, *In the High Yemen.* London, 1942.
Serra, Correa da, *Colleção de Livros Inéditos de História Portugueza, etc.,* 5 vols. Lisbon, 1790–1824.
Silva, A. A. Baldaque da, *Notícia sobre a Náo S. Gabriel, etc.* Lisbon, 1892.
Silva, Luciano Pereira da, "Kamal, Tábuas da India," in *Lusitania,* Vol. 1. Lisbon, 1924.
Silveira, Francisco Rodriguez, *Memória de un Soldado da India,* compiled from British Museum MSS by A. D. S. S. Costa Lobo. Lisbon, 1877.
Sion, Jules, *Asie des Moussons, IIème Partie,* Vol. IX de *Géographie Universelle.* Paris, 1929.
Smithes, M., *Things Seen in Portugal.* London, 1931.
Sociedade de Geografia de Lisboa, *Boletim.* Many articles are to be found in the long series of Bulletins. Yearly indexes should be consulted.
Sousa, Fr. Luis de, *Anais de D. João,* 2 vols. Lisbon, 1938.
————, *Annaes de Elrei Dom João Terceireo,* ed. by A. Herculano. Lisbon, 1844.
Spears, John R., *Master Mariners.* London, n.d.
Stanley, Henry E. J., *The Three Voyages of Vasco da Gama, and His Viceroyalty,* from the *Lendas da India* of Gaspar Correa. London, 1869.
Stefansson, Vilhjalmur, ed., *Great Adventures and Explorations.* New York, 1947.
Stephens, H. Morse, *Albuquerque.* Oxford, 1912.
————, *Portugal* (the Story of the Nations Series). New York and London, 1891.
Stevens, William Oliver, and Allen Westcott, *A History of Sea Power.* New York, 1944.
Stevenson, Edward Luther, *Genoese World Map, 1457.* New York, 1912.
Stier, H. G. G., *Flämisches Tagebuch über Vasco da Gamas Zweite Reise.* Braunschweig, 1867.
Stigand, Capt. C. H., *The Land of Zinj.* London, 1913.
Strande, Justus, *Die Portugiesenzeit von Deutsch- und Englisch-Ostafrika.* Berlin, 1899.
Strong, S. A., "The History of Kilwa," in *Journal of the Royal African Society.* London, 1895.
Sulaymân, *Voyage en Inde et en Chine,* transl. from the Arabic by Gabriel Ferrand. Paris, 1922.

Sykes, Sir Percy, *A History of Exploration*. New York, 1934.
——, *The Quest for Cathay*. London, 1936.
Synge, M. B., *A Book of Discovery*. New York and London, n.d.
Tafur, Pero, *Travels and Adventures, 1435–1439*. London, 1926.
Tannenbaum, Frank, *Slave and Citizen*. New York, 1947.
Taylor, E. G. R., *Original Writings and Correspondence of the Two Hakluyts*, 2 vols. London, 1935.
Teixeira de Aragão, A. C., *Vasco da Gama a Vidigueira*, 3rd ed. Lisbon, 1898.
——, D. *Vasco da Gama e a Villa da Vidigueira*. Lisbon, 1871.
——, *Vasco da Gama e a Vidigueira* (2nd ed.), in *B.S.G.L.*, Ser. 6a. Lisbon, 1886.
Theal, George McCall, *History and Ethnography of Africa South of the Zambezi*, 2 vols. London, 1907.
Thomazi, A., *Histoire de la Navigation*. Paris, 1947.
Thurston, Edgar, *Castes and Tribes of South India*, 7 vols. London, 1909.
Tiele, Pieter Anton, "Oosten Voor de Komst der Portugeezen" in *De Gids*, Vols. XVIII, XIX. Amsterdam, 1874.
Tonneau, Albert, "Découverte de la Route Maritime des Indes," in *B.S.G.L.*, 1948.
Towle, George M., *Voyages of Vasco da Gama*. London, n.d.
Toynbee, Arnold J., *Civilization on Trial*. New York, 1948.
Trapier, Blanche, *Les Voyageurs Arabes au Moyen Age*. Paris, 1937.
Ulloa, Affonso de, *Historia dell' Indie Orientali*, comp. dal Sig. Fernando Lopes di Castagneda. Venetia, 1578.
Valle, Pietro Della, *Travels in India*, 2 vols. London, 1892.
Van Linschoten, John Huyghen, *Voyage to the East Indies*, ed. by Arthur C. Burnell and P. A. Tiele, 2 vols. London, 1885.
Varnhagen, Francisco Adolpho de (Visconde de Porto Seguro), *História Geral do Brasil*, 3rd ed. São Paulo, 1927.
Vars, Jules, *L'Art Nautique dans l'Antiquité*. Paris, 1887.
Varthema, Ludovico di, *Itinerario*, ed. Giudici, 2nd ed. Milan, 1929.
——, *The Itinerary 1502–1508*, ed. by Sir Richard Carnac Temple. London, 1928.
——, *The Travels of Ludovico di Varthema*, transl. by John Winter Jones, ed. by George Percy Badger. London, 1863.
Vasconcellos, Ernesto de, "Early Portuguese Explorations of the North American Coast," in *O Instituto*, Vol. 72. 1925.
Vasconcellos, Joaquim de, "O Retrato de Damião de Góis por Alberto Dürer," in *Lusitania*, Vol. L. Lisbon, 1924.
Vasconcelos, Dr. Antônio de, *Iñes de Castro*, 2nd ed. Barcelos, 1933.
Velho, Alvaro, *Diário da Viagem de Vasco da Gama*, ed. by Damião Peres, 2 vols. Lisbon, 1945.
——, *Journal du Voyage de Vasco da Gama*, French transl. by Arthur Morelet. Paris, 1864.
——, *Journal of the First Voyage of Vasco da Gama*, transl. by E. G. Ravenstein. London, 1898.

————, *Roteiro da Primeira Viagem de Vasco da Gama,* Preface, etc., by Fontoura da Costa. Lisbon, 1940.

————, *Roteiro da Viagem de Vasco da Gama em MCCCCXCVII,* 2nd ed., ed. by A. Herculano and Castello da Paiva. Lisbon, 1861.

Vespuccius, Albericus, *Voyage from Lisbon to India,* transl. by C. H. Coote. London, 1894.

Viana, Mário Gonçalves, *Vasco da Gama.* Oporto, 1937.

Vignaud, Henry, *Études Critiques sur la Vie de Colomb avant ses Découvertes,* 1ère série. Paris, 1905.

Viterbo, J. P. Sousa, *Trabalhos Nauticos dos Portuguezes,* 2 vols. Lisbon, 1898–1900.

Wagner, Henry R., *Sir Francis Drake's Voyage Around the World.* San Francisco, 1926.

Waldman, Milton, ed., *The Omnibus Book of Traveller's Tales.* New York, n.d.

Watson, Foster, *Richard Hakluyt.* London, 1924.

Weber, Albrecht, *The History of Indian Literature.* London, 1892.

Welch, Sidney R., *Europe's Discovery of South Africa.* Cape Town and Johannesburg, 1935.

————, *South Africa Under King Manuel, 1485–1521.* Cape Town and Johannesburg, 1946.

Whiteway, R. S., *The Rise of Portuguese Power in India, 1497–1550.* Westminster, 1899.

Wilbur, Marguerite Eyer, *The East India Company.* New York, 1945.

Williamson, James A., *Europe Overseas.* London, 1925.

Wroth, Lawrence C., *The Early Cartography of the Pacific,* Vol. 38 of the *Papers of the Bibliographical Society of America,* No. 2. New York, 1944.

Wyndham, H. A., *The Atlantic and Slavery.* Oxford, 1935.

Yule, Henry, *The Travels of Marco Polo,* 3rd ed., 2 vols. (with supp. vol. by Henri Cordier). London, 1921.

————, *Cathay and the Way Thither,* 2nd ed., 4 vols. London, 1915.

Yule, Henry, and A. C. Burnell, *Hobson-Jobson,* new ed. by William Crooke. London, 1903.

Zain ed Din, *Tohfut-Ul-Mujahideen,* transl. into English by Lieut. M. J. Rowlandson. London, 1833.

Zimmermann, Alfred, *Europäischen Kolonien,* Vol. I, *Die Kolonialpolitik Portugals und Spaniens.* Berlin, 1896.

Zinadim (Zain al Din al Ma'bari), *História dos Portuguéses no Málabar,* transl. from Arabic MSS by David Lopes. Lisbon, 1898.

Zurara, Gomes Eanes de (see also Azurara), *Crónica dos Feitos de Guiné* (extracts ed. by Alvaro J. Da C. Pimpão). Lisbon, 1942.

Zurla, Ab. D. Placido, *Di Marco Polo e Degli Altri Viaggiatori Veneziani,* 2 vols. Venice, 1818.

INDEX

CPSIA information can be obtained at www.ICGtesting.com
Printed in the USA
BVOW08s1148290713

327229BV00015B/549/P

9 781258 476441